The Sword and the Cross

THE SWORD
AND THE CROSS

Reflections on Command and Conscience

JAMES H. TONER

PRAEGER

New York
Westport, Connecticut
London

Library of Congress Cataloging-in-Publication Data

Toner, James Hugh, 1946–
 The sword and the cross : reflections on command and conscience /
James H. Toner.
  p. cm.
 Includes bibliographical references and index.
 ISBN 0-275-94212-0 (alk. paper)
 1. War—Religious aspects—Christianity. 2. Conscience. 3. Christianity
and politics. I. Title.
BT736.2.T65 1992
172'.42—dc20   91-32209

British Library Cataloguing in Publication Data is available.

Library of Congress Catalog Card Number: 91-32209
ISBN: 0-275-94212-0

First published in 1992

Praeger Publishers, One Madison Avenue, New York, NY 10010
An imprint of Greenwood Publishing Group, Inc.

Printed in the United States of America

The paper used in this book complies with the Permanent Paper Standard
issued by the National Information Standards Organization (Z39.48—1984).

10 9 8 7 6 5 4 3 2 1

To my father, James H. Toner, of Monson, Massachusetts, and to the memory of my mother, Catherine Leahy Toner (1911–1977)

Deo gratias

Where there is no vision, the people perish:
but he that keepeth the law, happy is he.

Without wise leadership, a nation is in trouble;
but with good counselors there is safety.

The beginning of wisdom is the fear of the Lord,
and knowledge of the Holy One is understanding.

—Proverbs 29:18; 11:14; 9:10

CONTENTS

Preface   ix

1 Introduction   1

2 The Etiology of War   15

3 The Avatars of Power: War and Politics   37

4 On the Just War Tradition   61

5 Command and Conscience   85

6 The Political Christ of the Synoptic Gospels   105

7 On Pacifism   129

8 The Sword and the Cross   153

Selected Bibliography   173

Index   183

PREFACE

[Captain Vere, speaking about the death penalty which, however reluctantly, he is about to impose on the hapless Billy Budd:] But do these buttons that we wear attest that our allegiance is to Nature? No, to the King. Though the ocean, which is inviolate Nature primeval, though this be the element where we move and have our being as sailors, yet as the King's officers lies our duty in a sphere correspondingly natural? So little is that true, that in receiving our commissions we in the most important regards ceased to be natural free-agents. When war is declared, are we the commissioned fighters previously consulted? We fight at command. If our judgments approve the war, that is but coincidence.

—Herman Melville, *Billy Budd, Foretopman*

As the twentieth century segues into the twenty-first, we are left with a terrible statistic: About *100 million people* have died as a result of well over one hundred wars in this century alone. Recently when Pope John Paul II called for a day of prayer for peace, wars or insurrections were then raging in forty-three countries around the globe, including Guatemala, El Salvador, Nicaragua, Colombia, Ecuador, Peru, Suriname, Northern Ireland, Spain, Lebanon, Kurdistan, Iran-Iraq, Afghanistan, India, Western Sahara, Angola, Namibia, South Africa, Mozambique, Southern Sudan, Ethiopia, Sri Lanka,

Cambodia, and the Philippines.[1] Command (the political and legal power to initiate and to conduct war) and conscience (the moral and ethical power to decide whether and how to fight) *must* become more than, as Melville had Captain Vere put it, mere "coincidence."

But ensuring symbiosis of sword and cross requires no mean or minor effort. In World War II, some accounts have it, Winston Churchill and his advisers received word from code-breakers that in about two days the Germans were planning massive aerial raids on Coventry. If the British took the kinds of protective measures (including major evacuation of the civilian populace) indicated, the Germans would thereby certainly know that their codes had been broken, thus compromising a valuable British intelligence weapon. According to the accounts,[2] Churchill decided not to warn Coventry. The subsequent German bombing is described as massive and successful. One author quotes President Franklin D. Roosevelt, who supposedly knew of Churchill's dilemma, as saying: "War is forcing us more and more to play God. I don't know what I should have done." Another author said that "This was the sort of terrible decision that sometimes has to be made on the highest levels in war. It was unquestionably the right one, but I am glad it was not I who had to take it."[3] Intriguing and instructive as this episode may be, it very likely never took place.[4] But that does not derogate from the power of the *story*, however apocryphal it may be.

Ivo D. Duchacek has written compellingly of seven World War II case studies involving what might be termed "command and conscience" problems. He describes the dilemmas of the September 1938 Munich settlement; the August 1939 Soviet-Nazi pact; the 1941 British alliance with the Soviets; Eisenhower's willingness in 1943 to deal with French Admiral Darlan, who had reneged on his promise in 1940 to bring the French fleet over to the British, and was thus hated as a Nazi puppet; the Nazi offer to trade concentration camp prisoners for trucks in 1944; the raid on Dresden in February 1945; and the use of the atomic bombs against Japan. In these, and other matters he examines, Duchacek writes that the leaders "had to find their own human way in a labyrinth of conflicting norms, values, necessities, orders, and possible sanctions."[5]

Problems of command and conscience have disturbed me since high school. Because I was in college in the 1960s, having graduated in the fateful year of 1968, and served subsequently as a U.S. Army officer, these kinds of problems have been especially haunting for me. After four years of military service, I earned my doctorate in political science and international relations and began my teaching career, most of which has been spent at Norwich University, a military college; there proved to be no escape for me from the problems of "command and conscience."

Research for this book has been done principally at four libraries: The Hesburgh Library at the University of Notre Dame; the main campus library at the University of Massachusetts (Amherst), during a National Endowment for the Humanities Summer Institute on "War and Morality"; the Chaplin Memorial Library at Norwich University; and at the Fairchild Library at the U.S. Air University. An independent study leave from Norwich University afforded me the time to organize twenty years of notes and reflections. The cordial and creative atmosphere I encountered at the U.S. Air War College (Maxwell Air Force Base, Montgomery, Alabama), where I serve at present as a two-year visiting Professor of Political Science, has been immensely stimulating. I have profited a great deal from lengthy talks with the class members there (mostly senior officers of the Air Force, as well as selected officers from other services, some civilians from U.S. government agencies, and selected officers from foreign states), as well as from discussions with my Air War College colleagues. I thank in particular Dr. Grant Hammond and Dr. Robert Wendzel, both of whom have been most generous with advice and assistance, but neither of whom is responsible for any errors of fact or judgment in this volume. I also gratefully acknowledge the generous encouragement of my editor at Praeger, Dan Eades, with whom I have worked before and with whom I hope to work again.

At the Air War College, a book known as *Tongue and Quill* (Air Force Pamphlet 13-2 [2 January 1985]) is used as an aid to speaking and writing improvement. One of the suggestions offered there about writing is this: "As you begin your first draft, *put your last line first!*" (p. 51). This is not a first draft; and this is not, exactly, my last line. But to be very clear about the point of this book, I might make allusion to an old idea. Someone once said that there are three things that endure: God, Whom we will never fully understand on this earth; human error and egotism, which we will never fully eradicate on this earth; and modest laughter, signifying our ability to deal as best we can with the circumstances in which we find ourselves. This book argues that, like Sisyphus, we must spend our lives making decisions the full consequences of which are hidden from our eyes; but we must move ahead. We must do the very best we can.

Commanders and leaders must appreciate the reality that lack of preparation is unethical as well as unprofessional. In discussing the origins of war, war and politics, the tradition of the just war, the idea of "command and conscience," the image of Christ in the synoptic Gospels, the mirage of pacifism, and finally the "sword and the cross," I have as a last line the argument that conscience consists in our doing our level best to ensure that what we do is virtuous; that virtue consists of sound education complemented by grace; that command is the leader's art of bringing to bear on a given problem the values of studied wisdom, pondered experience, and judicious judgment. No one is truly fit to lead unless he can blend the cardinal philosophical virtues of wisdom, courage, temperance, and justice with the enduring religious virtues of faith, hope, and charity.

And no one can fully ensure the harmony of all those desiderata, for we are human; and to be human means to fail. But more: To be fully human means to try, to do our utmost to be and to do and to act as we ought to—in imitation of our image of the Good. Because modern society so often tells us either that there is no Good or that all we have is our own autistic image of the Good, we deprive our leaders of precisely that element which will bond command with conscience: the understanding and application of *civic virtue*. We live in two worlds, as Augustine told us: the heavenly (that of the cross) and the earthly (that of the sword). To attend to the well-being of our neighbor, we must have a vision of what ought to be, as well as a vision of what is. That vision is the product of the ethics which informs politics; politics is then imbued with meaning and purpose and clarity about ends and means; such clarity about objectives and opportunities is itself the heart of the statesman's education.

But our modern education says little or nothing about wisdom or virtue. Too many of our politicians, consequently, have no understanding of the symbiosis between ethics and politics. Thus, while there may be some understanding of the positive (or civil) law, there is little understanding of the natural law, which is justice, and hardly any discernment of the common good, which it is, after all, the statesman's task to prosper.

That is the thesis, the last line, of this book. One thing only should be added. Our human dignity derives, not from great success (which is, in any case, but momentary), but rather from tenacity of effort. Our lot, as private citizens or as public leaders or commanders, is to do the very best we can on the basis of intelligent consideration of the evidence we have at hand. To expect an end to trouble is to expect the "days of miracles." Those days will come—but not now. Thus we, "poor banished children of Eve," prudently and prayerfully resolve to determine what is the best (if not the perfect) course to choose, to follow that path with perseverance (but not with arrogance), and to reflect often (yet not with trepidation) upon our motives and our means and our probable results so that, in the end, "we may be made worthy of the promises of Christ." If we stumble again and again, as we will, we know that we as a human race have fallen far; such sepulchral knowledge is assuaged by the faith and the hope that we are, at the same time, graced by nature's grace. We do all we can. Do less and we violate the canons of ethics. Do more, such as trying to create a heaven on earth, and we make of politics an instrument of hell.

The bonding of command and conscience is civic virtue, best seen in the United States in the soul and mind of Abraham Lincoln. It is a lugubrious—but I fear entirely accurate—observation that Lincoln today would stand no chance of election to any post of influence or authority. If that observation gives us pause to think and to worry, it is offered as no reflection *on Lincoln*.

This book was conceived, researched, written, and produced with the gracious help of my wife Rebecca, without whose inspiration it could never have been. No sweeter joy exists than the paradox of falling in love again with the same woman for the first time. My son Jamey, fledgling writer that he is, learned something about the time needed, in the library and at the keyboard, to finish a project of this sort. I am deeply grateful to them, and to my older sons, Chris and Pat, for enduring the querulous nature of someone who has spent a quarter of a century pondering the intractable problems of "Command and Conscience." After all that, I have fully and finally resolved hardly anything; but I know I have wrestled with the angels. Lord willing, I am the better for it, and they will see and share in that.

NOTES

1. *A Matter of Fact* (Ann Arbor, MI: The Pierian Press, 1986), p. 272. Since 1945, when the last great global war ended, up to ten million people have died in smaller, regional conflicts which have haunted every continent. *A Matter of Fact*, 1990, p. 508.

2. Anthony Cave Brown, *Bodyguard of Lies* (New York: Harper & Row, 1975); William Stevenson, *A Man Called Intrepid* (New York: Harcourt Brace Jovanovich, 1976); F.W. Winterbotham, *The Ultra Secret* (New York: Dell, 1974).

3. Roosevelt is quoted by Stevenson (above, n. 2), p. 153. The second quotation is from Winterbotham (above, n. 2), p. 95.

4. See F. H. Hinsley, *British Intelligence in the Second World War,* Vol. One: *Its Influence on Strategy and Operations* (London: Her Majesty's Stationery Office, 1979) in which he contends that there is no basis for the claims that Churchill knew in advance of the Coventry bombing (pp. 535–36). My colleague at the U.S. Air War College, Dr. Alexander Cochran, in calling this book to my attention, indicated that his own review of the materials surrounding this case persuaded him that Hinsley is correct.

5. Ivo D. Duchacek, *Nations and Men,* 3d ed. (Hinsdale, IL: The Dryden Press, 1975), ch. 8. The quotation may be found on pp. 309–10.

1 INTRODUCTION

For the life of me, I can't see what this God business has to do with
practical politics.

—an old-time Tammany Boss

"When are you going to stop killing people?" Lady Astor blatantly
asked Joseph Stalin in 1931, when he was murdering the kulaks (wealthy
farmers) in his drive to collectivize the land. His reply: "When it is no
longer necessary."

The thesis of this book may be plainly stated at the outset. It is that
the leader—whether politician, diplomat, or soldier—bereft of ethical values is likely *to commit* heinous acts of butchery or barbarity in
the name of political expediency. And more: that the leader—
whether politician or diplomat, or soldier—bereft of practical values[1]
is liable, ironically, *to condone* heinous acts of butchery or barbarity
in the name of moral purity. The leader who will murder to achieve
or to preserve power is given too much to the city of Man; the leader
who will ignore others' depredations lest he soil his own hands by
resisting them is given, in one sense at least, too much to the city of
God. As there can be remorseless violence, so there can be remorseless peace. With one foot, synecdochically, in the temporal and one
foot in the eternal, man endures a tension and turmoil never fully to

be resolved during his earthly sojourn. By attempting to end or to eliminate the tension which is consistent with his earthly existence, man is thus subject to a philosophical double jeopardy. On the one hand, he risks, by concentrating on consolidating earthly power, the danger of a created tyrant—the Hobbesian Leviathan; on the other hand, he risks, by wistfully ignoring those power configurations, an Auschwitz or the Gulag. In expecting himself to replace God, man sins against the divine, for man must understand that he is creature. In expecting, however, that God will resolve all problems despite man's insouciance, man sins against his neighbor, for man must understand that he is also creator.

Few today understand—and fewer would agree with—the idea that the human existence is essentially tragic. Even as man creates his own fate and the configurations of his political power on earth (confronting his duty in time), so must he "[r]ectify deformed human existence by developing order as orientation to the divine source"; so must man "[u]se experience of the divine as a norm to correct deformed theologies."[2] If *tragedy* is understood, as any dictionary might tell us, as "a serious drama with an unhappy ending," one is reminded of Anatole France's remark that man is born; he suffers; he dies. We aspire to the infinite but are locked into the finite. Our human existence is filled with serious problems, few of which will be satisfactorily resolved in the here and now—resulting in the tensions and drives and urges which are, in fact, part of the human condition. In expecting an imminent (or a human) end to the trials of a troubled human race, we expect what will not be, perhaps trusting, unwisely, in earthly powers rather than in the divine. Still, we are charged with doing all we can to do and to act as we should, insofar as we can descry the right. Thus we arrived at the core of politics as described by Augustine: Seeking, consciously or unconsciously, after the sacred city, we live, during and despite our quest, in the secular city. Our responsibility to love God is challenge enough for our fallen race; our challenge to love one another, in the absence of grace, is beyond the practicable. Thus obtains the tragic dimension of human life.

ON POLITICAL POWER

Understood in the light of the foregoing analysis, politics becomes the noble art of reconciliation. Not only should human interests be politically reconciled, but the politician must try to effect a conciliation between the sacred and the secular. The politician, the leader of the polis, must then be able to identify, that is, to merge, the political and the ethical. In the absence of an architectonic vision of the Good or of what ought to be, the politician can please only communities of power; he cannot affirm what is right but only what is expedient. Without vision, the politician can advance or defend no coherent teleological ethics but only the consequentialist or utilitarian. Politics and ethics are at one, or ought to be; but that unity demands of statesmen the ability wisely to choose the appropriate course of action, which should always blend the demands of Perfection with the counsels of Prudence, to the exclusion of neither. Politics is, as the shibboleth reminds us, the art of the possible. While not itself the divine, politics must be, as it were, in touch with the divine; for without the order suggested by the divine (in Revelation, in authentic Christian tradition, and in the Magisterium), one is at a loss to distinguish between right and wrong, honor and shame, truth and falsity. Thus does the representative of Caesar ask of Truth Incarnate, "What is truth?" (Jn. 18:38) Blinded to the eternal, Caesar will err in time.

If Heaven has no need of prudence, the secular city does. Again, the leader with a hardened heart cannot perform the twin duties of reconciliation which are at the heart of the political enterprise: to accommodate competing human interests where possible, and to harmonize, again where possible, all such activity with the divine order.[3] As Kissinger has put it, "Statesmanship requires above all a sense of nuance and proportion, the ability to perceive the essential among a mass of apparent facts, and an intuition as to which of many equally plausible hypotheses about the future is likely to prove true."[4] It is precisely this intuition Kissinger refers to with which the philosopher must be concerned. *Intuition* means perception of truth without reasoning. It is a kind of Burkean prejudice, beliefs derived from experience, an instinct, a gut feeling. St. Thomas Aquinas expressed it as *Quisquid recipitur secundum modum recipiensis* ("That which is perceived, is perceived according to the nature of the perceiver"). If we contend that the politician must exert his influence sagaciously, then we must concern ourselves not only with "the Good," but also with the way in which the politician is trained in perceiving that Good (i.e., with education). Indeed, politics and ethics and education must all be concerned with wisdom and with virtue; they are, or should be, inseparable. The educated, ethical leader can thus bring to bear on a particular problem the full force of a properly formed sense of nuance and proportion and his intuition. It is precisely in this sense that I will employ the noun *conscience* in this book.

A critical part of that education consists in recognition both of human potential and of human limitation. "I am a democrat," C. S. Lewis once wrote, "because I believe in the Fall of Man." He continued:

I think most people are democrats for the opposite reason. . . . [P]eople like Rousseau . . . believed in democracy because they thought mankind so wise and good that everyone deserved a share in government. The danger of defending democracy on those grounds is that they're not true. . . . The real reason for democracy is just the reverse. Mankind is so fallen that no man can be trusted with unchecked power over his fellows. Aristotle said that some people were only fit to be slaves. I do not contradict him. But I reject slavery because I see no men fit to be masters.[5]

Lord Acton's well-known apothegm that "power tends to corrupt; absolute power corrupts absolutely" is in keeping with Lewis's comment. So was Reinhold Niebuhr's astute comment in *The Children of Light and the Children of Darkness* (lectures originally presented in 1944) that "Man's capacity for justice makes democracy possible; but man's inclination to injustice makes democracy necessary." A political intuition formed along these lines leads to the inescapable conclusion that political power must be balanced if tyranny is to be averted; it is but a small step to endorse the concept of separation of powers in domestic politics and of balance of power in international politics. Such an intuition flows, as it ought to, from a strong, if unarticulated, concept of human nature itself. It was in this sense that Hans Morgenthau observed that "the history of political thought is the history of the moral evaluation of political power."[6]

But Niebuhr died in 1971 and Morgenthau, in 1980. One observer from the University of Virginia, W. L. Miller, has noted that, many years after his death, few students seem inspired by Niebuhr's thought, leading Miller to question what his "lasting place in the history of American thought, of theology, of political philosophy, will be."[7] Morgenthau, similarly, is little known among most undergraduates today. Students of mine recently attended a conference on international affairs at Mount Holyoke College in Massachusetts, where only a handful of the participants seemed to recognize Morgenthau's name and fewer still were aware of his approach to the study of international politics. Niebuhr and Morgenthau—important as they are—are not the issue. Rather, the vexatious question is whether their understanding of world politics is taught, thought about, and debated today.

In an atmosphere on so many campuses of late (as the popular press readily testifies) of "multiculturalism," of "political correctness," and of triumphant relativism, Morgenthau seems medieval in writing that "without. . . the assumption that objective, general truths in matters political exist and can be known, order and justice and truth itself. . . become the mere by-products of ever changing power relations."[8]

Even language itself, as Charles Krauthammer has observed, "has been bleached of its moral distinctions, turned neutral, value-free, 'non-judgmental.' "[9] George Orwell, of course, had testified along similar lines in his famous observation that corruption in language precedes corruption in politics; but Orwell, too, seems little known these days. Today there is no virtue and no vice; all depends upon one's perceptions, one's feelings, one's urges. The notion that truths exist, let alone *the* truth, is quaint, silly. One is reminded of Samuel Johnson's admonition: "If he does really think that there is no distinction between virtue and vice, why, sir, when he leaves our houses let us count our spoons." The first sentence of this chapter suggests that the leader bereft of ethical values is likely to commit butcheries and barbarities. But of course we ourselves cannot expect to distinguish such crimes unless we know right from wrong, honor from shame, vice from virtue.

POLITICS DEFINED

George Will is correct in his observation about the history (one hesitates to write *development*, *evolution*, or *progress*) of political philosophy:

Until Machiavelli, the task of political philosophy was to solve man's fundamental problem, which was to answer the question "How ought I to live?" With Machiavelli, political philosophy became concerned with solving the politician's problem, which was understood to be keeping order and keeping power.[10]

Thus *politics* itself is seen, in the customary definitions of Harold Lasswell (*Politics: Who Gets What, When, How?*) and of David Easton ("the authoritative allocation of values") as an enterprise involving the division of spoils. I can offer yet another definition:

politics is that action or process by which individuals or groups seek, competitively, to exalt their values and to legitimize their interests. Russell Kirk, however, gets to the gist: politics, he once wrote, is the "application of ethics to the concerns of the commonwealth." There it is. Kirk's definition succinctly joins ethics and politics; the three preceding definitions omit ethics. What, after all, does "God business" have to do with ward politics? If one says "nothing at all," one has nothing to say to Stalin (see the epigraphs to this chapter) by way of rejoinder when the Soviet leader implicitly admits killing millions of humans. He, after all, decided who got what and when and how.

Modern political science can offer no reply to the massacres of Stalin. In fact, politics (as Athens and Jerusalem used to tell us before the corruptions of Machiavelli and of modernity) is a function or division of philosophy, which is the studied search for wisdom. Political philosophy is the quest for the best regime, urgently calling us to evaluate the principality. In its refusal to determine right from wrong and virtue from vice, modern political science is at one with contemporary education, which stands mute about the greatest problems and challenges of our day, and thus contributes, as Leo Strauss once put it, "to the victory of the gutter." In a similar sense, Milton is thought to have observed that "When we can't measure the things that are important, we ascribe importance to the things we can measure." Niebuhr, who talked about God, and Morgenthau, who talked about objective reality, are often regarded as irrelevant in an educational climate of emotivism,[11] for there are no ultimate criteria in emotivism, and such moral autism has no place for thoughts about the permanent things.

THE COMPLEXITY OF POLITICS

What I refer to here as the permanent things (as Russell Kirk would have it) might well be called elsewhere a "frame of reference." The point is that unless leaders are schooled in what ought to be they can hardly expect to judge well what is. Leaders who do not have time to read and to reflect, as Kissinger has told us, "risk becoming the victims of the simplifiers—mindless pacifism on the left and on the right equally mindless insistence on treating the new technology as conventional."[12] There is value, to be sure, in the principle known as "Occam's Razor" (sometimes referred to as the "Law of Parsimony"): "Entities must not be multiplied beyond necessity." To oversimplify, of course, is to distort reality. In our natural human craving for certitude and security, we tend toward solutions and answers far too simplistic, whether of the Jim Jones or of the Hitlerian variety; we are uneasy with what Glenn Tinder has called "Humane Uncertainty."[13] The tension we experience as human beings, Tinder tells us, leads us at times to confuse the "politics of convenience" (that is, ordinary political life) with the "politics of redemption" (that is, the promise of an earthly fulfillment via human devices). Investing mundane reality with a transcendent character leads us, however, as Professor Voegelin so powerfully wrote, not to heaven but to hell. Our desire to clarify reality, commendable in some respects, can, if unchecked, lead to excess and to expectations inconsistent with the very reality one seeks to comprehend. In time, of course, one arrives at the "realization of what is hoped for and [the] evidence of things not seen [Heb. 11:1]," which is faith. Thus we come, full circle, back to the permanent things.

Still, many, perhaps most, of the educators of today would lampoon faith. That way lies the great simplification; the tensions of the moment are thus dissolved into the specious clarity of an apotheosized humanity. Education becomes, not the effort to inculcate into students the fruits of learning about wisdom and virtue, not a disciplined understanding and awe of the cosmos, but an end in itself, a call to employment, an exercise in utilitarianism. In such a modern enterprise, political activity need not be complicated by philosophical conjecture about what ought to be; analysis may be sheerly empirical and phenomenal rather than contemplative and noumenal. Despite the warnings of Michael Howard that "Political activity takes place in a two-dimensional field—a field which can be defined by the two coordinates of ethics and power. . . . [and that] Effective political action needs to take constant account of both dimensions,"[14] too many persist in their belief that one is either ethical or powerful. The two do not intersect. It is precisely with the intersection of the two dimensions that we ought to be principally concerned.

Yet once we allow for such an intersection, we encounter dramatic difficulty. Our desire to simplify, to have finished answers to apparently intractable problems, leads us away from the humane uncertainty of the politics of convenience and toward the siren-song of unidimensional redemptionist politics. That is, we seek salvation in the here-and-now promise of power uncomplicated by ethics or of ethics uncomplicated by power. The point of this book is that ethics requires concern about and perhaps judicious involvement in the messy world of politics. That is nothing new. Aristotle said as much

2,000 years ago. Moreover, wise politics demands education in and the practice of ethics, properly understood.[15] But this involves us in a world which frightens the great simplifiers who have left Aristotle, Augustine, and Anselm far behind. In their urgent need to escape from the intellectual anxieties endemic to life itself, the great simplifiers have ignored the permanent things, thus, ironically, creating (as Allan Bloom has told us) a sterile education, a corrupt politics, a charlatan ethics. Symptomatic of the disease is the use of the word *charismatic*, today meaning the power to influence or to charm; in fact, *Time* once referred to "Marilyn Monroe's unique charisma."[16] When we consider that the word is derived from the Greek for *favor* or *grace*, meaning a gift of the Holy Spirit, we return once again to the depravity of language around us. Was Hitler, then, a "charismatic" leader? Of course he was—*if* we corrupt the adjective; of course he was—if we refuse to concern ourselves with the intersection of ethics and politics.

ON CHRISTIAN REALISM

For many years a dichotomy has existed between *idealism* and *realism*. Those who favored idealism (rarely carefully defined) maintained that idealists were compassionate and loving, suggesting that politics itself must be the enterprise of charity in action. The opponents of idealism suggested that such arguments are bogus, contending that idealism was Micawber-like, or (in a kind of *tour d'horizon* of European literature) Panglossian, or Quixotic. *Soi-disant* realists thought of themselves as prudent or mature or seasoned. Their opponents thought them only calculating and cunning. Of course, close students of realists know that the writings of Niebuhr, Kennan, Morgenthau, Osgood, Kissinger, and others of that school are nowhere nearly as hard-hearted as their opponents describe them. The problem we must face occurs in recognizing that because *idealism* has come to mean being impractical or fainthearted in approaching world politics, "no one in his right mind would admit to being an idealist."[17] One perceptive observer suggests that realism can be divided into "positivistic realism" (in which morality has no application to problems in world politics) and "normative realism" (in which moral judgments about foreign affairs are permissible but, in one form, are not applied and, in a weaker form, are not regarded as decisive in foreign affairs matters).[18] The distinction is somewhat blurred, but the main point is that realists resist a utopian, sentimentalized approach to world politics. Hope, they know, is not an effective foreign policy management tool!

This book will present a view of what is called here "Command and Conscience" based upon the ideal of Christian realism. I use the expression "the ideal of Christian realism" quite deliberately. I will argue in these pages that a biblical truth, corroborated by historical experience, is that any statecraft devoid of a sense of limitation is bound inevitably to fail, for politics is not theology; one's soul is not saved by the devices of economics and diplomacy. Prudent statecraft is a product of sober reflection on the theological insight and on the historical example of man's proclivity to sin. The theologian Niebuhr:

Good and evil are not determined by some fixed structure of human existence. Man, according to the biblical view, may use his freedom to make himself falsely the center of existence; but this does not change the fact that love rather than self-love is the law of his existence in the sense that man can only be healthy and his communities at peace if man is drawn out of himself and saved from the self-defeating consequences of self-love.[19]

The politician Adlai Stevenson in Hartford, Connecticut, said on 18 September 1952, "Man has wrested from nature the power to make the world a desert or to make the deserts bloom. There is no evil in the atom; only in men's souls."

Christian realism counsels us, as Talleyrand (1754–1838) once put it, not to expect too much. "Above all else," the French diplomatist said, "not too much zeal!" At the same time, we are not released from the lifelong effort of loving God and our neighbor and thus in embroiling ourselves in the problems and passions of the day. One cannot, in good conscience, sigh, walk away from politics, and await Judgment Day. Christian realism is thus an exercise in true *civic virtue*. Keynes is supposed to have said, "In the long run, we are all dead." True as that may be, its unbridled cynicism is not an option the Christian realist may exercise. We do not expect to resolve all serious problems but, in the end, we know that, by divine devices, our success is certain (Jn. 16:33).

Our task, while awaiting the Parousia, is to temper our entirely proper sense of limitation by faith and by hope and by charity. These theological virtues married to the classical virtues of wisdom, courage, temperance, and justice are, or ought to be, the hallmarks of Christian realism.

Almost by definition, realists are practical, logical, and circumspect. Christians must be intent upon things and thoughts of heaven (as in Phil., chapters 3 and 4). The sense of the tragic emanates from understanding that, like Sisyphus, we mortals must struggle as best we can toward the heights, all the while knowing we will never attain our full goal. St. Thomas Aquinas instructed us that reason and faith are mutually constructive; so, too, are politics and religion, provided that each apprehends its proper powers and its appropriate limitations. As a hammer is not the right tool for driving a screw, politics is not the right instrument for effecting our salvation, and religion is not the right vehicle for providing effective foreign policy. Knowing the right tool for many jobs depends upon a knowledge of, say, carpentry. Knowing how to blend the counsels of faith and the dictates of reason requires a knowledge of politics. And the argument here, once again, is that politics comprehends ethics and genuine (that is, ordered, disciplined, classical) education.

PROSPECTUS

This book is divided into eight chapters, of which this, the introduction, is the first. The second chapter examines the etiology of war, asking where conflict originates. Frederick the Great in a 1742 letter to Voltaire held that "It is the fashion these days to make war, and presumably it will last a while yet." The greatest danger of politics is the liability of war. Statesmen must deal every day with the specter of war. The purpose of this chapter is to explore the origins of war from the vantage point offered by Christian realism. A Russian proverb has it that "Eternal peace lasts until the next war." There is far too much truth in that. Still, if we know the source of the pathology, we are more likely to deal effectively with it than if we merely accept the disorder, the disease, as inevitable. The book thus deals, at the outset, with the most difficult question in statecraft: why do wars occur?

Chapter 3 studies war and politics. To recognize, as Karl von Clausewitz (1780–1831) did, that "War is nothing but the continuation of politics with the admixture of other [i.e., violent] means," is necessary but insufficient. Christian realism suggests that warfare is a political instrument, never an end in itself. Because war is a political mechanism, it must always be understood in strategic context; thus Chapter 3 is an inquiry into strategy. It may well be in the field of geopolitics and military strategy that Christian realism has both the most to offer—and the most to learn!

Chapter 4 is a study of just war theory and international law. At a time when so many students of politics were willing (and eager) to relegate just war theory to the ash heap of history, along came Saddam Hussein and the Gulf War of 1990–1991, described correctly by President Bush as a just war. The idea of justice in warfare, both in going to war and in conducting the war itself, is exactly what Christian realism concerns: recognition of the hard truth that violence may well have to be employed in this vale of tears but insistence that there are military avenues which decent leaders, diplomats, and soldiers may not take in the prosecution of such wars. Of course, many regard "just war" as an oxymoron; not only is it a useful term but it must be as well a truly vital military concept and alternative. Tacitus knew as much centuries ago: "They make a desert," he said, "and call it peace." The notion that "all is fair in love and war" is ipso facto wrong both politically and ethically. There are things that we cannot and must not do, as Christian realism plainly adjures us.

Chapter 5 explores the soldier's ethos of "Command and Conscience." Philosophers have too little to say to soldiers, beyond a certain, apparently ethereal, exhortation to virtue. Soldiers, in their turn, have little to say to philosophers, beyond a smug conviction that philosophy is, after all, merely the stuff of the ivory tower, impossibly irrelevant to the profession of arms. But since Nuremburg and Tokyo and Manila—the sites of the war crimes tribunals after World War II—soldiers have had to learn, whether they liked it or not, that they had better comprehend, even in a tactical way, the basic adjurations and admonitions of the just war theorists. This chapter attempts to look at command (broadly construed to mean leadership, both military and civilian) and conscience (understood, as explained above, as intuition or a rightly formed predisposition to choose wise courses of action based upon a sense of right and wrong informed by science— or proper knowledge, the fruit of genuine education).

Chapter 6 explores the idea of the "political Christ" of the synoptic gospels. The idea of Christian realism, of course, takes Jesus as its model. The great question posed by Jesus himself is: "But who do you say that I am?" (Lk. 9:20). Clearly if Christ was an impostor, Christian realism is a specious enterprise. But the idea of Christian realism is based on the conviction that Jesus is the Son of God—and more, that he is God himself revealed to man in the Incarnation. If that is so, then to disregard the political Christ is not only cavalier but blasphemous, for clearly no one can teach us better about politics than God himself. This is not to say that there will not be many views of the teachings; but to ignore the core of the teachings merely because it is, and has been, subject to a constellation of exegeses, is ill advised.

Chapter 7 is an examination of pacifism. Erasmus once contended that "The most disadvantageous peace is better than the most just war." But is that true? It is odd, somehow, to think of war as glamorous, but we often do. So many movie characters seem to wallow in the horrors of war. Even Robert E. Lee himself, in a comment passed to General Longstreet in December 1862, reflected that "It is well that war is so terrible—we would grow too fond of it." Pacifism does humanity a service in reminding us that war is slaughter. One must wonder, however, whether war, which is always evil, is the greatest evil. The tragedy of human existence may, in fact, require choosing, not between good and evil, but among various degrees of evil.

Chapter 8 is an overview of the book, a conclusion and a summary. A major objective of all foreign and national security policy is to ensure the survival of the nation. But survival alone makes no sense unless it is in the service of fundamental values that imbue the nation's existence with meaning and purpose. Secretary of State Dean Acheson put it well: "the means we choose to overcome the obstacles in our path must be consonant with our deepest moral sense."[20] A few moments of reflection on this basic concept reveals its difficulties. It says, in essence, that there are things which the United States will not and cannot do, despite the possible concomitant sacrifice of geopolitical advantage. "If one fought against an enemy ostensibly *because* of his methods," wrote George Kennan, "and permitted oneself to be impelled by the heat of the struggle to adopt those same methods, who, then, could be said to have won?"[21] This chapter will contend that the sword (that is, politics, diplomacy, war, command itself) has its vital function on earth, much as the classical and Christian philosophers told us. The cross, however, is paramount. In *Brave New World*, Huxley tells us about the drug "soma," which he describes as "Christianity without tears." I believe it was Fulton J. Sheen who once said that there is no Easter without Good Friday. There is no final triumph from the sword; there is no purpose, redemption, or *telos* from the sword. In the end, the sword is much like the church. In Heaven there is no need for faith and no need for the church, for its premier purpose as shepherd and as moral cicerone has been fulfilled. But on earth, there is every need for the church as a community of faith (to guide and to inspire and to teach) and for the sword (to nourish and to protect and to preserve). In the end, the union of the sword and the cross amount to the prospect of civic virtue, which consists of the recognition that we are earnest citizens of our metropolis until the political order, through wanton and wicked policy, forfeits the allegiance we owe it under its flag and under our God. "We must," as we read in the Acts, "obey God rather than men" (5:29).

The imperative of divine obedience need not necessarily preclude civil obedience any more than it need invariably counsel civil disobedience. (Indeed, a very fair reading of the Gospels seems to suggest that the presumption should always be the need for civil obedience.) Christian realists must work sedulously for coincidence whenever and wherever possible between the demands of the secular city (the sword, command) and the sacred city (the cross, conscience). Knowing that tensions exist among the competing constituencies of our earthly existence—as well as between our human failings and the perfection to which we are called by a Heavenly Father—we find comfort and consolation in the promise of a divine mercy that is ours if, our pride in check, we can but bring ourselves to ask for it. That way lies "the peace of God that surpasses all understanding" (Phil. 4:7). Here on earth, however, as Kennedy put it in 1961, "God's work must truly be our own." To maintain and, where possible, to enlarge the intersection between the ethics of the cross and the politics of the sword is our burden and our glory and is the true test of the civic virtue to which we are called as Christians and as citizens. In turn, civic virtue consists in blending the theological gifts of faith and hope and love with the cardinal qualities of prudence, courage, temperance, and justice. That way lies as much peace of mind and peace of soul[22] as we can experience, this side of Paradise.

NOTES

1. As Alasdair MacIntyre points out, "for Aristotle stupidity of a certain kind precludes goodness" and "excellence of character and intelligence cannot be separated" in *After Virtue*, 2d ed. (Notre Dame, IN: University of Notre Dame Press, 1984), pp. 154, 155.

2. Paul G. Kuntz, "Voegelin's Four Decalogues," *The Intercollegiate Review* 26 (Fall 1990): 48. This is a useful review of the late Professor Eric Voegelin's book, *Autobiographical Reflections*, ed. Ellis Sandoz (Baton Rouge, LA: Louisiana State University Press, 1989).

3. As will be discussed later in the text, this is not meant to imply that leaders need, or should expect, some revelation from on high. Beware the political leader who announces himself as "God's chosen agent"! But as C. S. Lewis (see *The*

Abolition of Man) and others have pointed out, there is a sense of "right reason" (often called natural law) which people share, regardless of culture or class. When, for example, Jim Jones led people into the jungle, proclaiming the advent of the kingdom and anointing himself as the elect of God, people of reasonable judgment could unite, practically without exception, in an understanding that Jones was a grisly impostor. Some acts are so self-evidently evil that human beings recoil in horror from them. Could anyone—other than a Nazi—gaze with equanimity, for example, on the horrors of a concentration camp? And had not the Nazis forfeited legitimate claim to humanity? Is one of the reasons that advocates for choice in the abortion debate invariably consider the display of photographs of aborted babies in bad taste because they are evidence of a slaughter which sickens those who see them—and from which we, in our humanity, recoil?

4. Henry A. Kissinger, *White House Years* (Boston, MA: Little, Brown, 1979), p. 39.

5. C. S. Lewis, *Present Concerns*, ed. Walter Hooper (New York: Harcourt Brace Jovanovich, 1986), p. 17.

6. Quoted in Greg Russell, *Hans J. Morgenthau and the Ethics of American Statecraft* (Baton Rouge, LA: Louisiana State University Press, 1990), p. 151.

7. Quoted in "The Definitive Reinhold Niebuhr," *Time*, 20 January 1986: 71.

8. Quoted in Russell (above, n. 6), p. 60.

9. "The Moral Equivalent of . . . ," *Time*, 9 July 1984: 88.

10. George Will, *Statecraft as Soulcraft: What Government Does* (New York: Simon and Schuster, 1983), p. 29.

11. MacIntyre (above, n. 1), p. 33.

12. Henry A. Kissinger, *Years of Upheaval* (Boston, MA: Little, Brown, 1982), p. 1195.

13. Glenn Tinder, *Political Thinking: The Perennial Questions*, 3d ed. (Boston, MA: Little, Brown, 1979).

14. Michael Howard, "Ethics and Power in International Policy," *International Affairs* 53 (July 1977): 374.

15. See Alasdair MacIntyre, *Whose Justice? Which Rationality?* (Notre Dame, IN: University of Notre Dame Press, 1988).

16. Taken from *The World Book Dictionary*, 1989, Vol. I, p. 343.

17. Robert L. Holmes, *On War and Morality* (Princeton, NJ: Princeton University Press, 1989), p. 56.

18. Ibid., pp. 56–57.

19. Reinhold Niebuhr, *Christian Realism and Political Problems* (New York: Charles Scribner's Sons, 1953), p. 130.

20. Quoted in Robert Leckie, *Conflict: The History of the Korean War, 1950–1953* (G. P. Putnam's Sons, 1962), p. 399. "Ours is not a wicked country," Senator Frank Church once observed, "and we cannot abide a wicked government" (*Time*, 16 June 1975: 10).

21. George F. Kennan, *Memoirs, 1925–1950* (Boston, MA: Little, Brown, 1967), p. 198.

22. The phrase "peace of soul" was used by Fulton J. Sheen as the title of one of his many books.

2 THE ETIOLOGY OF WAR

History would not be what it is, the record of man's crimes and follies, if logic and decency governed its events and great decisions.[1]

—Ladislas Farago

It is becoming more and more obvious that it is not starvation, not microbes, not cancer, but man himself who is mankind's greatest danger because he has no adequate protection against psychic epidemics, which are infinitely more devastating in their effect than the greatest natural catastrophes.[2]

—C.G. Jung

The well-known strategist Bernard Brodie, asked about the origins of war, answered that "Any theory of the causes of war in general or any war in particular that is not inherently eclectic and comprehensive . . . is bound for that very reason to be wrong." But Geoffrey Blainey, another highly competent student of war is, by contrast with Brodie, reductionist. All war aims, he contends, "are simply varieties of power. The vanity of nationalism, the will to spread an ideology, the protection of kinsmen in an adjacent land, the desire for more territory . . . all these represent power in different wrappings. The conflicting aims of rival nations are always conflicts of power." In quoting both analysts, Michael Howard, for his part, contends that both Brodie and Blainey are right.[3] The cause, source, origin, or etiology of war is protean, kaleidoscopic. Although Blainey's single-factor analysis seems, on balance, too reductionist, the power factor itself is subject to myriad interpretations. Regrettably, the observation of Oliver Wendell Holmes (1841–1935) appears wholly justified: "As long as man dwells upon the globe, his destiny is battle."

But is that *it*? Is that all that can be said about the prodigious expenditure of blood and treasure which has haunted mankind since man first crashed club upon the skull of other men? Is it all we can do to say, "War is"? To catalogue the causes of war hardly resolves the problem; but it may be a start. To expect that war will disappear is foolish; but to acquiesce supinely in the supposed inevitability of war is despairing. The point, then, of this chapter is to sort and to classify some of the thought about the etiology of warfare. Because warfare is arguably the greatest threat to the survival of the human species, we need constantly and critically to inquire into the origins of war in order, one hopes, more effectively to prevent it.

In Walter Miller's brilliant novel about nuclear warfare (and the human condition), a priest who discerns an approaching Armageddon plaintively asks:

Listen, are we helpless? Are we doomed to [war] again and again and again? Have we no choice but to play the Phoenix in an unending sequence of rise and fall? Assyria, Babylon, Egypt, Greece, Carthage, Rome, the Empires of Charlemagne and the Turk. Ground to dust and plowed with salt. Spain, France, Britain, [and, perhaps, one day] America—burned into the oblivion of the centuries. And again and again and again.

Are we doomed to it, Lord, chained to the pendulum of our own mad clockwork, helpless to halt its swing?[4]

One would think not. After all, in Paris on 27 August 1928, the Kellogg-Briand Treaty was signed, and war was renounced as an instrument of national policy. About sixty-five years later, that treaty *is still in effect*, its existence serving as an unintended and unfortunate mockery of its original, admirable goals. Similarly, the United Nations Charter obliges its members to "refrain in their international obligations from the threat or use of force against the territorial integrity or political independence of any state, or in any other manner inconsistent with the Purposes of the United Nations."[5]

The promise of these Panglossian texts is betrayed by events both recent and ancient. Even the Bible, for example, contains multiple references to warfare,[6] and the Dupuys are clearly correct in their judgment that "the dawn of history and the beginning of organized warfare went hand in hand."[7] The ubiquity of war is thrown into relief by the decade-long controversy over Jonathan Schell's book *The Fate of the Earth*, which will be discussed at length later in this book. Schell's jeremiad about the danger of nuclear war (correct as far as it went) became a quixotic call for a new political order. Schell's analysis was correctly limned a decade ago by Michael Kinsley, who said that "To Schell, apparently, all considerations apart from the danger of nuclear war are mere distractions."[8] The deep concern about a nuclear winter thought certain to result as the consequence of nuclear warfare has, in the minds of most analysts, subsided,[9] but one finds such news about reduced dangers from nuclear winter somehow only marginally comforting. The lugubrious fact remains that war, whether conventional or nuclear, has stalked the human race all our days.

This is not the place to question at length the feasibility or the morality of the Strategic Defense Initiative. The terrifying scenario, in these days, is not the prospect of a nuclear exchange between the superpowers but the increasingly likely danger of nuclear proliferation among the world's less developed countries. One can only wonder how the Gulf War of 1991 would have turned out had Saddam Hussein controlled a nuclear arsenal. Some argue that an SDI defense could help avert a nuclear disaster in the event of an attack on the United States; others contend that SDI research only fuels nuclear arms races. One thing is certain: concern about the horizontal and vertical proliferation of weaponry (i.e., to more countries quantitatively and weapons development and improvement within single countries) is a lurid manifestation of the security dilemma. The more secure a given country may be, the more its neighbors express concern that if that secure country launches an attack on them, it may be able to do so with impunity—leading, one can argue, to the irresistible alternative of a preemptive (or anticipatory) attack.

"War," Heinrich von Treitschke (1837–1896) once observed, "is elevating, because the individual disappears before the great conception of the state." Although war-mongers such as Treitschke are, thankfully, rather rare these days, one need only consult the pages of the popular press to see the staggering cost, in lives and in money, of warfare and preparation for warfare. Doomsayers have long predicted the end of the human race as we struggle with our own mad inventions. One psychologist, Jerome Frank, contended that "the longer the risk [of nuclear war] continues, the greater the probability of war; and if the probability continues long enough, it approaches certainty."[10] Such lamentations, of course, do not readily translate into effective national security policy. To begin to understand war, one must define it as clearly as possible, for the better our grasp of war's logic, the better our prospects of limiting (if not eliminating) it. One cannot control a disease, after all, without understanding its peculiar pathology.

WHAT IS WAR?

War is a major armed conflict, usually between states. That is a useful, dictionary-type definition. Oddly, however, it says both too much and too little. Too much, because it incorporates such a broad-based understanding, resulting in (necessary) vagueness. (Compare Cicero's definition: "a contending by force.") Too little, because we must question what *major* means, what arms are referred to, whether saying *conflict* is merely circular, and whether war can be intra-national as well as international. Clausewitz defined war as "an act of violence intended to compel our opponents to fulfill our will." He wrote also, as alluded to in the introduction to this book, that "War is nothing but a continuation of political intercourse, with a mixture of other means." Quincy Wright's monumental study of war contains this definition: "the legal condition which equally permits two or more hostile groups to carry on a conflict by armed force."[11]

Webster's *Third New International Dictionary* offers this definition of *war*: "a state of usu[ally] open and declared armed hostile conflict between political units (as states or nations)." This is largely in keeping with Professor Wright's legalistic definition of war. But does it satisfy? Does it capture the essence of war? There is ample scholarly debate about the meanings of *force*, *violence*, *conflict*, and *war*.[12] But there is little agreement. When, for instance, did the Korean conflict become the Korean War? War may resemble pornography in that, even though war cannot precisely be defined, combat veterans know what it is, just as former Justice Potter said of smut, "I know it when I see it."[13] One analyst has written that

[F]orce is the controlled use of armed and other coercion to achieve a rational and potentially moral end. Violence is the irrational and uncontrolled use of armed coercion with the result that great evil is done and little if any proportionate good is accomplished.[14]

As Charles Lofgren explained, "Today, threatened or applied force is a rational instrument of policy only if it is used with restraint."[15] We thus approach a definition of war which Christian realism may be able to accept. I offer this: *War is the limited application of force— customarily by states—toward the achievement of reasonable and ethical political goals.*[16] In accepting the idea of just war (see Chapter 4), I must reject the notion of unlimited war and of warfare that ignores its properly political dimension (e.g., a crusade) or its ethical dimension (e.g., a massacre). Thus even in something as apparently easy as defining *war*, we find the Christian realist embroiled in an effort to integrate the sword and the cross. This is no mere intellectual distraction, for the manner in which we define a subject establishes its boundaries and helps us to isolate its principal properties.[17] For that reason, we must understand *war* in the context of its twin dimensions of politics and ethics. Reconciling these dimensions is a herculean task, but the scholar and soldier alike have no alternative to the responsibility of understanding that war's beginning, duration, and termination are more than merely "military"; they are essentially political and ethical. To deny or to disparage that is to invite havoc.

Single-cause explanations of events are invariably too simplistic— or too Procrustean. To interpret complicated matters by suggesting merely one cause (as opposed to suggesting a principal cause) is a fallacy[18] likely to result in confusion rather than clarification. Following are a number of causes of war, somewhat arbitrarily divided. Some will quarrel with the causes listed or with the classifications employed. To be sure, a number of possible causes of conflict are overlooked, for what appears below is illustrative rather than exhaustive. Finally, the listing is meant to be seminal, and its categories are certainly not mutually exclusive.

THE NONPOLITICAL CAUSES OF WAR

The Biological

In *Germany and the Next War* (1911), Friedrich von Bernhardi (1849–1930) contended that "War is a biological necessity of the first importance." That harsh judgment is supported by some biologists and by some quasi-biologists who contend that survival is the principal human instinct and that all forms of life are engaged in a constant struggle in which only the strongest survive. Social Darwinism is a political form of this controversial biological view. Ethologists—or those who study animal behavior—argue by analogy that man is innately aggressive, has a territorial instinct, and is governed by certain genetic predispositions. The views of such writers as Konrad Lorenz are regarded as mere polemics by some. In his well-known book *On Aggression*, Lorenz explains that

All [man's] trouble arises from his being a basically harmless, omnivorous creature, lacking in natural weapons with which to kill big prey, and, therefore, also devoid of the built-in safety devices which prevent "professional" carnivores from abusing their killing power to destroy fellow members of the same species.[19]

Lorenz argues, in effect, that because we humans have no natural means of killing (teeth, claws, and so forth), we have developed an external means of doing so (weaponry) which effectively prevents the evolution of what he calls "ritualization of aggression." Some animals within the same species, however, have a means of offering threatening gestures as well as of surrendering, thus often obviating the need for violence. Exacerbating the human inability to ritualize our aggression is the human lack of inhibitions against killing members of our own species. Perhaps, Lorenz argues, in time we can learn to channel our aggressive instincts into more socially acceptable paths than intraspecific aggression (which too often culminates, not only in the establishment of a "champion" of an area, but in the competitor's death).

Robert Ardrey, a playwright turned biologist, contends that "Man is a predator whose natural instinct is to kill with a weapon." He asks "Are we so far from being nature's most glorious triumph that we are in fact evolution's most tragic error, doomed to bring extinction not just to ourselves but to all life on our planet?"[20] In essence, Ardrey maintains that man is a weapons-bearing species and that some of our psycho-motor abilities derive from our employment of weapons, which we were forced to use because we could not outrun or outwrestle our prey.

Ashley Montagu believes that "the views of Ardrey and Lorenz . . . have no scientific validity whatever."[21] Sally Carrighar explains the deleterious aspects of belief in innate aggression:

Nothing could more effectively prolong man's fighting behavior than a belief that aggression is in our genes. An unwelcome cultural inheritance can be eradicated fairly quickly and easily, but the incentive to do it is lacking while people believe that aggression is innate and instinctive with us, as both Ardrey and Lorenz declare.[22]

The biological approach to war is important but is not, of itself, a basis for understanding, preventing, or even mitigating war.

The Psychological

Some psychologists argue that aggression is the product of frustration,[23] or that certain mental maladjustments or psychoses result in violence. A spate of psychohistories and psychobiographies (of such people as Woodrow Wilson, John Foster Dulles, Richard Nixon, and Lyndon Johnson) testifies to the popularity of examining warfare and political figures through the science of psychoanalysis.

Of course, the term *psychoanalysis* is that of Sigmund Freud (1856–1939), who believed that humans have a powerful aggressive drive. This macabre excerpt from *Civilization and Its Discontents* makes the point:

The element of truth behind all this [about man's aggressive tendencies], which people are so ready to disavow, is that men are not gentle creatures who want to be loved, and who at the most can defend themselves if they are attacked; they are, on the contrary, creatures among whose instinctual endowments is to be reckoned a powerful share of aggressiveness. As a result, their neighbour [*sic*] is for them not only a potential helper or sexual object, but also someone who tempts them to satisfy their aggressiveness on him, to exploit his capacity for work without compensation, to use him sexually without his consent, to seize his possessions, to humiliate him, to cause him pain, to torture and to kill him. *Homo homini lupus.* Who, in the face of all his experience of life and of history, will have the courage to dispute this assertion? As a rule, this cruel aggressiveness waits for some provocation or puts itself at the service of some other purpose, whose goal might have been reached by milder measures . . . . [M]an [is] a savage beast to whom consideration towards his own kind is something alien. Anyone who calls to mind the atrocities committed during the racial migrations or the invasions of the Huns, or by the people known as Mongols under Jenghiz Khan and Tamerlane, or even at the capture of Jerusalem by the pious Crusaders, or even, indeed, the horrors of the recent World War [I]—anyone who calls these things to mind will have to bow humbly before the truth of this view.[24]

A related suggestion by Anthony Storr is that humans have a physiochemical system that responds to frustration or to perceived danger by violent reaction.[25] Erich Fromm has suggested that certain leaders (e.g., Hitler and Stalin) suffered from necrophilia, and that their sick love of death and destruction was a major cause of the grief and havoc in Europe in the 1930s and 1940s.[26] It is quite serious enough to find a warped, twisted personality in any human being; but when that is the personality of a critical world leader, the world may well have a price to pay. Not for nothing have the U.S. armed services long insisted upon psychological screenings for those dealing with nuclear weapons.

The famous experiments of Stanley Milgram[27] indicated that people may well be willing to accept the authority of leaders (in his experiment, "scientists" dressed in lab smocks) asking them to inflict pain and suffering on hapless victims. In light of Fromm's thesis about sick personalities, one finds Milgram's experiments (suggesting sycophancy in the face of authority) to be reason for anxiety. Comfort, to the extent that it is available at all in this area, may be derived, in small part, from Arthur Schlesinger, Jr., who argues that we must not fall victim to substituting psychiatry for politics:

The life of affairs is not just the projection of internal maladjustments. Public issues are not just figments in the imagination of politicians. Problems exist. They are real. One must add that politics is fully as sophisticated a field as psychiatry. It requires quite as much specialized knowledge and trained instinct, even if politicians, unlike psychiatrists, do not choose to dress up their black arts in a technical vocabulary.[28]

Morton A. Kaplan agreed: "In general, the psychologists who have been talking loudly about international politics make ridiculous and misleading assertions that they attempt to cloak beneath a certificate of professional skill."[29]

Thus, while psychological and psychiatric insights are important and should not be dismissed cavalierly, they are not, of themselves, sufficient to explain the genesis of war. In politics, moreover, there is an adage: *Quis custodiet ipsos custodes?* (Who will guard those who are themselves the guardians?) That question might be posed profitably to any self-appointed board of psychiatric governors seeking to exercise political power.

The Anthropological/Sociological

This school sees war, not as a result of instinct or psychological need, but as a cultural phenomenon, emerging out of social structures. Margaret Mead, for example, considered warfare to be a simple social invention. Bronislaw Malinowski contended that war is not biological: "Human beings," he said, "never fight on an extensive scale under the direct influence of an aggressive impulse."[30] Some anthropologists believe that, through careful study of peaceful societies, the industrial world might be able to eliminate much of its violence.

Others in this area view war as useful, if not as good. British sociologist Stanislav Andreski argues that "without war civilization would still be divided into small bands wandering in the forests and jungles."[31] Arnold Toynbee's view of history as a cyclic pattern of challenge and response is well known. It is obvious that war is a societal occurrence, for, according to the definitions advanced at the beginning of this chapter, war is group conflict normally between organized political entities. What this school may overlook at times is that the motivation or maladjustment of leaders, written large (i.e., transformed into national imperative), can lead to war. John Stoessinger, for example, has argued cogently that "With regard to the problem of the outbreak of war, the case studies [in his book] indicate the crucial importance of the personalities of leaders."[32] There can hardly be doubt that the next edition of his book will offer a profile of the War in the Gulf (1990–1991), which almost certainly would not have occurred without the pathological personality of Saddam Hussein.

This is not offered to denigrate the anthropological approach to war, which, indeed, offers useful research about primitive societies. There is value, to be sure, in such work and in some of its possible applications to advanced industrial societies. But the idea that war emerges from cultural or social causes *alone* seems not to square with the evidence of military history.

The Ecological

Representative of the ecological approach to warfare is the work by Dr. Arthur H. Westing, which he did under the auspices of the

Stockholm International Peace Research Institute.[33] This volume offers extensive analysis of the effects of war on the environment. This book and similar efforts document the dangers posed to the continued survival of the human race by both civil and military abuse of our finite planetary resources. The ecological approach does not see the environment as causing war (unless, in a Malthusian sense, nations must struggle desperately over diminished or depleted resources) but as a cause for human confraternity—should we recognize in time that, as Westing says, "the situation in which man finds himself today is a grave one" (p. 192). Under this heading one might also install a number of the geographic/geopolitical theories about warfare, a few of which will be referred to in Chapter 3 of this book.

The critical importance of the ecological element of warfare was made clear in late January 1991, during the Gulf War, when the largest oil slick in history was discovered fouling the waters of the Persian Gulf. Regarded as an act of "environmental terrorism," the oil slick was denounced by the United States on 25 January as a deliberate act by the Iraqis under Saddam Hussein (*Facts on File*, 31 Jan. 1991). The long-term environmental impacts of that kind of terrorist tactic are impossible to predict. One thing is certain: all humans are likely to suffer from this new kind of war crime.

Thus war seems to come from—or perhaps could be cured by effective work with—our genes, our mental aberrations, our social structures, or our abused environment. But these views largely ignore what Aristotle, the father of political science, tried to tell us about 2,300 years ago—that man is a fully political being, and not merely a response to stimulus.

THE POLITICAL CAUSES OF WAR

Personal Pathology

Students of international relations know that a principal approach to the study of war is the examination of what is called "levels of analysis,"[34] usually beginning with the decision-maker. As we have already determined above, it obviously makes a major difference who is in charge in a country, either before or during a crisis. The 1962 Cuban missile crisis might not have been resolved peacefully had someone other than John F. Kennedy been president. Count Axel Oxenstierna (1583–1654) of Sweden knew the importance of having prudent leaders. He once advised his son: "*Quantula sapientia regitur mundus*" ("With how little wisdom is the world governed"). There is more to the study of decision-making than some psychologists might admit. In 1971, for example, Kenneth B. Clark suggested that psychotechnology might produce a "peace pill" that world leaders could take to prevent them from using their political power destructively.[35] As I have previously suggested, savage or stupid leaders can certainly cause wars. But war can be caused as well by good-hearted leaders who misjudge or misperceive or misunderstand world politics. One thinks of Neville Chamberlain, the British prime minister noted for his policies of appeasement, at Munich in 1938.

There are those who would argue that war is the result of men's boredom. A number of veterans have expressed the opinion that their military service, especially in combat, was the most intense and curiously enjoyable time of their lives. In his novel, *The War Lover*, John Hersey has the lover of his hero (a World War II U.S. Air Force combat pilot) say to him:

"Why do you men have a conspiracy of silence about this part of war, about the pleasure of it?" . . . She said men pretended that battle was all tragedy—separation, terrible living conditions, fear of death, diarrhea, lost friends, wounds bravely borne, sacrifice, patriotism. "Why do you keep silent about the reason for war? At least what *I* think is the reason for war: that some men enjoy it, some men enjoy it too much. . . . I don't know what we can do about these men, how you can educate this thing out of them, or stamp it out, or heal it out—or whether you can get rid of it at all." She just had a feeling, a woman's feeling, that this was where all the trouble came from. We couldn't have a real peace while these men had that drive in them.[36]

The late Barbara Tuchman offered a similar analysis:

Males, who so far in history have managed government, are obsessed with potency, which is the reason, I suspect, why it is difficult for them to admit error. I have never known a man who, with a smile and a shrug, could easily acknowledge being wrong. Why not? *I* can, without any damage to self-respect. I can only suppose the difference is that deep in their psyches, men somehow equate being wrong with being impotent.[37]

Although hyperbolic, Tuchman's remarks do make the point that the individual matters. At the first level of analysis, psychology and biology once again come into play.

Societal Tensions

On 5 September 1919, speaking in St. Louis, President Woodrow Wilson asked: "Is there any man here or any woman—let me say, is there any child—who does not know that the seed of war in the modern world is industrial and commercial rivalry?" The old notion of the merchants death[38] continues to manifest itself, despite the fact that twenty years after Wilson's implied criticism of such industrialism, Franklin Roosevelt was praising the "great arsenal of democracy." (Twenty years after *that*, Dwight Eisenhower was warning us about the "military-industrial complex." Twenty years after *that*, President Bush was waxing eloquent about the superior American technology which helped to defeat the Iraqis so handily!) But if Americans, generally, are ambivalent about the blessings or curses of industrial power, they do seem to accept somewhat uncritically the notion that if the right leader has power, everything will be all right. That viewpoint is hardly universally shared.

Marxists in particular customarily reject the idea that war is caused by—or at least is intimately related to—personality disorders or leadership failures. Rather, most Marxists view war as a consequence of a diseased social order marked by the economic tension of the class struggle. They would contend that once the privileged classes of history are eliminated (either by bullet or by ballot), the nation's tensions will be reduced, its social harmony assured, its foreign policies pacified. If the power elite, the profit motive, and the exigent need for overseas markets will give way to the grandeur of socialism, it is likely (or certain in the judgment of certain members of this school) that warfare, too, will be eliminated. Still, Falk and Kim, who are hardly apologists for conservative economics, say that

While economic causes have been an important factor in the past wars, there is no firm empirical evidence that they have been most prominent or decisive. Economic causes have figured directly in less than 29 percent of the wars from 1820 to 1929, according to Lewis Richardson's statistical study of war.[39]

Structural Liabilities

In their iconoclastic book *The War Ledger*,[40] A. F. K. Organski and Jacek Kugler contend that relative rates of growth in the gross national product are linked to the outbreak of a number of wars; to them a crisis takes place when a challenging nation threatens to surpass in economic power a dominant nation. Their theory of the "power transition" sees political growth and development as being far more influential on war than war is on growth. Power, to Organski and Kugler, derives from the nation's political organization and the ability of central governmental elites to penetrate all aspects of society and to extract resources therefrom.

Along with societal tensions, structural liabilities make up the second level of analysis, which concentrates upon politics within the state (rather than upon the decision-maker or upon the international system). Organski and Kugler, for example, discuss a Phoenix factor at work in world politics: "Within a relatively short period of time [after the war], all nations return to the levels of national capabilities they would reasonably expect to have held had there been no war" (pp. 106–107 [One will be watching Iraq in the 1990s]). The tendency to go to war increases as great power involvement increases and the possibility that nuclear weapons may be used becomes more likely (pp. 161, 176, 215). "One is led to the bizarre conclusion that nuclear weapons do not deter the opponents of the nuclear powers, but deter only their possessors" (p. 178). There is no arms race between the U.S. and the U.S.S.R.[41] (p. 199). Deterrence does not exist (p. 216), and war is neither a rational nor an effective instrument of policy (p. 220). Essentially, Organski and Kugler contend that, for one to understand world politics, he must study the structure and class stratifications of each society and learn that the tensions of global affairs result more from intranational bureaucratic competition than from international political motives.

This book offers a strong argument in behalf of the importance of economic analysis in considerations about the etiology of war. Clearly, one cannot ignore domestic structure and financial exigencies in investigating the outbreak of war. But these authors carry their arguments too far. They contend, for example, that, despite its victory in World War II, England is in the economic situation (behind Germany) it fought to avoid. Although this may be true economically, Britain does not have a swastika on its flag—and surely that counts for something. Modern political science has begun to examine more closely the competitive natures of governmental bureaucracies and fiefdoms, and the study of structural impetus to violence is important.[42] But the second level of analysis, important as it is, cannot provide the full explanation for the causes of war.

Systemic Pressures

A number of political analysts would say that wars do not derive from individual idiosyncrasies, or from the ostensible deficiencies of social organizations or bureaucratic competition, or even from the greed of the power elite or industrial barons; rather, the source of war is the essentially anarchic condition of the state system in world politics.

At least one analyst, Werner Levi,[43] has concluded, however, that because sovereignty is diminishing, because internationalization is increasing, because "economics is international politics by other means" (p. 118), and because warfare may now "be useless for the achievement of most conceivable or national purposes" (p. 78), no nuclear war will be fought, and "developed states are unlikely to engage in a modern war with each other directly" (p. 15). This is all very reassuring—until one recalls that Sir Norman Angell (1872–1967) published his book *The Great Illusion* in 1910. He argued essentially that it was illusory for one to think that victory in war could lead to one nation's absorbing the economic strength of another nation. The world, he wrote, was so interdependent in trade and in economics that war was senseless. Four years later World War I erupted (but Angell still received the Nobel Peace Prize in 1933).

Some would cure war by personal psychology; some would cure it by introducing socialism; some would eliminate it by eliminating social stratification and bureaucracy. Those who see the source of war in the dimension of international relations would solve war by one of two devices: they might seek to eliminate all power through ardent pacifism (see Chapter 7 in this book), or to consolidate all power through world government and law. Inis Claude once explained why law is not mankind's savior:

Law is a key word in the vocabulary of world government. One reacts against anarchy—disorder, insecurity, violence, injustice visited by the strong upon the weak. In contrast, one postulates law—the symbol of the happy opposites to those distasteful and dangerous evils. Law suggests properly constituted authority and effectively implemented control; it symbolizes the supreme will of the community, the will to maintain justice and public order. This abstract concept is all too readily transformed, by worshipful contemplation, . . . into . . . a magic word for those who advocate world government. . . . Most significantly, it leads them to forget about *politics*, to play down the role of the political process in the management of human affairs, and to imagine that somehow *law*, in all its purity, can displace the soiled devices of politics.[44]

There is, then, no simple, single cause of war; neither is there an elementary remedy for it. Americans in particular have difficulty in accepting this because it suggests that there is no warless millennium on the horizon. Because Americans are used to a relatively painless existence, they expect happy endings in all their books and movies and generally have precious little understanding of the symbiotic relationship between power and politics (see Chapter 3). Balance of power—the Christian realist reply to the persistent question of how we may be able to prevent or to contain war—appears to be an anathema. For balance of power implies that, in international affairs, there is no human end to the struggles and tensions among peoples. We therefore must inquire into reasons for war that transcend those already sketched, for they do not adequately answer the question, why do men and nations fight?

TRANSPOLITICAL CAUSES OF WAR

Philosophical Approaches

Political scientist Morton Kaplan stated that "evil will never be eliminated from the world nor will good ever reign supreme."[45] That assessment is part of our intellectual heritage from Saint Augustine, Machiavelli, Hobbes, Luther, Malthus, Jonathan Swift, Dean Inge, Spinoza, Bismarck, Metternich, Freud, Nathaniel Hawthorne, Joseph Conrad (*Heart of Darkness*), and William Golding (*The Lord of the Flies*), among many others. Consider this passage from *The Federalist*:

[M]en are ambitious, vindictive, and rapacious.
    The causes of hostility among nations are innumerable. There are some which have a general and almost constant operation upon the collective bodies of society. Of this description are the love of power or the desire of pre-eminence and dominion—the jealousy of power, or the desire of equality and safety [No. 6: Hamilton].

But the notion that war is an *ultima ratio*—the last or final argument—has seemed generally inconsistent with the American experience. American power, as political realists have so long tried to tell us, has always had to be righteous power if it were to be used at all. Our wars have had to be all or nothing; and we have alternated between crusades and pacifism, neither of which is practicable—or ethical, I will argue—today. Yet, as William O'Brien has pointed out:

One of the lasting lessons of history is that force is a perennial necessity, at the international as well as at the national or subnational level. Justice and order must be preserved by force when all other means fail. Thus even an optimistic view of the future of mankind should probably envisage the continuation of the institution of war in the form of armed coercion applied on behalf of the international order against rebellious elements rather than the total elimination of armed coercion, which has not been achieved within the most advanced national or subnational societies.[46]

To be sure, all decent humans want an end to war, but to desire is not necessarily to obtain. In this nation of relatively spectacular wealth and achievement, we too often indulge ourselves in the mirage that merely because we want an end to human misery we shall have it. In the cited John Hersey novel, the American hero is told by an English woman, "Darling, you're so American. You get what is and what you want all mixed up together in your head."[47] The Christian realist philosophy informs us that the problems of world politics— preeminent among them that of war—will never fully or finally yield to human solutions. Cecil Crabb has explained this succinctly:

Americans have found it difficult to accept *partial solutions* to age-old problems disturbing the peace and security of the international community. Their usual expectation is that such problems will be "solved" within a relatively short time and that the tensions between nations will be "eliminated" by some dramatic development like an East-West summit conference or a new nonaggression treaty. For reasons that are not altogether apparent, Americans have been slow to apply a lesson that emerges from their own experience with countless internal problems like divorce, delinquency, alcoholism, traffic accidents, crime, poverty, and many other issues. That is that few problems in human affairs are ever "solved" in a final sense. They are ameliorated, softened, mitigated, made endurable, adjusted to, outlived—but seldom eliminated.[48]

Spiritual Approaches

The Christian fathers and the scholastics are, in many ways, the spiritual progenitors of Reinhold Niebuhr. But they, in turn, depended upon the scripture and teaching of the early church. The New Testament explains the cause of war in these words:

Where do the wars and where do the conflicts among you come from? Is it not from your passions that make war within your members? You covet but do not possess. You kill and envy but you cannot obtain; you fight and wage war. You do not possess because you do not ask. You ask but do not receive, because you ask wrongly, to spend it on your passions (James 4:1–3 [NAB]).

Historian Bernard Norling has contended that only the most saccharine observer can fail to note the ubiquity of human weakness:

Among the more disagreeable things he sees are hordes of venal politicians; prostitution; drug addiction; organized crime which touches businessmen, labor unions, politicians, policemen and judges, and which nobody seems able to do much about; millions of "workers" who work little indeed and then steal from their employers in the bargain; widespread "sharp practice" in business and advertising that approaches outright fraud; systematic tax evasion under a thousand guises; robberies; muggings; riots; murders—one could extend the list indefinitely. And these manifestations of man's willingness to cheat and abuse his fellows have existed in all societies, at all times, at all economic, social, and educational levels. . . . Christian theologians have had a simple explanation for this somber condition: they have charged it to Original Sin.[49]

Utopians of all stripes—including, of course, Marxists—promise the perfectibility of mankind and the elimination of war. The spiritual testimony of orthodox Christianity counsels skepticism in the face of such specious promises. The confusion of the eschatological promises of religion with the practical concerns of statecraft is likely to lead to something of the horrors found in Iran under the late Khomeini. As Niebuhr told us, "The New Testament does not . . . envisage a simple triumph of good over evil in history. It sees human history involved in the contradictions of sin to the end."[50]

The Christian realist views concentrations of power with great trepidation. In the Madisonian tradition of American politics, one could say that "the accumulation of all powers, legislative, executive, and judiciary, in the same hands, whether of one, a few, or many, and whether hereditary, self-appointed, or elective, may justly be pronounced the very definition of tyranny" (*Federalist* 47). Thus, the Christian realist regards *separation of powers* in domestic affairs and *balance of power* in international affairs as means of preserving both order and peace. The idea of divided and checked power, to the Christian realist, is in accord with the verities of human nature. Niebuhr, as always, puts it well:

A balance of power is something different from, and inferior to, the harmony of love. It is a basic condition of justice, given the sinfulness of man. Such a balance of power does not exclude love. In fact, without love the frictions and tensions of a balance of power would become intolerable. But without the balance of power even the most loving relations may degenerate into unjust relations and love may become the screen which hides the injustice.[51]

Those who expect the easy (and the earthly) triumph of the millennium; the end to war; the establishment of legal, political, or social utopia; the reign of full international or interpersonal harmony—are pursuing a chimera. Although *balance of power* is a nebulous term,[52] the notion does convey the idea of resolute pursuit of peace and harmony, but always with the kind of appropriate prudence and circumspection which history and Proverbs 27:1 advise: "Boast not of tomorrow, for you know not what any day may bring forth."

CONCLUSION

One suspects, then, that war has many causes—and no cure. Although war cannot be eliminated by human science or statecraft, it can perhaps be arrested if we can remember that internationally as well as domestically, "ambition must be made to counteract ambition." As Madison goes on to ask, in the fifty-first *Federalist*, "what is government itself but the greatest of all reflections on human nature?" To study war is to study human nature, the first level of analysis. To study human nature is to know the awesome mosaic of our human potentials—and of our human perils. How are we to save humankind from the scourge of war? Each person must answer the question in his own way. As I do not expect an end to political tension and turmoil, neither do I expect an immediate end to human life on earth through nuclear warfare—provided we can avert the dangers of unused,[53] unknown,[54] and undistributed[55] power. But, as Inis Claude has written, "We must be aware that power will always be with us, and thus the possibility of the violent disruption of order."[56]

But, then, if there is no utopia on the horizon, whom do we trust? Whence comes eternal peace? Some would trust genetic engineering; some, psychological research; others, socialist politics. I reject these as largely irrelevant. I look elsewhere for that full and final peace which humanity, unaided by a higher power, can never wholly achieve. And I recall the ancient petition: *Agnus dei, qui tollis peccata mundi, dona nobis pacem.* (Lamb of God, who takes away the sins of the world, grant us peace.)

NOTES

1. Epigraph to Bernard Norling, *Timeless Problems in History* (Notre Dame, IN: University of Notre Dame Press, 1970).

2. Epigraph to Morris West, *Proteus* (New York: Bantam, 1979).

3. Michael Howard, "The Causes of Wars," *The Wilson Quarterly* 8 (Summer 1984): 95. In his book *The Causes of War* (New York: The Free Press, 1973), Blainey contends that "War is a dispute about the measurement of power" (p. 114).

4. Walter M. Miller, Jr., *A Canticle for Leibowitz* (New York: Bantam, 1959), p. 245. Emphasis in original.

5. See Article 2(4) but note Article 51. Israel has been a member of the United Nations since 11 May 1949. Consider Menachem Begin's remark that the 7 June 1981 raid on the Iraqi nuclear facility was a "morally supreme act of self-defense. No fault whatsoever on our side" (*Time*, 22 June 1981: 30). A little more than ten years after that remark, many Americans may have been better disposed to accept its logic!

6. See, for example, Joshua 8, Judges 15, Sirach 12:10, Matthew 24:6, Mark 13:7, Luke 21:9. In Chapter 7 of this book, a lengthy textual analysis is presented.

7. R. E. Dupuy and T. N. Dupuy, *The Encyclopedia of Military History*, revised ed. (New York: Harper and Row, 1977), p. 1.

8. "Press: Second Thoughts on Schell," *Time*, 3 May 1982. Another useful *Time* piece is in its issue of 19 April 1982: 20–21.

9. See, for example, Russell Seitz, "In From the Cold: 'Nuclear Winter' Melts Down," *The National Interest* 5 (Fall 1986): 3–17.

10. *Time*, 9 March 1970, p. 47.

11. Much of the preceding, and this definition, is based upon Quincy Wright, *A Study of War*, abridged by Louise L. Wright (Chicago, IL: University of Chicago Press, 1964), ch. 1, p. 7.

12. See, for example, Herman Kahn, *On Escalation* (New York: Praeger, 1965), Henry Eccles, *Military Concepts and Philosophy* (New Brunswick, NJ: Rutgers University Press, 1965), Richard A. Falk and Samuel S. Kim, eds., *The War System: An Interdisciplinary Approach* (Boulder, CO: Westview, 1980), and Julian Lider, *On the Nature of War* (Swedish Institute of International Affairs, 1977; distributed in the U.S.A. by Renouf USA, Inc., Brookfield, VT).

13. "Surprise from the Swing Man," *Time*, 29 June 1981: 48.

14. Thomas E. Murray made the distinction. *New Catholic Encyclopedia*, 1967, s.v. "War," by W. V. O'Brien.

15. Charles Lofgren, "How New is Limited War?" *Military Review* 47 (July 1967): 18.

16. The distinguished military historian Theodore Ropp says simply that "War is a violent conflict between states" in *The Encyclopedia Americana*, 1980, s.v. "War." But there can be internal or guerrilla war.

17. To pursue this subject, see the extremely useful study by James E. Dougherty and Robert L. Pfaltzgraff, *Contending Theories of International Relations*, 3d ed. (New York: Harper & Row, 1990); Francis A. Beer, *Peace Against War* (San Francisco, CA: W. H. Freeman, 1981); and Patrick Morgan, *Theories and Approaches to International Relations*, 3d ed. (New Brunswick, NJ: Transaction Books, 1981). The bibliography of the present book contains a number of references which can be profitably consulted.

18. See David Hackett Fischer, *Historians' Fallacies: Toward a Logic of Historical Thought* (New York: Harper & Row, 1970).

19. Konrad Lorenz, *On Aggression*, trans. Marjorie K. Wilson (New York: Bantam, 1966), p. 233.

20. Robert Ardrey, *African Genesis* (New York: Atheneum, 1963), pp. 316, 318. See also his book *The Territorial Imperative* (New York: Atheneum, 1966).

21. Ashley Montagu, ed., *Man and Aggression*, 2d ed. (New York: Oxford University Press, 1973), p. xix.

22. Sally Carrighar, "War Is Not in Our Genes," *The New York Times Magazine*, 10 September 1967: 74 et seq. Reprinted in Montagu (above, n. 21), pp. 122–35. (Quotation on p. 135.)

23. For example, see John Dollard, Leonard Doob, Neal Miller, et al., *Frustration and Aggression* (New Haven, CT: Yale University Press, 1939).

24. Sigmund Freud, *Civilization and Its Discontents*, trans. and ed. James Strachey (New York: Norton, 1961), pp. 58–59.

25. See Anthony Storr, *Human Aggression* (New York: Atheneum, 1968), pp. 11–14. See also Storr's book *Human Destructiveness* (New York: Morrow, 1972).

26. Erich Fromm, *The Anatomy of Human Destructiveness* (New York: Holt, Rinehart and Winston, 1973).

27. Stanley Milgram, *Obedience to Authority: An Experimental View* (New York: Harper & Row, 1974).

28. Arthur Schlesinger, Jr., "Can Psychiatry Save the Republic?" *Saturday Review/World*, 7 September 1974: 15.

29. Morton A. Kaplan, in his review of *Old Myths and New Realities*, by J. W. Fulbright, in *World Politics* 17 (January 1965): 361.

30. Based upon Dougherty and Pfaltzgraff (above, n. 17), pp. 317–20.

31. "The Case for War," *Time*, 9 March 1970: 46.

32. John G. Stoessinger, *Why Nations Go to War*, 5th ed. (New York: St. Martin's Press, 1990), p. 209. Original in italics.

33. Arthur H. Westing, *Warfare in a Fragile World* (New York: Crane, Russak, & Co., 1980).

34. See Kenneth Waltz, *Man, the State, and War: A Theoretical Analysis* (New York: Columbia University Press, 1959).

35. See James A. Stegenga, "The Physiology of Aggression (and of Warfare?)" *International Journal of Group Tensions* 8 (1978): 65.

36. John Hersey, *The War Lover* (New York: Bantam, 1959), p. 376.

37. Barbara W. Tuchman, "An Inquiry into the Persistence of Unwisdom in Government," *Parameters* 10 (March 1980): 6–7. This particular passage is filled with so many fallacies that one could fill a page merely by citing them. One suspects that Tuchman, a highly intelligent and disinterested historian, if pressed, would have conceded the weakness of this passage, which is cited for illustrative purposes only.

38. For background information, see John E. Wiltz, *In Search of Peace: the Senate Munitions Inquiry, 1934–1936* (Baton Rouge, LA: Louisiana State University Press, 1963).

39. Falk and Kim (above, n. 12), p. 376. For a different view, see Richard Barnet, *Roots of War* (Baltimore, MD: Penguin Books, 1972).

40. A.F.K. Organski and Jacek Kugler, *The War Ledger* (Chicago, IL: Univer-

sity of Chicago Press, 1980). Cf. Paul Kennedy, *The Rise and Fall of the Great Powers: Economic Change and Military Conflict from 1500 to 2000* (New York: Random House, 1987).

41. For a similar judgment, see Grant T. Hammond, *Plowshares into Swords* (Columbia, SC: University of South Carolina Press, 1992).

42. For more details, see Falk and Kim, eds. (above, n. 12), Part VI. A decade ago, Arno J. Mayer, in *The Persistence of the Old Regime* (New York: Pantheon, 1981) looked at social stratification before World War I.

43. Werner Levi, *The Coming End of War* (Beverly Hills, CA: Sage, 1981).

44. Inis L. Claude, Jr., *Power and International Relations* (New York: Random House, 1962), pp. 260–61.

45. Kaplan (above, n. 29), p. 341.

46. *New Catholic Encyclopedia*, 1967, s.v. "War," by W. V. O'Brien.

47. Hersey (above, n. 36), p. 381.

48. Cecil Crabb, Jr., *American Foreign Policy in the Nuclear Age*, 3d ed. (New York: Harper and Row, 1972), p. 31.

49. Norling (above, n. 1), p. 102.

50. Reinhold Niebuhr, *Christianity and Power Politics* (New York: Scribner, 1940; reprint edition, Archon Books, 1969), p. 20.

51. Ibid., pp. 26–27.

52. As Claude (above, n. 44) says, "The immediate task [of world politics], in short, is to make the world safe for the balance of power system, and the balance system safe for the world" (p. 284).

53. One is reminded of Sir Robert Thompson's equation: national power equals manpower plus applied resources times *will*. See Richard Nixon, *The Real War* (New York: Warner, 1980), pp. 43, 306. *The Almanac of World Military Power*, 4th ed. (San Rafael, CA: Presidio Press, 1980) defines military power as "the capability of a nation to employ armed forces effectively in support of national objectives by exerting influence on the performance of other nations." Military power is never, by itself, the answer to a political challenge; but failure justly and wisely to use military power may be as dangerous, in some circumstances, as adventurism.

54. For a good analysis, see Blainey (above, n. 3): "War is a dispute about the measurement of power" (p. 114).

55. "In a world whose moving force is the aspiration of sovereign nations for power, peace can be maintained only by two devices. One is the self-regulatory mechanism of . . . the balance of power. The other consists of normative limitations . . . in the form of international law, international morality, and world public opinion." Hans J. Morgenthau, *Politics Among Nations*, 5th ed. (New York: Knopf, 1973), p. 24.

56. Claude (above, n. 44), p. 285.

3 THE AVATARS OF POWER: WAR AND POLITICS

War is a matter of vital importance to the State; the province of life or death; the road to survival or ruin. It is mandatory that it be thoroughly studied.[1]

—Sun Tzu (early fourth century B.C.)

[W]ar is not a mere act of policy but a true political instrument, a continuation of political activity by other means. What remains peculiar to war is simply the peculiar nature of its means.[2]

—von Clausewitz (1780–1831)

To this point in the book, I have argued that the leader of a country must be wise enough to fashion prudent political policies to meet the exigencies of statecraft; simultaneously, however, he must have sufficient moral vision to understand, in addition to what *is* being done, what *ought* to be done. The fusion thus achieved is true civic virtue. The contradictions and conflicts of our human condition will lead to ruin a leader, very likely with his nation in tow, who fails to understand both the immanent and the transcendent planes of magisterial responsibility. To the degree that the leader misapprehends human nature and congregated human nature (that is to say, the state), he puts at risk the political health of the society he directs. If, for example, Niebuhr is right that "all justice in human society rests upon some kind of balance of power,"[3] and if the leader does not grasp that reality, he has failed in the first instance: He does not know the foundation of politics. How, then, can he inspire his people to build the edifice of the state?

The purpose of this chapter is to inquire into what I call the "avatars" of power. *Avatar* is from Hindu mythology, meaning the incarnation of a god. Politics, especially Tinder's "politics of redemption," can take on the aspects of a god; that god can display its might through the means of force and violence. Hobbes's "Leviathan"— the mortal god—has practically unchecked power. Without the anchor of balanced power, the ship of state will drift into the shoals of totalitarianism. The wars of such states admit of no scheme of proportion, for there is no higher authority (save other nations' power) that it will respect. Here we will examine the idea of the nation and the state, the concept of tradition and fundamental values, the notion of leadership, the dilemmas of political responsibility, and the application of these concepts to limited war.

NATION AND STATE

To define a state in the usual manner—as a delimited area of territory administered by a competent government in charge of people and resources—may satisfy some juridical and onomastic purposes, but it conveys practically nothing to those seeking some understanding of the phenomenon of nationhood. "State," after all, is a legal fiction; "nation" is a socio-political fact. In modern times, the nation precedes the state;[4] that is, the state may be said to come into existence only when the people commonly subscribe to some ordered and purposeful association, and thereafter develop those institutions which promise to preserve and protect that association. For, as Stanley Hoffmann has said, "Unless the nation is a mere fiction, a territory with central power but not really a community, there must be some common values, if not about the polity, at least about society."[5]

Expressed most simply, a nation is an idea, a fundamental agreement, a heritage created by and shared among the population. Of all the theories of revolution which seek to explain why revolution occurs, perhaps the most discerning is the idea that revolution is the product of disenchantment: the sentiment grows that a trust has been violated, an ancient promise broken, a certain bond of faith betrayed. As Ernest Renan expressed it more than a hundred years ago, a nation is "a daily plebiscite."[6] When the popular concord which gave rise to the nation finally dissolves, the state cannot long be expected to survive.

A nation cannot be understood as a *product*. A nation is, rather, a *process* whereby a people's past, present, and future find some expression. The people of the nation are not merely the living, because the nation is comprised as well of those who have gone before and those who will come long after, both the dead and the unborn. There is, then, a corporate being which, while intangible, binds, in Edmund Burke's words, a man to his country with "ties which though light as air, are as strong as links of iron." As Walter Lippmann comments, "That is why young men die in battle for their country's sake and why old men plant trees they will never sit under."[7] There is no more powerful expression of this idea than that provided by President Lincoln on the eve of the Civil War:

We are not [he told southerners] enemies but friends. We must not be enemies.

Though passion may have strained, it must not break our bonds of affection. The mystic chords of memory stretching from every battle-field and patriot's grave to every living heart and hearthstone all over this broad land, will yet swell the chorus of the Union, when again touched, as surely they will be, by the better angels of our nature.[8]

"A nation," Ernest Renan said, "is a soul, a spiritual principle. Two things . . . make up this soul . . . a rich heritage of memories; and . . . the desire to make the most of the joint inheritance . . . . To share the glories of the past . . . and [to] desire to do more—these are the essential conditions of a people's being." Renan concludes: "to have suffered, rejoiced and hoped together; these are things of greater value than identity of customs-houses and frontiers in accordance with strategic notions."[9]

To be sure, one can carry all this too far, but the idea is a sound one. The "mystic chords of memory" which tie together those who share a nationality are not easily created—or broken. One does not wish a nation (or a global government, for that matter) into existence. Although it may well have been true about 1648 or so that the state (that is, the institutions of inchoate government) created the nation (that is, pulled people together, to some extent), the reverse has been the case, as we have seen, since about 1789. A nation, therefore, must, in fact, understand itself. As George Kennan put it:

[E]ach [sovereign entity] has had some overall purpose, going beyond just the routine chores of government—some purpose to which the total of its political life was supposed to be dedicated and by which its existence as a separate political entity was supposed to be justified. The purpose may often have been crude and not too clearly formulated. It may in some instances have been more felt than expressed. It may at times have been repressed and temporarily forgotten under the stress of some great external danger. But I suspect it has always been there.[10]

In order to feel worthy of itself, and in order to justify its continued existence, a state develops for itself some role, some mission, some series of ideals which it takes upon itself, through a national mythology, to represent. It could not be otherwise. Even as people need a purpose to impart some meaning to their lives, so do nations. Even as people create customs and concepts to imbue their daily life with purpose, so do nations develop customs, laws, and institutions to embody their national experience. As journalist Max Ways put it, "No society can exist without some fixed points of truth, held in common. The points can change; they can be the subject of conflict; they can be more or less consciously held. But they are the indispensable web of co-operation."[11]

NATIONAL INTEREST

That "indispensable web" has another name: the national interest. Whether an a priori national interest exists for a nation-state[12] is, of course, a debatable question.[13] Some hold that the national interest amounts to no more than what those in power say it is. But one must think it absurd that Hitler could have told the Germans what their national interest was. (It would have made no difference, by the way, had he won; the Nazi creed would have been no less a monstrous perversion regardless of any successes it might have enjoyed on the battlefield.) Some have suggested a way around this quandary. Abandon the idea of the national interest, they recommend, and concentrate instead on the idea of national interests. Although this is a sensible notion, it unfortunately overlooks (as is the wont of modern political science) the normative question: How are we to judge the worth, the merit, the value, of a state's actions? To hold that there is merely a cluster of competing interests at work within a state is to dismiss the notion that there is a transcendent national cause to which all parochial or provincial concerns are (or should be) subordinate. As Charles O. Lerche has written, "[T]here seems to be some danger in relegating the more general term to the discard and in concentrating entirely on what 'the decision-making group' in a state thinks is important." The national interest, he suggests, "might well be made in terms of a generalized version of interest rooted in mass tradition."[14]

In short, while it is hardly correct to say that in refereeing the national interest, the decision-making group is acting as arbitrarily as the dictator, neither view adequately examines or explains against what measure or provision or standard the decided-upon national interest (of the competing interests) is to be judged. Lerche does come close in referring to "mass tradition."

The national interest, to the Christian realist, has three tiers, as in a pyramid. The highest tier is that of material well-being. The second is the somewhat larger segment of national security. The third and largest tier is composed of those national core values to which Lincoln and Burke referred. Of course, these three tiers are complementary. But their order is significant. The nation's financial health obviously matters, for a nation in economic ruin cannot hope to effect its security. Although some would rank physical security as most important, this judgment appears to discount or to disregard the fact that a nation exists by common subscription to fundamental values. Sir Harold Nicolson once explained:

There does exist such a thing as international morality. Its boundaries are not visibly defined nor its frontiers demarcated; yet we all know where it is. If other countries transgress these frontiers, we at least should respect them. *Allis [sic] licet: tibi non licet.* That is to say, what is right for others is not right for us. That should be our motto; by that we shall in the end prevail.[15]

Should the nation consistently and substantially violate its own values in order to continue to exist, its very existence would thereby become counterfeit, and the nation will have betrayed the first "compact" under which that association was begun, as well as the traditions by which that association was continued.[16]

Two considerations in particular require brief comment. First, the national interest is exactly that: it refers to the physical and psychological well-being of the people in question. For that reason, the "interest" takes place over the "national." There is no requirement whatever that the concern of statesmen to serve the national interest demands of them an abandonment of the interests of others, a

renunciation of international fellowship, or a 'dismissal of the purposes and prospects of international organization. Without entering
here into all the philosophical nuances of the question, one may say
that the profound task of all statesmen is to guide their nations toward
the good and just life.

But it is precisely the good and just life about which logical
positivism and empirical political science have nothing to say. It
should come as no surprise, therefore, that scholars in those fields
must stand mute before the question of the national interest. They
can quantify and calculate the great questions of the avatars of power
(Who won the election? Who rules? for how long? with what
percentage of the populace in support?) and of war (What are the
probable causes of the conflict? What is the most efficient strategy to
win?), but they cannot weigh the great moral questions of the good of
power (Who should win? Who should have power? Why?) or the
good of war (Is going to war just? How can the war be waged
ethically?). It is with these kinds of questions that the national
interest has the most to do. Robert Osgood:

In its broadest sense, the interdependence of universal ideals and national
self-interest is simply a reflection of the fact that a man has a moral sense as
well as an ego and that both parts demand satisfaction. Consequently,
nations act with the greatest consistency and stability when their actions are
based upon a balance of egoism and idealism. For this reason most
compelling national ends are those self-interested ends, like survival, which
are most easily reconciled with idealistic ends, and those idealistic ends, like
the minimum standard of decency, which are most compatible with national
self-interest.[17]

A similar, classical rendition of this view is that of Montesquieu
(1689–1755), in *The Spirit of the Laws*: "The law of nations is
naturally founded on this principle, that different nations ought in
time of peace to do one another all the good they can, and in time of
war as little injury as possible, without prejudicing their real interests
[Book I, 3]."

It is literally vital for statesmen to realize, as Raymond Aron has
put it, that there is a "morality of responsibility," or, to use Adam
Ulam's phrase, "an immorality of unrealism."[18] A state's national
interest ought to imply both those things which can be compromised
and those things which cannot be compromised. To be aware of such
things is a mark of political maturity. Peremptorily to dismiss the idea

of national interest because of its necessarily nebulous qualities is to trivialize political science (knowledge of the polis), which is at its heart concerned with the nature of the best regime. A regime cannot be good, that is, worthy of respect, unless it knows both its history and its ethics. "It is only if we are aware of how our selection of goals, our vision, reflects our character that we may become truly free," wrote Stanley Hoffmann.[19] There is a great deal of sense, in terms of the national interest, in the famous promise that "You will know the truth, and the truth will set you free" (Jn. 8:32). Epistemologically, one cannot know what to do until one knows what ought to be done; similarly, a nation cannot choose a wise course of diplomacy until its leaders divine what ought to be done. Thus, the national interest may well exist independent of a ruler's perception, for the health of a nation consists in economic strength and in physical security; but, beyond that, the ultimate vitality of the nation is its moral integrity. And too many leaders lose that faculty on the way to the forum.

CRUCIAL, OR CORE, VALUES

To discuss balance of power as a panacea is, of course, mistaken, for it is no such thing. The notion of balance of power is a political rubric, not a chemical formula. It is opportunistic, not deterministic. It is no magical, mythical, or mystical philosopher's stone to resolve the enigmas of statecraft. There is, in short, no replacement for the statesman's trained acumen and learned intuition. But a statesman wholly out of joint with the norms, mores, and traditions—that is, the core values—of his society can be no leader. Certainly the leader can and must exert a healthy and hortatory effect on his citizenry; he can urge them to accept his judgments according to the circumstances and challenges of the moment. But the leader normally cannot effect resounding change in the very fabric of the society he leads. To some considerable extent, the leader reflects the treasury of principles he inherits. As three scholars put it, a nation's principles "are deeply imbedded in the general culture and political philosophy of a society and are powerful, if intangible and subjective, guides to action."[20]

A nation of down-to-earth, practical people, Americans find discussion along these lines too ethereal—that is, too "mushy"—for comfort. Realists like to think of the national interest in relatively clear ways, pretty much dictated by the kind of geopolitical analysis which Mackinder or Spykman or Mahan might have done.[21] And there is much point and purpose to those kinds of studies. They are necessary; they are not sufficient. The Christian realist will want to know the purpose factors as well as the power factors. What can we do? What should we do? What are the probable results? Cook and Moos explain the reasons:

The United States is the heir and standard-bearer of a culture begotten and bred in Europe. That culture rests on the twin foundations of Greco-Roman politics and law and Judaeo-Christian ethics and religion. Our own tradition and history give us a unique position as modern champions of those ancient insights.[22]

"It was not for nothing," commented Denis Brogan, "that the founders of the Republic adopted a proud Latin motto: 'Novus ordo seclorum,' a new order of the ages."[23] The Christian, as I will argue in Chapter 7, must guard against excesses of idealism and of enthusiasm. The realist must guard against excesses of pessimism. The Christian realist must season a reasonably positive outlook with the condiment of canniness. As Kissinger expressed it, "Our moral convictions must arm us to face the ambiguity inseparable from the long haul or else they will wind up disarming us."[24]

Choosing the right course between the sword and the cross is no easy chore. Examples could be multiplied but one of interest, given the labyrinth of Middle Eastern politics, is the comment in 1967 of then Soviet Premier Aleksei Kosygin, who asked President Lyndon Johnson at Glassboro to explain the American commitment to Israel. "I don't understand you Americans backing Israel. There are 80 million Arabs and only 3 million Israelis. It does not make sense. Why do it?" Replied Johnson: "Because it is right."[25] Accepting hardheaded geopolitical advice is wise, provided that it not frustrate what is "right." The cynic could dismiss Johnson's line, asking how many Jewish voters there are in the United States. Still, in this instance, the inveterate politico Lyndon Johnson was, at least in my view, reacting precisely as an American leader of the time should have reacted. But such an opinion would have dumbfounded Machiavelli (1469–1527); as he put it in the *Prince*: "But so wide is the separation between the way men actually live and the way that they ought to live, that anyone who turns his attention from what is actually done to what ought to be done, studies his ruin rather than his preservation [Chapter 15]."

Tension is at the heart of balance, whether on a tightrope or in politics. One must manage the affairs of state. Those who dismiss ethics as flighty at least resolve tension. Similarly, those who dismiss reason of state as villainous incur no tensions. "Saints," Arthur Schlesinger, Jr. wrote, "can be pure, but statesmen must be responsible." And because most of the "raw material of foreign affairs is . . . morally neutral or ambiguous . . . [in] the great majority of foreign policy transactions, moral principles cannot be decisive."[26] But the leader, true to his national principles and to those truly crucial values which endow his country with purpose can ignore neither ethics nor politics, for in their appropriate harmony is to be found the real national interest. Hans Morgenthau, incorrectly considered by many to be the most intransigent apostle of *Realpolitik*, had it exactly correct in this appraisal:

A foreign policy that does not permit mass extermination as a means to its end does not impose this limitation upon itself because of considerations of political expediency. On the contrary, expediency would counsel such a thorough and effective operation. The limitation derives from an absolute moral principle . . . [and] sacrifices the national interest where its consistent pursuit would necessitate the violation of a moral principle, such as the prohibition of mass killings in times of peace.[27]

Dean Acheson, Truman's Secretary of State, said that the "means we choose to overcome the obstacles in our path must be consonant with our deepest moral sense."[28] Journalist Max Ways asked, "Who would dare explain American policy as derived from our 'sacred honor'? The phrase has become worse than hallowly archaic; moderns find it downright offensive." Such a phrase, of course, is not to be found in the contemporary lexicon of political science. "Yet it is with 'sacred honor' that the political function of the people has most to do."[29] As the war in Vietnam finally ended, the editor of *Time* said simply that, "we also expect our foreign policy to enable us to feel good about being Americans."[30] More than fifteen years later, as the Gulf War of 1991 ended, the same magazine reported that President Bush believed that the war had "nothing to do with religion per se. It has, on the other hand, everything to do with what religion embodies: good vs. evil, right vs. wrong."[31] Bush clearly believed that he had a moral imperative to wage that war, which he believed (as did the vast majority of Americans) to be wholly just.[32] What is morally correct *can* also be politically wise. A nation's history and mores can serve as a beacon light to the statesman whose task it is to forge the chains linking the sword and the cross.

THE ORDEAL OF LEADERSHIP

The statesman has the responsibility of conducting a dialogue of sorts with the traditions he represents. To be sure, the statesman must be aware of the character of the people, but he cannot be intimidated by it; he must be faithful to the precepts and purposes of his nation, but he cannot be overcome by them; he must master the customs and mores of his nation, yet he must not be mesmerized by them. In short, the logic of the national experience provides the statesman with knowledge of what he must do to preserve and to promulgate his country's core values, but nowhere does it tell him how it is to be done. "What a political leader wants to do," explained Max Ways, "and what he can do are determined as much by the basic beliefs of a society as by considerations of technical power."[33] Irving Kristol's succinct explanation merits quotation:

If foreign policy is to be judged (as it must) by public opinion, this can have reference only to its moral dimension—the people are not in a position intelligently to analyse the intricacies of military technology or economic development, whereas they can (or so the American system assumes) take a fair reading of this policy's more general aspects, and especially can express its opinion whether it is "in the American grain." It is absurd to ask the public to do more; it is folly to ask it to do less.[34]

The notion that something "just isn't right" can fill a social scientist accustomed to exactitude with unspeakable horror. But values cannot always be articulated; many must be felt. Those values which are born of the national experience, and inculcated into the citizenry by the national customs and mores, may never be expressed exactly in the polls and may take time to mature, but they are there nonetheless. And it is these which set the parameters within which democratic politicians have the freedom to exercise their authority. "The function of the public in a democratic policy-making process," says Gabriel Almond, "is to set certain policy criteria in the form of widely held values and expectations."[35]

During the Cuban missile crisis, Robert F. Kennedy argued that the United States could not launch a surprise attack on the Cubans because it would destroy the American moral position at home and around the world.[36] Not only must the leader refrain from choosing unjust ends; he must also refrain from choosing unjust means. The central burden of Christian realist leadership lies in the statesman's twin responsibilities of discerning what he ought to do (and then balancing that with what he, in fact, can do) and then organizing a coherent, cogent program to implement his evaluation. "But the responsibility of leaders is not simply to affirm an objective," writes Kissinger. "It is above all to endow it with a meaning compatible with the values of their society."[37] The statesman must do what is right, insofar as he is empowered to do so; but first he must see the right, insofar as he is empowered to do that. President Lincoln told his southern countrymen, as he assumed his high office, that the government would not attack them: "You have no oath registered in Heaven to destroy the Government, while I shall have the most solemn one to 'preserve, protect, and defend' it."[38] Kennedy would not do something; Lincoln could not forbear doing something—both in the name of justice, both in the name of the national interest. Both were right.

Leaders can err, of course, by being too aggressive, too egocentric. That is well known. Less known is another kind of leadership failure—the failure of moral cowardice. "Democratic politicians," said Walter Lippmann, "rarely feel they can afford the luxury of telling the whole truth to the people." Although his case may be overstated, there is entirely too much truth to this ringing indictment:

With exceptions so rare that they are regarded as miracles and freaks of nature, successful democratic politicians are insecure and intimidated men. They advance politically only as they placate, appease, bribe, seduce, bamboozle, or otherwise manage to manipulate the demanding and threatening elements in their constituencies. The decisive consideration is not whether the proposition is good but whether it is popular—not whether it will work well and prove itself but whether the active talking constituents like it immediately.[39]

Dean Acheson has a partial explanation for this unhappy phenomenon:

[The American people] can never do what is necessary until they understand what is necessary, and why; and they will never understand that until their leaders in government, business, and labor are willing to tell them. This takes more courage—and vision too—than most leaders, trained and aspiring to succeed in a special and limited constituency, have at their command.[40]

The point here is not that leaders are liars, although some are. Rather, the problem is the natural tendency of leaders to tell the people what they want to hear. The people want to hear that their sons and daughters are at war for a holy reason; tell them that. The people want to believe that peace is at hand; tell them that. The people want to believe that a given problem has been eternally resolved; tell them that. The people want to believe that their country always represents exalted purpose; tell them that. Merely because, to use Kennan's phrase, "[T]he truth about external reality will never be wholly compatible with those internal ideological fictions which the national state engenders and by which it lives,"[41] does not and cannot excuse the leader from telling the citizenry the truth: that Americans fight wars for political advantage; that peace is the fortuitous product of skillful diplomacy, prudent military policy, and damned good luck; that problems may take on new shapes but are hardly ever solved; that America, while it may have some legitimate claims to success and virtue, is as prone to "sin" as any other nation in the world. Those are the principal tenets of Christian realism; they do not square with the demotic mind, for

[O]ne of the main purposes of society is to conceal these truths [about power] from its members. That concealment, that elaborate and subtle and purposeful understanding of the nature of political man and of political society, is one of the cornerstones upon which all societies are founded.[42]

The leader must have a sense of human limitation; he must not have too much zeal. To dissemble or to deceive about the need either for ethical concern or for political expediency, properly balanced, is to fail in the premier task of leadership, which is education—thus once again tying politics, ethics, and education together.

Morgenthau succinctly captures the gist of the preceding by saying simply that "The statesman, then, is allowed neither to surrender to popular passions nor disregard them. He must strike a prudent balance between adapting himself to them and marshaling them to the support of his policies. In one word, he must lead."[43] More than seventy years ago, Elihu Root (1845–1937) wrote that

[T]here is a human way to prevent the people from having an erroneous opinion. That way is to furnish the people, as a part of their ordinary education, with correct information about their relations to other peoples, about the limitations upon their own rights, about their duties to respect the rights of others, about what has happened and is happening in international affairs, and about the effects upon national life of the things that are done or refused as between nations; so that the people themselves will have the means to test misinformation and appeals to prejudice and passion based upon error.[44]

I define *leadership* as the ability to inspire appropriate action beyond the expectable. "The expectable" is the routine suggested by national mores. This routine of belief or deed may at times be all right as such. When the belief or deed emanating from the national mores is, in the leader's judgment, somehow inadequate or defective, he must be able to inspire, that is, to teach, in order to transcend the routine. The fallacy here is clear, of course: Lincoln is dead. In order to instill civic virtue, the leader must be virtuous. And while some leaders may correctly sometimes be so described, we recognize as Christian realists that all leaders are prone to error and to excesses of ego. The vicious leader (and they abound in history) teaches, by word or deed, vice. The ancient wisdom of political science warns us not to trust too much: *Quis custodiet ipsos custodes?* "Who will guard those who are themselves the guardians?" The modern political arena is not the bailiwick of moral philosophers intent upon learning, and then effectively teaching, virtue. One greets adjurations to have the leaders enlighten us with the wry smile of seasoned cynicism.

VOX POPULI, VOX DEI?

The obverse part of the "Great Man" Theory of history suggests that, if most progress and significant events are the products of great leaders, most perversity and corruption are also the results of the machinations of puissant personalities. The solution to the problem is democratization. The people, it is sometimes argued, are not responsible for the depredations of venal leaders.

It is a somewhat gratifying idea, after all, that good people are seduced by bad leaders, that good citizens are shamefully represented by odious governments. But that such is often mere fiction is suggested by Fouad Ajami, who points out, in an essay about Saddam Hussein, that "Deep in the Arab psyche there is an attraction, a fatal attraction, to the swagger of the strongman . . . . Despots always work with a culture's yearnings, with its sins of omission and commission." He quotes the Prophet Muhammed: "You will get the rulers you deserve."[45] Are the Germans, and the Russians, and the Japanese, and the Italians, and many Latin Americans (and many others) *culturally* responsible for the tyrants that have arisen in their midst? Daniel Boorstin has suggested that while, on the one hand, we like to say that we had no quarrel with the Iraqi people (nor with the German or Japanese people in World War II), at the same time our Lockean political tradition counsels us to believe that rulers govern with the consent of the governed. People everywhere ought to be reminded, Boorstin says, that "their dictators are only their servants."[46] Christian realism instructs us plainly that there is no necessary virtue in numbers. In the first public opinion poll, Bishop Fulton Sheen once wrote, the crowd chose Barabbas over Jesus.

Part of our suspicion of democracy consists in the fear that it will degenerate into ochlocracy. Public opinion is always just that: public, which can mean ordinary (having both positive and negative connotation) and opinion, possibly suggesting mere conjecture rather than knowledge. As Walter Lippmann once wrote:

The rule to which there are few exceptions . . . is that at the critical junctures, when the stakes are high, the prevailing mass public opinion will impose what amounts to a veto upon changing the course on which the government is at the time proceeding. Prepare for war in time of peace? No. It is bad to raise taxes, to unbalance the budget [a dated book!], to take men away from their schools or jobs, to provoke the enemy. Intervene in a developing conflict? No. Avoid the risk of war. Withdraw from the area of conflict? No. The adversary must not be appeased. Reduce your claims on the area? No. Righteousness cannot be compromised. Negotiate a compromise peace as soon as the opportunity presents itself? No. The aggressor must be punished. Remain armed to enforce the dictated settlement? No. The war is over.
The unhappy truth is that the prevailing public opinion has been destructively wrong at the critical junctures.[47]

Walter Lippmann lived long enough (1889–1974) to see his idea of the strong executive emerge—only to become corrupted into the "imperial presidency"!

If we must be suspicious of individual leaders, as well as of the nation they represent (whether in honor or in shame), can we resolve our problem by ratcheting the whole thing up a notch? If nationality groupings can be dangerous, either because of or despite their leaders (whose power they anoint or acquiesce in), can we rely upon the peace instinct of an emerging global community, which, some write, will ordain peace if sovereign governments will so permit? It is, of course, generally not true. Michael Howard suggests that these kinds of assumptions mar the thinking of many of those in "peace research," in which many tend to assume a homogeneity of thought-process and value-systems through-out the world, and posit the essential artificiality of national barriers to free communication. Governments and state-mechanisms are seen, by these schools, not as the representatives and the spokesmen of their peoples, but as their gaolers [jailers], inhibiting rather than fostering international understanding.

Professor Howard compares this kind of thinking to that of Cobden (1804–1865), one of "optimism based on ignorance":

[T]he belief that if only *peoples* could get together behind the backs of their *governments*, peace would be no problem. There is, they believe, a world community latent which is basically their own writ large; and it is only the archaic and self-interested apparatus of national governments and bureau-cracies and armed forces which stands in the way of its realisation.

Howard points out that the chief fallacy behind all this is the specious notion that "approaches and techniques that may be valid in creating peace *within* a particular culture can be transferred to an interna-tional, culturally heterogeneous environment."[48] As one interna-tional law scholar put it, "Common sense and a hard look at the world as it is appear to dictate the view that such conceptions [about an inchoate global community] are little more than lovely mirages."[49]

THE QUANDARY

Christian realism understands, with Morgenthau, that we have largely lost those objective criteria which allow us to distinguish between good men and scoundrels, between art and trash. "What the crowd desires and tolerates becomes the ultimate standard of what is good, true, beautiful, useful, and wise. What you can get away with . . . is morally permitted."[50] Fearful of untutored opinion, we must at the same time be leery of consolidated power. To the extent that any solution exists on this earth to this perennial problem, it derives from the classic Madisonian formulation:

Ambition must be made to counteract ambition . . . . It may be a reflec-tion on human nature that such devices should be necessary to control the abuses of government. But what is government itself but the greatest of all reflections on human nature? If men were angels, no government would be necessary. If angels were to govern men, neither external nor internal controls on government would be necessary. In framing a government which is to be administered by men over men, the great difficulty lies in this: you must first enable the government to control the governed; and in the next place oblige it to control itself [*Federalist* 51].

No better statement of Christian realist political wisdom exists. We know that leaders *and* people can err. That a check-and-balance system be instituted is no guarantee of wise public policy; but it is a better bet than a concentration of power in one man's hands, for that can lead to tyranny, or unrelieved power in the hands of the masses, for that can lead to mobocracy. One author tried to resolve the leader-people impasse by defining democracy as a government of the people by an elite sprung from the people.[51] The essential truth of human government is this: it offers, at its best, a temporary balancing of competing political forces so that the public order might be preserved and the genuine national interest advanced; it offers, at its worst, a monopoly of power wielded for the selfish ends of the tyrant or the horde, irrespective of the legitimate national interest. Finally, we must recapture the truth that the national interest, natural law, "right reason," Lippmann's "public philosophy," and the civic virtue are one. A national interest prosecuted in behalf of the selfish lusts of the tyrant or in behalf of the equally selfish desires of the throng is by no measure a "national interest." But how are we to judge unless we can determine, not just what is, but what *ought to be*? (See Chapter 8 for discussion.)

RELEVANCE TO WAR

When the statesman fails to appreciate the need for balanced power within his society, he imperils the nation; when he fails to understand the same logic in the international arena, he endangers his region—or the globe. Kant was right in saying that a state of peace had to be established. But, as Michael Howard suggests, "What perhaps even he did not discern was that this is a task which has to be tackled afresh every day of our lives; and that no formula, no organisation and no political or social revolution can ever free mankind from this inexorable duty."[52]

As I will argue later in this book, there is *no solution to the problem of war*, which is not to say that certain wars cannot be prevented or their effects, at minimum, assuaged. Reinhold Niebuhr knew, as one scholar expressed it, that "the limits of human imagination, the easy subservience of reason to the passions, and the persistence of collective irrationalism and egoism make social conflict inevitable in human history, probably to its very end."[53] Despite the admonitions of Niebuhr and others, Americans seem still to be waiting for a political Godot. "Perhaps no major nation," as Kissinger wrote, "has been so uncomfortable with the exercise of vast power as the United States. We have tended to consider war as 'unnatural,' as an interruption of our vocation of peace, prosperity, and liberty."[54] Consider another secretary of state (Cordell Hull) who, returning from the 1943 Moscow conference, declared that, "there will no longer be need for spheres of influence, for balances of power, or any other of the special arrangements through which, in the unhappy past, the nations strove to safeguard their security or promote their interests."[55]

As Greg Russell has written: "Americans have typically regarded the struggle for power as a social aberration—the consequence of ignorance, faulty institutional arrangements, or the suppression of the public voice."[56] In fact, war, as was discussed in the preceding chapter, emanates from three levels of analysis: the interstate system, intranational politics, and from individual mental or moral aberrations. What is frequently not perceived is that, at all three levels, there is a striking similarity: the contest for mastery and self-exaltation, which are the product of unrestrained personal (or national) ego.

LIMITED WAR

In his plaintive memoirs, General William Westmoreland contends that "The intellectual community and some who represented it in government . . . had no comprehension of the use of force." In this regard, he quotes with approval the Duke of Wellington's admonition to the House of Lords: "A great country cannot wage a little war."[57] If many of our generals and politicians have had trouble with the idea of limited war (stretching back to the Korean War), there can be no doubt that war, to be just, *must* be limited. One U.S. Navy officer had it right in saying that "unlimited war has become suicidal—so that, like it or not, we must be prepared to fight limited wars."[58] Limited war is not a new idea; in fact, limited wars have been fought throughout history. Most wars have been fought for objectives that were far short of total domination or annihilation of the enemy. In a sense, even World War II was limited. Robert Osgood contends that

A limited war is now broadly defined as a war that is fought for ends far short of the complete subordination of one state's will to another's and by means involving far less than the total military resources of the belligerents, leaving the civilian life and the armed forces of the belligerents largely intact and leading to a bargained termination.[59]

A close student of international law, William O'Brien, says simply that a limited war is one in which "political ends always determine military means" and in which the civilian authority "controls the use of the military instrument." "This is," he says, "the first and foremost guideline of limited war."[60] Thus a limited war is an international conflict in which both ends and means are circumscribed—both politically and militarily. In a word, the idea of limited war is "compellence,"[61] which implies the application of military coercion in order to achieve a political objective.

If, however, we conceive of politics, not as a means of resolving and accommodating competing interests, but as an end in itself (see Chapter 8 for full discussion), then war must be total and the enemy must be evil incarnate. We become the crusaders; the enemy becomes the infidel. T. R. Fehrenbach provides this insight into the traditional American understanding of war:

War could never be part of a system of checks and balances; the view seemed immoral. War must always be for a cause, a transcendental purpose: it must not be to restore the Union, but to make men free; it must not be to save the balance of world power from falling into unfriendly hands, but to make the world safe for democracy; it must not be to rescue allies, but to destroy evil.[62]

This is not the place to explore this theme at length. But one can point out that Americans responded with insouciance to Churchill's ideas about seizing Berlin and Prague before the Russians as the war wound down, with Eisenhower expressing reluctance to risk American soldiers' lives "for purely political purposes."[63] A similar notion existed as the Gulf War of 1991 erupted, with some protestors asserting, "No blood for oil!" Although the notion of a "political war" is anathema to many Americans, there is no alternative, save the crusade or absolute refusal to fight.

The idea of limited war flows naturally from the idea of balanced powers, an idea which, in turn, owes its genesis to a circumscribed understanding of politics. Clearly, if the state itself is man's telos and reason for being, then the state's wars are invested with a totality which admits of no limitations. Wise people and sage leaders, however, understand, with Clausewitz and with Sun Tzu, that politics and war are means to the end of the preservation of the national interest. To quote T. R. Fehrenbach, "It was hard for a nation and a people who had never accepted the idea of power, not as something in itself, but as a tool to whatever ends they sought, to fight and die for limited goals. In short, it was hard to grow up."[64]

CONCLUSION

"The remedy [for our present problems]," James MacGregor Burns wrote, "is the same as in 1776 and 1787—to rediscover our overarching values, to recommit ourselves to them, to restructure our institutions to fulfill them, and to support and sustain leaders who will serve them."[65] This chapter's principal thesis might well be put this way: In the beginning was the Agreement, and the Agreement was among the People who shared a common subscription to certain core values; all traditions, in time, sprang forth from these core values. And then there were leaders: they came as witnesses to give testimony to the traditions, that the best of them might be preserved. They themselves were not to usurp the traditions but to give testimony to those traditions.

This political adaptation of St. John is meant to underscore the central theme of this chapter: although a vigorous American leadership can and should dispel certain national myths in the service of realism in order to carry on viable diplomacy, there are core values about the nation (in whose name that nation explains its existence and purpose) which must never be abandoned. To make an avatar of politics in the belief that thereby all problems may be solved or averted is to idolize the profane at the expense of the truly sacred; what is more, in a world in which only limited wars can be just, a politics without limit invites wars without limit. If we are to deal effectively with politics and with war, we must understand the limitations each has and we must rediscover those axiomatic values which imbued our nation with meaning and purpose more than two centuries ago. Matthew Arnold, in *Self-Dependence*, once put it this way:

> O air-born voice! long since, severely clear,
> A cry like thine in mine own heart I hear,—
> "Resolve to be thyself; and know, that he
> Who finds himself loses his misery!" [Stanza 8]

Our national task, then, is to re-establish those values which we have neglected or forgotten, for wise politics proceeds, first of all, from a sense of who we are and what we value, that we might know, in turn, what we must do. Finally, understanding that politics is about proportion and limitation (and not about immoderation and zeal), we may learn, with Kissinger, that "Morality without security is ineffectual; security without morality is empty. To establish the relationship and proportion between these two goals is perhaps the most profound challenge before our government and our nation."[66]

NOTES

1. Sun Tzu, *The Art of War*, trans. Samuel B. Griffith (New York: Oxford University Press, 1963), p. 63.

2. Carl von Clausewitz, *On War*, ed. and trans. Michael Howard and Peter Paret (Princeton, NJ: Princeton University Press, 1976), p. 87. (Bk. I, Sec. 24).

3. Quoted in Arthur M. Schlesinger, Jr., *The Politics of Hope* (Boston, MA: Houghton Mifflin, 1963), p. 113

4. As Sir Ernest Barker has pointed out, "[Since the beginning of the nineteenth century], it is the nation which makes the State, and not the State which makes the nation. The creation of the State by the nation was an achievement of the French Revolution; it was the secret of the unification of Germany and Italy; it is the basis of 'succession' States that have issued from [World War I]." *National Character and the Factors in its Formation* (New York: Harper & Brothers, 1927), p. 125.

5. Stanley Hoffmann, *Gulliver's Troubles, or The Setting of American Foreign Policy* (New York: McGraw-Hill, 1968), p. 89.

6. Ernest Renan, "What is a Nation?" in *World Politics: The Writings of Theorists and Practitioners, Classical and Modern*, 2d ed., ed. Arend Lijphart (Boston, MA: Allyn and Bacon, 1971), p. 90.

7. Walter Lippmann, *Essays in The Public Philosophy* (Boston, MA: Little, Brown, 1955), p. 36.

8. *The New York Times*, 5 March 1861: 8.

9. Renan (above, n. 6), p. 89.

10. George Kennan, *The Realities of American Foreign Policy* (Princeton, NJ: Princeton University Press, 1954), p. 5.

11. Max Ways, *Beyond Survival* (New York: Harper and Brothers, 1959), p. 16.

12. Woodrow Wilson wanted to marry each nation to its own state, a logical, if probably impracticable, goal. Where does one stop? Should each tribe have its own country? Perhaps the most troubling aspect of modern world politics, next to proliferation, is the nationalities question. See "Whose America?" *Time*, 8 July 1991: 12–21, for discussion.

13. See James N. Rosenau, "The National Interest," in *The Scientific Study of Foreign Policy*, ed. Rosenau (New York: The Free Press, 1971), pp. 239–49 for a useful essay. See also Fred A. Sondermann, "The Concept of the National Interest," Orbis 21 (Spring 1977): 121–38.

14. Charles O. Lerche, *Foreign Policy of the American People*, 3d ed. (Englewood Cliffs, NJ: Prentice-Hall, 1967), pp. 12–13.

15. Sir Harold Nicolson, *Diplomacy*, 3d ed. (New York: Oxford University Press, 1963), p. 147.

16. By "compact," I do not mean to refer to the Lockean notion so much as to the understanding among the people of a state whereby political order was created to achieve particular ends and is continued by tacit agreement of successor generations.

17. Robert E. Osgood, *Ideals and Self-Interest in America's Foreign Relations* (Chicago, IL: University of Chicago Press, 1953), p. 17. See also Alan Tonelson, "What is the National Interest?" *The Atlantic*, July 1991: 35–52.

18. Raymond Aron, *Peace and War: A Theory of International Relations*, trans. Richard Howard and Annette Baker Fox (Garden City, NY: Doubleday, 1966), p. 634; Adam Ulam, *The Rivals* (New York: Viking, 1971), p. 383.

19. Hoffmann (above, n. 5), p. xv.

20. William Reitzel, Morton Kaplan, and Constance Coblenz, *United States Foreign Policy: 1945–1955* (Washington, DC: Brookings Institution, 1956), p. 473.

21. See, for example, Colin S. Gray, *The Geopolitics of Super Power* (Lexington, KY: The University Press of Kentucky, 1988). An excellent overview may be found in chapter 2 of James E. Dougherty and Robert L. Pfaltzgraff, Jr., *Contending Theories of International Relations*, 3d ed. (New York: Harper & Row, 1990).

22. Thomas Cook and Malcolm Moos, *Power through Purpose: The Realism of Idealism as a Basis for Foreign Policy* (Baltimore, MD: The Johns Hopkins Press, 1954), preface.

23. Denis Brogan, *America in the Modern World* (New Brunswick, NJ: Rutgers University Press, 1960), p. 8.

24. Henry A. Kissinger, *Years of Upheaval* (Boston, MA: Little, Brown, 1982), p. 242.

25. "American Jews and Israel," *Time*, 10 March 1975: 18.

26. Arthur Schlesinger, Jr., "The Necessary Amorality of Foreign Affairs," *Harper's*, August 1971: 73.

27. Hans J. Morgenthau and Kenneth W. Thompson, *Politics Among Nations*, 6th ed. (New York: Knopf, 1985), p. 252

28. Quoted in William H. Vatcher, *Panmunjom* (New York: Praeger, 1958), p. 220.

29. Max Ways, *Beyond Survival* (New York: Harper & Brothers, 1959), p. 5.

30. Hedley Donovan, "America and the World Out There," *Time*, 19 May 1975: 20.

31. "White Flags in the Desert," *Time*, 11 March 1991: 20.

32. "Why the President Hung Tough," *U. S. News & World Report*, 11 March 1991: 21.

33. Ways (above, n. 29), p. 111.

34. Irving Kristol, "A Matter of Fundamentals," *Encounter*, April 1960: 56.

35. Gabriel Almond, *The American People and Foreign Policy* (New York: Praeger, 1960), pp. 5–6.

36. Robert Kennedy, *Thirteen Days* (New York: New American Library, 1969), pp. 38–39.

37. Kissinger (above, n. 24), p. 979.

38. *The New York Times*, 5 March 1861: 8.

39. Lippmann (above, n. 7), p. 27.

40. Dean Acheson, *Power and Diplomacy* (Cambridge, MA: Harvard University Press, 1958), pp. 27–28.

41. George Kennan, "History and Diplomacy as Viewed by a Diplomatist," in *Diplomacy in a Changing World*, ed. S. D. Kertesz and M. A. Fitzsimons (Notre Dame, IN: University of Notre Dame Press, 1959), p. 108.

42. Hans Morgenthau, "The Nature and Limits of a Theory of International Relations," in *Theoretical Aspects of International Relations*, ed. William T. R. Fox (Notre Dame, IN: University of Notre Dame Press, 1959), p. 22.

43. Morgenthau (above, n. 27), p. 591.

44. Elihu Root, "A Requisite for the Success of Popular Diplomacy," *Foreign Affairs* 1 (September 1922): 5.

45. "Into the Dangerous Twilight," *U.S. News & World Report*, 11 March 1991: 25. Joseph de Maistre (1753–1821) entertained a similar view: "Every country has the government it deserves."

46. "The Point of the Spear," *U.S. News & World Report,* 4 March 1991: 41.

47. Lippmann (above, n. 7), pp. 19–20.

48. Michael Howard, "The Concept of Peace," *Encounter*, December 1983: 21, 23–24.

49. Gerhard von Glahn, *Law Among Nations*, 3d ed. (New York: Macmillan, 1976), p. 726.

50. Quoted in Greg Russell, *Hans J. Morgenthau and the Ethics of American Statecraft* (Baton Rouge, LA: Louisiana State University Press, 1990), p. 90.

51. See Maurice Duverger, *Political Parties*, 2d ed., revised, trans. Barbara and Robert North (New York: Wiley, 1964), p. 425.

52. Michael Howard, *War and the Liberal Conscience* (Oxford, England: Oxford University Press, 1981), p. 135. I thank my colleague at the Air War College, Dr. David Skaggs, for calling this to my attention.

53. Quoted in Kenneth W. Thompson, "Beyond the National Interest: A Critical Evaluation of Reinhold Niebuhr's Theory of International Politics," in *The Image of Man*, ed. M.A. Fitzsimons, Thomas T. McAvoy, and Frank O'Malley (Notre Dame, IN: University of Notre Dame Press, 1959), p. 441.

54. Kissinger (above, n. 24), pp. 37–38.

55. Quoted in Russell (above, n. 50), p. 113.

56. Greg Russell, "The Ethics of American Statecraft," *Journal of Politics* 50 (May 1988): 504.

57. William Westmoreland, *A Soldier Reports* (Garden City, NY: Doubleday, 1976), pp. 105, 359.

58. James A. Barber, "War: Limitations and National Priorities," *Naval War College Review* 23 (January 1971): 5. After MacArthur's relief from command in Korea, the Congress held a joint investigation. The minority report contained this sobering analysis: "We believe that a policy of victory must be announced to the American people in order to restore unity and confidence. It is too much to expect that our people will accept a limited war. Our policy must be to win. Our strategy must be devised to bring about decisive victory." *The New York Times*, 28 June 1951: 3. See also Morton Halperin, "The Limiting Process in the Korean War," *Political Science Quarterly* 78 (March 1963): 24–26.

59. *International Encyclopedia of the Social Sciences*, 1968, s.v. "Limited War," by Robert E. Osgood. See also two of Osgood's other works: *Limited War: The*

Challenge to American Strategy (Chicago, IL: University of Chicago Press, 1957) and *Limited War Revisited* (Boulder, CO: Westview Press, 1979).

60. William V. O'Brien, "Guidelines for Limited War," *Military Review* 59 (February 1979): 66.

61. The term is that of Thomas Schelling, in *Arms and Influence* (New Haven, CT: Yale University Press, 1966), p. 71; see also his book *The Strategy of Conflict* (New York: Oxford University Press, 1960).

62. T. R. Fehrenbach, *This Kind of War* (New York: Pocket Books, 1963), p. 286.

63. See, for example, John Lewis Gaddis, *The United States and the Origins of the Cold War, 1941–1947* (New York: Columbia University Press, 1972), p. 209. See also pp. 13, 68, 80, and 108. Bernard Brodie has asked, "To avoid hazarding American lives is bound to be commendable, but if it was not to be done for 'purely political purposes,' what then was that or any other war all about?" *War and Politics* (New York: Macmillan, 1973), p. 44. Paul Johnson, in *Modern Times*, quotes General Montgomery: "The Americans could not understand that it was of little avail to win the war strategically if we lost it politically" (New York: Harper & Row, 1983), p. 436.

64. T. R. Fehrenbach (above, n. 62), p. 44.

65. James MacGregor Burns, *Uncommon Sense* (New York: Harper & Row, 1972), p. 181.

66. Quoted in Stephen M. Millett, "The Moral Dilemma of Nuclear Deterrence," *Parameters* 10 (March 1980): 38.

4   ON THE JUST WAR TRADITION

There never was a good war or a bad peace.
—Benjamin Franklin (letter to Josiah
Quincy, 11 September 1773)

Moderation in war is imbecility.
—Lord Fisher (1841–1920)

War is now utterly preposterous.
—Dwight D. Eisenhower (speech in Rio
de Janeiro, 24 February 1960)

In remarks prepared for delivery to the National Press Club on 28 November 1984, then Secretary of Defense Caspar W. Weinberger presented a speech entitled "The Use of Military Power." Weinberger contended that "when our vital interests or those of our allies are threatened, we are ready to use force, and [to] use it decisively, to protect those interests." He proposed a six-part test to be applied whenever the American decision-makers contemplated the use of force overseas:

- Force should not be used unless "the particular engagement or occasion is deemed vital to our national interest or that of our allies."

- If the decision is made that combat troops should be committed, then "we should do so wholeheartedly and with the clear intention of winning."
- If and when forces are committed overseas, "we should have clearly defined political and military objectives."
- "The relationship between our objectives and the forces we have committed—their size, composition and disposition—must be continually reassessed and adjusted if necessary."
- Before troops are committed, "there must be some reasonable assurance we will have the support of the American people and their elected representatives in Congress."
- "The commitment of U.S. forces to combat should be a last resort."[1]

The Prussian soldier-scholar von Clausewitz (who died in 1831), argued in his classic text *On War* that "No one starts a war—or rather, no one in his senses ought to do so—without first being clear in his mind what he intends to achieve by that war and how he intends to conduct it. The former is its political purpose; the latter its operational objective."[2] As Secretary Weinberger observed, "War may be different today than in Clausewitz's time, but the need for well-defined objectives and a consistent strategy is still essential." *Strategy* is "the art of distributing and applying military means to fulfill the ends of policy."[3] (Of course, *strategy* can also refer to the skillful planning and management of, say, diplomacy; it can mean judicious choice and thoughtful administration of, say, political resources. When I employ the noun *strategy* here, I refer to the fundamental notion of the term: scrupulous planning.) The point of this chapter is to argue that the just war tradition and prudent strategy are more than merely compatible; they are symbiotic.

STRATEGY

Weinberger's criteria for the employment of United States' combat power are not found in an ethics textbook. Indeed, as Secretary of Defense, Weinberger could not, primarily, be concerned with advocating a scheme of ethics; his fundamental duty lay in effecting the national security of his country. To be sure, I have just argued in the preceding chapter that it does matter, of course, whether the leaders of a country are themselves decent, humane people. But what about the case, say, of a pacifist Secretary of Defense intent upon ensuring that American military power not be used at all? Does he have the right—indeed, the ethical obligation—to do all within his power to ensure the triumph of his view (in this admittedly very unlikely scenario)? Louis Halle has a succinct answer:

As an agent—and in his official capacity he is only that—he is not free to resolve the nation's problems by reference only to his own conscience, his own ethics. Although he is . . . a pacifist, he is not free to use his official position to institute pacifist policies for a nation that is not pacifist. His position is, rather, like that of the corporate director who, however much he believes in charity, is not entitled to give away the stockholders' assets as if they were his own.[4]

"The individual," observed Hans Morgenthau, "may say for himself: *'Fiat justitia, pereat mundus* (Let justice be done, even if the world perish),' but the state has no right to say so in the name of those who are in its care."[5] This is not to say that conscience is irrelevant for the leader (see Chapter 5 for discussion), but only that he has "corporate" as well as personal responsibility. When the two clash, as they sometimes will, he has the responsibility of choosing between the two and of acting accordingly; but he has not the right to try to give away national defense assets (or national monies) in the name of his private conscience.

Thus Weinberger, quite properly, is concerned with maintaining the national security, an enterprise evolving from a perception of the national interest. That perception must be rooted in his reading of the nation's traditions, its core values, its cherished beliefs. In the last chapter, I argued that a nation's material well-being, its physical security, and its treasury of fundamental convictions constitute its vital national interest. Knowing how to reconcile one's appraisal of these imperatives within the geopolitical context of the day is the art of statesmanship. Henry Kissinger:

But the responsibility of leaders is not simply to affirm an objective. It is above all to endow it with a meaning compatible with the values of their society. If peace is equated simply with the absence of war, if the yearning for peace is not allied with a sense of justice, it can become an abject pacifism that turns the world over to the most ruthless. To build peace on reciprocal restraint; to suffuse our concept of order with our country's commitment to freedom; to strive for peace without abdication and for order without unnecessary confrontation—therein lies the ultimate test of American statesmanship.[6]

As uncomfortable as we may be with the imprecision of it all, the national interest, the strategy that may effect that interest, and the idea of just war must be filtered through the minds and experiences of our national leaders who, in turn, must interpret and respond both to those ineffable values which they inherit and which they must conserve.

If one reads carefully through Weinberger's tests, one discovers that, however seriously and sincerely the Secretary intended them, they are frustratingly vague. The tests gloss over the nebulous nature of what is "vital" to our national interest. Indeed, no discussion at all exists of the argument, prominent in the scholarly literature, that the national interest (as a singular) may well amount to no more than what a given clique of leaders says it is at a given time. When we commit troops to combat, we ought to have a clear intention of winning. But what is that? Does it entail unconditional surrender? Even in the Gulf War of 1991, Saddam Hussein had the temerity to suggest that the Iraqis had won. Should the United States have bombed the Iraqi leader into a free, full, and open confession of defeat? Does winning mean military victory—or wise political settlement after the combat?

What is more, Weinberger discusses "clearly defined political and military objectives." Clausewitz, who is quoted earlier, argued for such clearly defined objectives in the early nineteenth century. But how often are those definitions provided? by whom? and to whose satisfaction? When we reassess our commitments, do we continue to upgrade them if necessary? Should the United States *still* be in Vietnam *today*, demonstrating our resolve? Should we have withdrawn our forces from Vietnam well before 1973? Or should we have bombed North Vietnam "back to the stone age" (as one general once suggested), being determined to "stay the course," if necessary, for decades? When the United States began the air war against Iraq, it did so only after Congress explicitly authorized the use of force (on 12 January 1991). But even after that authorization and the beginning of the air war, about 25,000 antiwar protesters marched on the White House.[7] Even the Gulf War, clearly one of the most militarily successful wars in history, was strongly objected to by thousands of American citizens. In fact, the Senate vote authorizing the use of American combat power was 52–47, hardly a clear mandate for war, even in a conflict seen by many as obviously just, both politically and military.[8] What does "last resort" mean and, even more significantly, when is that plateau reached?

The idea of just war has been debated, quite literally, for centuries. That its meaning is hardly crystal clear has been, for some, ample reason to impugn the entire notion. We often assume, however, that, by comparison at least, the idea of strategy is more lucid. Weinberger's tests, read carefully, suggest the opposite. However laudable and diligent the effort to make clear those ingredients necessary in the recipe of commitment of American combat power, it is still, understandably, a turbid concept. To amplify this, consider strategy, the ingredients of which have been defined by Seabury and Codevilla:

To make war strategy . . . is to answer five sets of questions. First, what do I want out of this situation? . . . Second, Whom or what do I have to kill, destroy, besiege, intimidate, or constrain to get what I want? . . . In other words, at what point do I win? Third, what can my enemy do to keep me from killing, destroying, or constraining as I must? . . . Fourth, what forces are available to me to defeat the best opposition that my enemy can throw at me, and how can I use them? . . . Fifth, am I willing to do what is necessary in good time to win? Do I have a realistic estimate of the costs? Is the whole thing worth the trouble?[9]

One scholar at the Naval War College, Philip Crowl, had a similar list, worth mentioning here:

The first and most fundamental question . . . is What is it about? Or in the words of Marshal Foch, *"De quoi s'agit il?"* . . . [Second,] Is the national military strategy tailored to meet the national political objectives? . . . [Third,] What are the limits of military power? . . . [Fourth,] What are the alternatives to war? . . . [Fifth,] How strong is the home front? . . . [And sixth,] Does today's strategy overlook points of difference and exaggerate points of likeness between past and present?[10]

Crowl ended his article with this advice to the fledgling strategist: "After all your plans have been perfected, all avenues explored, all contingencies thought through, then ask yourself one final question: What have I overlooked? Then say your prayers and go to sleep— with the certain knowledge that tomorrow too will bring its share of nasty surprises." But that is precisely the point of all this! To know that the "fog of war" will occur; that mistakes will happen; that the unprovided for can result—none of these things constitutes incontrovertible argument against the necessity of planning. To devise perfectly wise, moral strategy requires a perspicacity not given to humans, save Cassandra. All of Crowl's questions—all of Seabury and Codevilla's questions—result, necessarily, in answers that simply must be unsure, tentative, experimental. One thinks through one's own, or one's nation's, situation as prudentially as one can in the circumstances of the day. That much is demanded by any code of honor or integrity; but the guaranteeing of results (beyond a certain fair expectation of probable likelihood) is not something of which we finite mortals are capable. Strategy, like the insurance business, is the art of risk management. We return once again to the idea of *balance*, for strategy necessarily entails the weighing of alternative courses of action and the choice, almost invariably, not between certain success and certain failure, but between or among calculated and calibrated estimates of possible national vindication in the selection of one path over another. The lugubrious conclusion of Henry Kissinger:

The outsider thinks in terms of absolutes; for him right and wrong are defined in their conception. The political leader does not have this luxury. He rarely can reach his goal except in stages; any partial step is inherent morally imperfect and yet morality cannot be approximated without it. The statesman's test is not only the exaltation of his goals but the catastrophe he averts.[11]

CONSERVATIVE CONNECTION

More than thirty years ago, Samuel Huntington discussed the "military ethic," which he said emphasizes "the permanence, irrationality, weakness, and evil in human nature."[12] Those traits, which Huntington thought part of "conservative realism," must be contrasted with Rousseau's outlook on human nature, which was that "man is a being naturally good, loving justice and order: that there is not any original perversity in the human heart . . . ."[13] Students of philosophy will recognize that this is simply a reprise of the intellectual argument between Augustine and Pelagius, or even between Hamilton and Jefferson. Strategy—and the just war tradition—come down squarely on the side of conservative realism. In a recent remarkable book, Thomas Friedman suggested that "American statesmen must know how to play hardball" if they are to deal with Middle East politics. The American statesman "must also be a real son-of-a-bitch. He must understand that he is dealing with grocers who often play by their own rules, and that their own rules are Hama rules." Primary among these is "Rule or Die." (Hama is in Syria and is the site of the wanton slaughter of anywhere from 10,000 to 25,000 Syrians by the Syrian government in 1982.)[14] If we misperceive the nature of our enemy or of our ally, we run the very real risk, not only of bad strategy, but of bad ethics as well.

I argued in Chapter 2 that the ultimate cause of war is exactly what authors like Hawthorne, Melville, Cooper, Brownson, Golding or Conrad wrote about—the evil in the human heart. If that evil exists and, further, if it manifests itself, ultimately, in macropolitical form as state policy, we have a terrible choice to make: do we refuse to resist that evil, preferring, instead, our own moral purity (the *pereat mundus* position referred to previously); do we resist by nonviolent means, believing in the efficacy of those means (even in the face of the "Hama rules" referred to above); or do we use measured military power to deter or to compel (with all the moral ambiguity which that entails)? "It is of the essence of geopolitics," says Paul Johnson, "to be able to distinguish between different degrees of evil."[15] The just war proposition, and the very idea of strategy, suggest not only that we can make such distinctions—but that we must.

As St. Augustine (354–430) expressed it, "He, then, who prefers what is right to what is wrong, and what is well-ordered to what is perverted, sees that the peace of unjust men is not worthy to be called peace in comparison with the peace of the just" (*The City of God*, Bk. 19, Ch. 12). Augustine's philosophical position was given point fifteen hundred years later. The testimony of journalist Arthur Hadley as he entered a concentration camp in 1945:

I was the first or second tank in the column that liberated a major concentration camp, Magdeburg. When I came round the corner of that pine forest lane and saw the human skeletons hanging from the barbed wire enclosing the camp, I thought, how barbarous of men to string up corpses. Then some of the skeletons moved slightly and I realized I was looking at the starving living. There was a horror beyond the horror of all the dying I had seen. I learned a lesson that day. There are worse events than battle. When they come to take you off to the camp, fight. And people who tell you that you will be better off in the camps than resisting are not your friends.[16]

Several years ago, I was invited to be one of several panelists discussing the philosophical aspects of war at a conference in Vermont. I was the sole "realist" on the panel, and I was getting rather more than I was giving. My position, pretty much along the lines outlined by Augustine and Hadley, was being attacked on all sides as unenlightened and medieval. (That I did not take the second adjective as pejorative excited my opponents all the more!) I thought I was the only person in the fairly large crowd prepared to uphold the idea that force *could* be morally justifiable when an older man stood, hesitantly at first. "I have heard this young man [pointing to me] assailed from all sides for daring to suggest that force can be moral. I am not a historian or a philosopher. I am only a musician. But I have spent my life with music. I wish to tell you which music in my life has meant the most to me. I was a prisoner in [I cannot recall the name now of the Nazi concentration camp he mentioned], but the sweetest sounds I have ever heard were the sounds of U.S. Army tanks attacking that compound. It meant that I would grow to adulthood." The audience had the grace to sit a moment in respectful silence. I felt like Edward Everett at Gettysburg.

POLITICAL CONTEXT

In *Tranquillitas Ordinis*, a brilliant book by George Weigel, one reads that the Catholic tradition of moderate realism is based on three core convictions. The first to which Weigel refers is that political life "is an arena of rationality and moral responsibility." The political community is good, a wholesome reminder of the "sociability that is part of the God-given texture of human life." To complement that, however, we have the Augustinian tradition, which is "a continuing reminder that sin marks all the days of our lives, and that politics is always subject to corruption." Second, "the exercise of power is under moral judgment." The issue is not whether power will be exercised but how. Power, he writes, "like governance, has a positive dimension; it is an expression of the human creativity that is analogically related to the abiding creativity of God the Father, Jesus the Logos, and the Spirit brooding over the waters of the created order." Third, "the biblical vision of *shalom* will never be achieved in this world." Finally, he offers this adjuration:

The Catholic tradition of moderate realism knew that there could be a morally unworthy peace—under a particularly efficient tyrant, for example. But between the peace of tyranny and the eschatological peace of *shalom* is the peace of dynamic, rightly ordered political community. And it is to this third option that the Catholic tradition patiently but resolutely points us, urging that we never lose heart, but that we not lose our sense, either.[17]

In 1968, as student radicalism began to escalate, George Kennan offered this observation:

I have seen more harm done in this world by those who tried to storm the bastions of society in the name of utopian beliefs, who were determined to achieve the elimination of all evil and the realization of the millennium within their own time, than by all the humble efforts of those who have tried to create a little order and civility and affection within their own intimate entourage, even at the cost of tolerating a great deal of evil in the public domain.[18]

Exactly how much evil can be tolerated in the public domain? George Will once wrote that "All politics takes place on a slippery slope. The four most important words in politics are 'up to a point.'"[19] When we seek to find snappy shibboleths to use as absolute guides to the daily enigmas of life, we err. We can follow rule-oriented (or deontological) prescriptions, to a point; we can follow goal-oriented aspirations (consequentialism), up to a point; we can follow circumstantially oriented advice (situation ethics), up to a point. But as one observer pointed out,

When followed inflexibly, any of the three approaches to understanding the bases for our ethical judgments can result in moral aberration: exclusive attention to rules can result in legalism; rigid adherence to Mill's utilitarian goal of the greatest good for the greatest number can promote a tyranny of the majority; and preeminent attention to situations can result in loss of directives and moral chaos.[20]

Thus political and strategic ethics must be eclectic. "Every intervention [a strategic choice] requires a just cause [an ethical choice]," wrote Charles Krauthammer. "That doesn't mean that every just cause warrants intervention . . . . Foreign policy is an exercise in discrimination."[21] The very notion that such judgments must be based upon a palette of choices is upsetting to some. The success of fundamentalism in our time is due in substantial part to our natural human desire to have one simple choice rather than an array of options or opportunities. In refusing to be seduced by the tyranny of easy choices (to lean either toward despair on the one hand or toward presumption on the other), the Christian realist knows that, while he must have the courage to decide and to act in this imperfect world, he is not alone (Mt. 28:20) and that the deposit of faith and the promise of grace are ever with him in the Valley of the Shadow of Death.

INGREDIENTS OF THE JUST WAR DOCTRINE

"[T]he essence of war," write Seabury and Codevilla, "consists of the political decision that a given cause is worth killing and sacrificing for."[22] That is correct as far as it goes. But there is more. The essence of war consists of the *ethical* decision that a given cause is worth killing and sacrificing for. St. Augustine certainly thought that such causes existed.[23] In modern times, so did Henry Kissinger:

If the desire for peace turns into an avoidance of conflict at all costs, if the just disparage power and seek refuge in their moral purity, the world's fear of war becomes a weapon of blackmail by the strong; peaceful nations, large or small, will be at the mercy of the most ruthless.[24]

As Philip Lawler put it, "War is not hell. Hell is hell. War is bad enough in itself; it needs no exaggeration." And: "A Christian leader confronts a paradox: every human life is immeasurably valuable, and yet some other things are more valuable still."[25] The rudimentary idea of just war is, once again, balance. To ignore our neighbors' lives by thoughtlessly snuffing them out in the name of our political greed or in the name of our "Great Leader" is no Christian ethic, for it is remorseless war. But to ignore our neighbors' plights as they are brutalized by savage regimes when, strategically, there is something we both should and can do to assuage that situation is no Christian ethic, for it is remorseless peace. As I wrote in the Introduction, a leader bereft of ethics is likely to *commit* heinous deeds; but a leader bereft of practical values (i.e., strategic sense) is likely *to condone* heinous acts, excusing that apathy in the false name of moral purity. The just war doctrine instructs us—nay, it demands—that we love God and our neighbor. And if and when we ask, "What, then, is love?" we return to the anxiety of the human condition; to the awareness that we have little epistemological certitude in life; to the conviction that, by the grace of God, we will choose our strategic paths ethically and our ethical paths strategically. "We are, in the end, the image of God in history, and the task of history is one we cannot lay down. The issue is to take it up wisely, gracefully, well."[26] From such conviction evolve the tenets of the just war doctrine.

One can, of course, argue, as John Mueller has, that "Too often the quest for the 'just war' has led instead to what might be called the 'nice' war—wars in which the only people who die are young men in uniform . . . ." Mueller also argues that "it seems at least possible that, on balance, wars would be less frequent and less murderous if moral and religious precepts had never been applied to them"; therefore "belief in the existence of a guiding and an instrumental God has helped to facilitate the sacrificial, uncertain, masochistic, improbable, and fundamentally absurd activity known as warfare."[27]

But war is not always "fundamentally absurd"; there are values worthy of defense. And if one can agree with Mueller that crusades and inquisitions and Savonarola-like mentalities are evils, must we inevitably equate Jim Jones of Guyana with Mother Teresa of Calcutta? George Washington was stupidly bled to death in 1799 in the name of medicine; is that a reason imperiously to dismiss all health sciences as inimical to life? Mueller does well to remind us that religion and the idea of God can become perverted by scoundrels. Yet one must regard Mueller's indictments, on the whole, not only as transparently fallacious, but as contentiously ignorant of the genuine good that religious and ethical convictions have accomplished. Medicine has its quacks and placebos; so, too, does religion. But no fair and sensible person is prepared to inculpate or dismiss all of medicine because, in the end, we all die; and no fair or sensible person is prepared to inculpate or dismiss all of religion because, in the end, we all sin.

JUS AD BELLUM

Ethically governing the determination of *when* to go to war are the elements comprising what is known as *jus ad bellum*, which outline why and when recourse to war is permissible.

1. Just Cause: War is permissible only to confront "a real and certain danger," such as protecting innocent life, preserving conditions necessary for decent human existence, and securing basic human rights. The medieval notion of retributive war is generally regarded as impermissible today in view of the high risks of modern warfare.

2. Competent Authority: The decision to begin a war must be made by appropriate politically empowered (or constitutionally ordered) officials, not by private groups for private gain.

3. Comparative Justice: War is permissible only in light of prudent and prayerful consideration that the rights and values of the warring nation that will be advanced through the war outweigh or justify the killing and suffering certain to result from the initiation of hostilities. "Far from legitimizing a crusade mentality," observe the American

Catholic Bishops, "comparative justice is designed to relativize absolute claims [by one side about its 'just cause'] and to restrain the use of force even in a 'justified' conflict."[28]

4. Proportionality: Complementing the idea of "comparative justice" is the tenet of proportionality, meaning that the damage to be inflicted and the costs to be incurred must be balanced or consistent with the good expected by resort to arms.

5. Right Intention: This tenet insists that peace and reconciliation are the ultimate aim of the war. The classic statement in this regard is Lincoln's (4 March 1865):

> With malice toward none; with charity for all; with firmness in the right, as God gives us to see the right, let us strive on to finish the work we are in: to bind up the nation's wounds; to care for him who shall have borne the battle, and for his widow and orphan, to do all which may achieve a just and lasting peace among ourselves, and with all nations.

6. Last Resort: This tenet insists that all peaceful remedies must be exhausted before recourse to war can be permitted.

7. Probability of Success: This tenet is an effort to prevent irrationally resorting to war or even hopelessly and futilely resisting.

The notion of a just war, an obscene oxymoron to some, *is* medieval, or scholastic, or classical. Dating to the early fathers of the Church and extending now into nearly the twenty-first century, it implies that life is not the highest good; that some things are worth both dying for *and* killing for; that people or nations cavalier about such things sin grievously against God and man; that the sword and the cross, in this imperfect world, can be parallel. The idea of just war repudiates the notion of pacifism (which will be discussed in Chapter 7). It also repudiates the notion of jingoism, manifesting itself in a crusade mentality. The flag, as Jehovah's Witnesses tell us, *can* become a graven image, an idol. The just war tradition informs us that we have duties to the state; it also implicitly reminds us of the last words attributed (perhaps apocryphally) to Sir Thomas More, as he was put to death (1535) for supposed lack of fealty to the monarch: "I die the King's good servant—but God's first."

Because the just war doctrine attempts to reconcile the sword and the cross, it is subject to obloquy and vilification. Chauvinists may see this doctrine as unpatriotic; pacifists may see it as an endorsement of fascism, as Church sycophancy to the power of the state. There is hardly any doubt that the just war doctrine is being eroded at both ends. The idea that there is *anything* worthy of protection; the idea that there is *anything* truly sacred, deserving of defense; the idea that there is *anything* of such enduring and fundamental value that it can justify both killing and dying; the idea that *anything* can exceed in importance the worth of our own skins—these ideas hardly square with the force and function of modernity, of contemporary solipsism, of the narcissism which deny the notion of a genuine national interest and of a compelling public philosophy. Seabury and Codevilla had it exactly right in this searing passage:

[O]ne does not wonder that in 1861 an American public accustomed to biblical injunctions to fight for right, and led by Abraham Lincoln, should have fought even its own brothers for the abstract ideals of the Union and against slavery, while singing "The Battle Hymn of the Republic." Nor is it surprising that in the 1970s another American polity, accustomed to the *Playboy* philosophy, and led by presidents of somewhat ambiguous moral standing who repeatedly and emphatically refused to identify the enemy, label him evil, and call for his defeat should have stood by and watched the peoples of Southeast Asia—on behalf of whose freedom it had made a half-hearted commitment—sink wholly into slavery.[29]

A basic theme of this chapter is the problem of exegesis, or of hermeneutics. The more important the text, the more important interpretation of that text is.[30] The elements of the just war doctrine are subject to a variety of interpretations. As the mosaic of strategy requires skillful assembly by those versed in the matters of the sword, so does the mosaic of just war require scrupulous attention by those versed in matters of the cross. The very notion of *civic virtue* means that those doing the interpreting (of bible, Christian tradition, Church teachings; of Constitution, national traditions, fundamental values)— that is, the leaders—be prepared personally and professionally to be worthy of an oath of office normally ending with the prayer, "So help me God."

Thus did George Bush, in 1991, employ "archaic" language in saying, as the United States began its war against Iraq: "We know that this is a just war, and we know that, God willing, this is a war we will win."[31] Sixteen decades before Bush spoke, von Clausewitz wrote in *On War*: "the moral elements are among the most important in war. They constitute the spirit that permeates war as a whole, and at an early stage they establish a close affinity with the will that moves and leads the whole mass of force, practically merging with it, since the will is itself a moral quantity" (Bk. 3, Ch. 3). A leader devoid of ethical sense will commit barbarities; a leader devoid of practical sense will acquiesce in the barbarities perpetrated by others. There are fewer better examples of a truly just war than the 1991 Gulf War in which the American president was able to merge ethics and strategy—and thus prove worthy of his office and of his oath.

Practically all of the elements of the *jus ad bellum* are ambiguous, it is true. The idea of just cause can certainly be viewed in remarkably different ways. In the United States, one must compare the Constitution's Article I, Section 8, Clause 11 (empowering Congress to declare war) with Article 2, Section 2 (making the president the commander-in-chief), which has led to the obfuscation of the 1973 War Powers Act, which is a kind of awkward compromise between the two clauses. The ideas of comparative justice and of proportionality are hinged to a foresight with which we humans are, unfortunately, not endowed; for we cannot with certitude predict the consequences of war not yet initiated. If the notion of "right intention" seems clear enough, one recalls that practically every war in history was begun by nations "shooting *back*" at their enemies, and no aggressor in history has ever grandly announced that there was no ethical basis for his state's action, that the war was merely an exercise in self-aggrandizement. Even probability of success is necessarily turbid, as even the bishops admit that "at times defense of key values, even against great odds, may be a 'proportionate' witness." But as James Childress has pointed out, these criteria "are not designed to answer the question of the justification of war in general but the question of the justification of particular wars."[32]

One is left with the illusion that in politics and in morality alike there is mere confusion, such a range of amorphous choice that one person's preference is as good as another's. There is, or so it appears, no structure; all is protean. But in fact that is not true. In the realm of strategy, the statesman is free neither politically nor ethically to disregard the power factors relatively clearly associated with geopolitical realities, which substantially influence, even to the point of dictating, policy. Similarly, in the realm of ethics, there are abiding values, however much modernists may decry them, which are a function of right reason, natural law, and the public philosophy. Lincoln knew them, even if some of our contemporary leaders do not. Osgood and Tucker explain the idea that what appears as "choice without structure" is mistaken:

Only when the issues confronting the statesman do not affect—or at least do not vitally affect—a state's security and independence does it become possible to speak in a meaningful way of freedom to choose among alternative courses of action. To be sure, even when a state's security and independence are vitally affected the appearance of choice may result from uncertainty over the path necessity dictates. But choice in such instances is itself the result of one of those limitations that invariably determine the conduct of statecraft. What appears as choice therefore turns out, on closer analysis, to be little more than the limitation imposed by men's ignorance. The more the statesman knows the more he will appreciate the necessities that govern his actions and the less he will believe in the illusion of choice.[33]

Thus we return to the notion of an overarching national interest that transcends the wish or the whim of the statesman who is its temporary custodian. But this demands agreement that an objective standard obtains; that there is an appeal beyond the will of the politician of the moment; that neither war nor peace is always right (although the presumption *is* always toward the former); that duty and not right reigns supreme.

Permit two homely illustrations of that. If one believed that using narcotics was good for him, despite the abundant evidence to the contrary, does he have the freedom of choice to indulge himself? No. Positive law—civic statutes—prevent him from so doing. But even in the absence of such statutes, I would argue, he is not, in fact, free to use dope. Indeed, the idea of freedom demands that he not destroy himself by using dope; *license*, however, might so permit him. Freedom refers to our educated ability to choose as we ought. Imagine a boy given to gluttony and with the material means to indulge himself. Is he free to eat as he chooses? If we understand by *freedom* that it consists in the liberty to choose as one ought to choose, then the boy does not enjoy the freedom to eat endless junk food, for such is self-destructive license. To be free, one must be virtuous.

By the same token, the statesman who pursues a political chimera, exercising his "freedom of choice," is engaging in license. If he fails to appreciate the overarching geopolitical realities of his country's situation and thus fashions a policy out of delusion, he does not lead, but blunders. In that context, consider this assertion, by Seabury and Codevilla: "From time immemorial people have learned that if they did not take up arms and risk their lives in battle, quick death or mild slavery was the best fate they could expect."[34] In the text preceding, I quoted from Arthur Hadley: "And people who tell you that you will be better off in the camps than resisting are not your friends." Neither are they your leaders. In such situations, there is no choice, either ethically or strategically. Know first the truth, for that way lies real freedom—the liberty to choose as we should. The just war tradition brings us face to face with the national interest, which, in turn, compels us to ask questions of civic virtue.

JUS IN BELLO

Supreme emergency; military necessity; *kriegsraison; inter arma silent leges* (in time of war the laws are silent); all's fair in love and war—these and similar notions accompany the idea that, once war is embarked upon, there are no holds barred. "War strips away our civilized adornments and reveals our nakedness," says Michael Walzer, who goes on to discuss the famous Melian Debate (described so cogently by Thucydides), and concludes that "The clearest evidence for the stability of our values over time is the unchanging character of the lies soldiers and statesmen tell."[35] All decent people can agree, I believe, that one of the tragedies of our time is the triumph of movies that laugh at human sorrow and suffering, suggesting that war and gore are the fulfillments of the male—and female—psyche. Thus the very idea of a "war crime" seems silly. But if soldiers and statesmen have lied through the ages (as indeed, *mea culpa*, we all do), so, in particular today, do so many in our entertainment industry who suggest that war is a football game "written large." In this connection, and others, one must agree with Childress that "pacifists and just-war theorists are actually closer to and more dependent on each other than they often suppose."[36] We need to remind ourselves, constantly, that war, indeed, is a last resort.

At the same time, we must be ever aware that although we may accede to the initiation of hostilities, we are not bound to maintain support of a war if its conduct is contrary to the very principles inspiring its undertaking.[37] The elements of *jus in bello* can be listed this way:

1. Proportionality: The quantity of force employed or threatened must always be morally consistent to the ends being pursued in and by the war. Note that this is similar to the idea of the same name under *jus ad bellum* except that one can determine the effects of the war relatively more easily during its prosecution than at its outset.

2. Discrimination: Force cannot be applied so that noncombatants and innocents are the deliberate targets of attack. Combatants are the only appropriate targets in war.

3. Genocide is prohibited.

4. The positive laws of law (treaties, conventions, general principles of law accepted as comity, and the writings of publicists broadly accepted) must be observed.

To discuss the third and fourth item would involve us in international law debate, which is not the point of this chapter. One should note, however, that the old idea of *Respondeat Superior*, meaning that senior officers are answerable for war crimes but that junior officers following orders are not has not been an acceptable defense since the war crimes tribunals at the end of World War II. (See Chapter 5 for more discussion.)

The concepts of proportionality and discrimination—accompanied by the idea of "collateral damage"—bring their own problems to the just war tradition. One manner in which moral theology attempts to resolve the dilemmas inherent in fighting wars justly is by the invocation of the "Principle of Double Effect." One can never deliberately sin. But in a situation where the use of force can be foreseen to have a number of effects, either actual or probable, some of which are evil, the agent does not incur culpability, provided that he meets the following conditions: (1) the action must carry the intention to produce morally worthy consequences; (2) the evil effects are not *intended* to be ends in themselves or means to other ends, whether good or bad; and (3) the commission of collateral evil must be justified by considerations of proportionate moral weight.[38]

A number of people have criticized these elements of the just war tradition as casuistry. The Principle of Double Effect, for example, appears to be no more than sophistry, permitting attacks on innocents, so long as the attacks are incidental to the intention of the attacker. To be sure, there are those who will argue that the idea of limiting the conduct of warfare is simply impracticable—Lord Fisher, for example (in the epigraph to this chapter). Worth particular attention, however, are the arguments of those who see the just war tenets as too permissive—as mere sophistry. Donald Wells, for example, says:

Suppose that, instead of national war, we were discussing battles of Aryans against Jews. Suppose we approached this subject with medieval language and modern skill. We would . . . grant to Aryans the right to wage the war of extermination of the Jews, provided of course that the pogrom be declared by the duly constituted authority, be carried out with due decorum proportional to the threat, and with a just end in view. With this much granted, citizens would then see that they must kill Jews if their prince commanded it in the name of national defense (not unlike the Aryan concern with racial defense) . . . . Our means would naturally be humane gas chambers and sanitary ovens. If we put it this way, then the doctrine of the "just war"—like that of the "just pogrom"—would justify too much.[39]

That *is* an objection. Should it be taken seriously? Yes, if leaders and people are wholly without discriminatory powers (as, admittedly, they—and we—sometimes are). The just war tradition offers us, not a formula to be followed to ensure a perfect war "experiment," not a warranty to assure us flawless moral performance of men and machines in combat, but a collection of adjurations and admonitions, a treasury of reflections and meditations, a heritage of sacred deliberation, about mankind's most perplexing, and horrifying, problem: war.

"Slaves, be subject to your masters with all reverence, not only to those who are good and equitable but also to those who are perverse" (1 Pt. 2:18[NAB]). "Wives should be subordinate to their husbands as to the Lord" (Eph. 5:22[NAB]). Do these imperatives invalidate the Bible or Christianity? Or must their interpretation be taken in a broader context, both in terms of sacred literature and in terms of the times during which they were composed?

CONCLUSION: NOW THE BARBARIANS

John Courtney Murray, now more than thirty years ago, despaired about the advent of the new barbarian:

The barbarian need not appear in bearskins with a club in hand. He may wear a Brooks Brothers suit and carry a ball-point pen with which to write his advertising copy. In fact, even beneath the academic gown there may lurk a child of the wilderness, untutored in the high tradition of civility, who goes busily and happily about his work, a domesticated and law-abiding man, engaged in the construction of a philosophy to put an end to all philosophy, and thus put an end to the possibility of a vital consensus and to civility itself.

Father Murray continued:

This is perennially the work of the barbarian, to undermine rational standards of judgment, to corrupt the inherited intuitive wisdom by which the people have always lived, and to do this not by spreading new beliefs but by creating a climate of doubt and bewilderment in which clarity about the larger aims of life is dimmed and the self-confidence of the people is destroyed, so that finally what you have is the impotent nihilism . . . now presently appearing on our university campuses.[40]

A generation after that, Alasdair MacIntyre wrote that "This time however the barbarians are not waiting beyond the frontiers; they have already been governing us for quite some time. And it is our lack of consciousness of this that constitutes part of our predicament. We are not waiting for Godot, but for another—doubtless very different—St. Benedict."[41] Those who can discern no values worthy of protection, who can descry no social or political values worthy of the congregation of beliefs we call patriotism, who can divine no transcendent values in the temporal order (and thus reveal themselves as morally autistic) are the new barbarians, for civic virtue is not on their minds and certainly not on their agendas. It is not only St. Benedict whom we await—but St. Augustine and St. Thomas as well.[42]

On the eve of war against Iraq—now pretty universally seen as a strategically sensible and ethically eminently justifiable war—there was very strong reaction against it. One self-proclaimed liberal wrote that "I have found myself among the minority of liberal Democrats who have favored . . . his [Bush's] decision to go to war . . . [for] some wars are indeed worth fighting . . . ."[43] Exactly so: some wars are worth fighting. Because prudent strategy is ineffably linked to ethical wisdom, the national interest evolves from, and then transcends, those national values which the people with heart and mind and soul find worthy of protection because those core beliefs endow their national life with dignity and purpose. Thus did Pope Pius XII say in 1948: "A people threatened with an unjust aggression, or already its victim, may not remain passively indifferent, if it would think and act as a Christian."[44]

John Stuart Mill (1806–1873), in opposing England's siding with the Confederacy during the Civil War, wrote:

War is an ugly thing, but not the ugliest of things. The decayed and degraded state of moral and patriotic feeling which thinks nothing *worth* a war is worse . . . . A man who has nothing which he cares about more than he does his personal safety is a miserable creature who has no chance of being free, unless made and kept so by the exertions of better men than himself.[45]

NOTES

1. Caspar W. Weinberger, "The Uses of Military Power," *Defense/85*, January 1985: 2–11; and "The Use of Military Power," *Aerospace Speeches* (Washington, DC: Secretary of the Air Force, Office of Public Affairs), 84–85.

2. Karl von Clausewitz, *On War*, ed. and trans. Michael Howard and Peter Paret (Princeton, NJ: Princeton University Press, 1976), p. 579 (Bk. 8, Ch. 2).

3. B. H. Liddell Hart, quoted in *The Art and Practice of Military Strategy*, ed. George E. Thibault (Washington, DC: National Defense University, 1984), pp. 140–41.

4. Louis J. Halle, "Morality and Contemporary Diplomacy," in *Diplomacy in a Changing World*, ed. Stephen D. Kertesz and M. A. Fitzsimons (Notre Dame, IN: University of Notre Dame Press, 1959), p. 32.

5. Hans Morgenthau and Kenneth W. Thompson, *Politics Among Nations*, 6th ed. (New York: Knopf, 1985), p. 12.

6. Henry A. Kissinger, *Years of Upheaval* (Boston, MA: Little, Brown, 1982), p. 979.

7. "Week One." *U.S. News and World Report*, 11 March 1991, p. 60.

8. The vote in the House of Representatives was 250 to 183.

9. Paul Seabury and Angelo Codevilla, *War: Ends and Means* (New York: Basic Books, 1989), p. 98.

10. Philip A. Crowl, "The Strategist's Short Catechism: Six Questions Without Answers," in *The Harmon Memorial Lectures in Military History*, ed. Harry R. Borowski (Washington, DC: United States Air Force, Office of Air Force History, 1988), pp. 377–87. The material quoted is found on pp. 380–86. The same article may be found in Thibault (above, n. 3), pp. 28–35.

11. Henry A. Kissinger, *White House Years* (Boston, MA: Little, Brown, 1979), p. 55.

12. Samuel Huntington, *The Soldier and the State* (Cambridge, MA: Belknap Press, 1957), p. 79.

13. Quoted in Walter Lippmann, *Essays in The Public Philosophy* (Boston, MA: Little, Brown, 1955), p. 74.

14. Thomas L. Friedman, *From Beirut to Jerusalem* (New York: Farrar Straus Giroux, 1989), pp. 76–77, 104, 505, 508.

15. Paul Johnson, *Modern Times* (New York: Harper & Row, 1983), p. 351. See also the essay by Lance Morrow, "Evil," in *Time*, 10 June 1991: 48–53. See also Chapter 8 in this book, section entitled "The Persistence of Evil."

16. Arthur T. Hadley, *The Straw Giant* (New York: Random House, 1986), p. 207.

17. George Weigel, *Tranquillitas Ordinis* (New York: Oxford University Press, 1987), pp. 42–45. I am grateful to my friend and colleague Professor Fred Mokhtari of Norwich University for the gift of this book.

18. George F. Kennan, *Democracy and the Student Left* (Boston, MA: Atlantic Monthly Press, 1968), p. 9.

19. George Will, *Statecraft as Soulcraft* (New York: Simon and Schuster, 1983), p. 93.

20. Samuel D. Maloney, "Ethics Theory for the Military Professional," in *Concepts for Air Force Leadership*, ed. R. I. Lester and A. G. Morton (Maxwell Air Force Base, AL: Air University Center for Aerospace Doctrine, Research, and Education, 1990), p. 51.

21. Charles Krauthammer, "Must America Slay All the Dragons?" *Time*, 4 March 1991: 88.

22. Seabury and Codevilla (above, n. 9), p. 12.

23. St. Augustine, *The City of God*, Book four, Chapter fifteen.

24. Kissinger (above, n. 6), p. 238.

25. Philip F. Lawler, *The Ultimate Weapon* (Chicago, IL: Regnery Gateway, 1984), pp. 61, 68.

26. Weigel (above, n. 17), p. 45.

27. John Mueller, "Deterrence, Nuclear Weapons, Morality, and War," in *After the Cold War: Questioning the Morality of Nuclear Deterrence*, ed. Charles W. Kegley, Jr., and Kenneth L. Schwab (Boulder, CO: Westview Press, 1991), pp. 84, 92, 94. Mueller also glibly contends that "If war can still be meritorious, if it remains an accepted method for settling issues, it is reasonable to anticipate that eventually it will come about" (p. 86). If we regard war as meritless, if we proclaim it unacceptable as a means of settling disputes, does that mean war will never again come about? One wishes it were that easy.

28. National Conference of Catholic Bishops, *The Challenge of Peace: God's Promise and Our Response* (Washington, DC: United States Catholic Conference, 1983), p. 29. The account noted draws heavily on this pastoral letter. For comments on this letter, see Dean Curry, ed. *Evangelicals and the Bishops' Pastoral Letter* (Grand Rapids, MI: Eerdmans, 1984); James E. Dougherty, *The Bishops and Nuclear Weapons* (Hamden, CT: Archon Books, 1984); Judith A. Dwyer, ed. *The Catholic Bishops and Nuclear War* (Washington, DC: Georgetown University Press, 1984).

29. Seabury and Codevilla (above, n. 9), p.48.

30. For one perspective, see Robert H. Bork, *The Tempting of America* (New York: The Free Press, 1990).

31. *Time*, 11 February 1991: 42. See also Michael Novak, "Of War and Justice," *Forbes*, 4 March 1991: 58.

32. James F. Childress, *Moral Responsibility in Conflicts* (Baton Rouge, LA: Louisiana State University Press, 1982), p. 92. For a very useful, succinct analysis of these criteria, see Douglas P. Lackey, *The Ethics of War and Peace* (Englewood Cliffs, NJ: Prentice-Hall, 1989). His case studies showing the application of these concepts are exceptionally well done.

33. Robert E. Osgood and Robert W. Tucker, *Force, Order, and Justice* (Baltimore, MD: The Johns Hopkins Press, 1967), p. 257. In a footnote on that same page they quote Friedrich Meinecke: "Only so long as the statesman is uncertain which is the true *raison d'etat* is it possible for him to choose."

34. Seabury and Codevilla (above, n. 9), p. 7.

35. Michael Walzer, *Just and Unjust Wars* (New York: Basic Books, 1977), pp. 4, 19. Probably the finest work in the field of *jus in bello* is that of William V. O'Brien, *The Conduct of Just and Limited War* (New York: Praeger, 1981). See also Sheldon Cohen, *Arms and Judgment* (Boulder, CO: Westview Press, 1989). A little-known volume that offers some interesting exchanges is *Just War Theory in the Nuclear Age*, ed. John D. Jones and Marc Griesbach (Lanham, MD: University Press of America, 1985). Of course, James Turner Johnson, *The Just War Tradition and the Restraint of War* (Princeton, NJ: Princeton University Press, 1981) is by now a standard reference. See pp. 20–30 for an interesting commentary on Walzer's book. The notes and bibliographies in these books will fruitfully absorb the most serious reader and researcher for years.

36. Childress (above, n. 32), p. 93. See also Gordon C. Zahn, "Pacifism and the

Just War," in *Catholics and Nuclear War*, ed. Philip J. Murnion (New York: Crossroad, 1983). For a "Methodist" view, see Todd Whitmore, ed., *Ethics in the Nuclear Age* (Dallas, TX: Southern Methodist University, 1989). The statement of the Methodist bishops is on pp. 167–68.

37. See the interesting piece by and about Dale Noyd, "An Unjust and Immoral War," in *War and Peace*, ed. Edward K. Eckert (Belmont, CA: Wadsworth, 1990), pp. 376–80. William O'Brien took a different view. See *U.S. Military Intervention: Law and Morality* (Beverly Hills, CA: Sage, 1979).

38. Robert L. Phillips, *War and Justice* (Norman, OK: University of Oklahoma Press, 1984), p. 13. For a useful overview of these criteria in a hypothetical setting, see James L. Carney, "Is It Ever Moral to Push the Button?" in *The Parameters of Military Ethics*, ed. Lloyd Matthews and Dale Brown (Washington, DC: Pergamon-Brassey's, 1989), pp. 39–52. In Osgood and Tucker (above, n. 33), one finds another useful explanation of "double effect," which "attempts to reconcile the injunction against doing evil that good may come with the taking of certain acts that are known . . . to entail evil effects. In the case of war it is evident that this attempted reconciliation is mandatory if war is to be sanctioned at all . . ." (p. 310n).

39. Donald A. Wells, "How Much Can the 'Just War' Justify?" *Journal of Philosophy* 66 (4 December 1969): 829.

40. John Courtney Murray, *We Hold These Truths* (New York: Sheed and Ward, 1960), p. 12. One wonders what the late Father Murray would have thought about the "political correctness" of many American campuses in the 1990s!

41. Alasdair MacIntyre, *After Virtue* (Notre Dame, IN: University of Notre Dame Press, 1981), p. 263. I am indebted to George Weigel (above, n. 17), pp. 424–25, for the idea of the connection between Murray and MacIntyre.

42. "For prayer is not only the profoundest realism; if sincere, it is also the most and best that anyone can do for peace." John Finnis, Joseph Boyle, and Germain Grisez, *Nuclear Deterrence, Morality, and Realism* (Oxford, England: Oxford University Press, 1987), p. 388. Because this book is principally concerned with nuclear deterrence, it is largely peripheral to the issues here, but is an exceptionally well-argued book, leading, however (I think mistakenly), to a conclusion of recommended unilateral western disarmament.

43. Paul Starr, "No Vietnam," *The New Republic*, 18 February 1991: 8, 10.

44. Quoted in *The Challenge of Peace* (above n. 28), p. 24. Original in italics.

45. Quoted in James Turner Johnson, "Does Defense of Values by Force Remain a Moral Possibility?" in Matthews and Brown, eds. (above, n. 38), p. 7. Johnson also quotes Erasmus (c. 1466–1536): "Think . . . of all the crimes that are committed with war as a pretext, while 'good lawes fall silent amid the clash of arms'—all the instances of sack and sacrilege, rape, and other shameful acts . . . . And even when the war is over, this moral corruption is bound to linger for many years. Now assess for me the cost—a cost so great that, even if you win the war, you will lose much more than you gain. Indeed, what realm . . . can be weighed against the life, the blood, of so many thousand men?" (p. 8). As I mentioned in the text noted, I once heard a Jewish musician answer that question.

Johnson argues that "There is ultimately no way to get to the truth or falsity of various perceptions of value" (p. 8). Then, of course, there *is* no point to war, for we would never know what it protects. Then, of course, there would be no point to pacifism, for we would never be able to evaluate its wisdom or folly: there would be no evaluation at all, for there would be no way to distinguish truth from falsity—or honor from shame, or right from wrong. Some of the new barbarians dress well; they have ways to choose their wardrobes, but not their ethics.

5 COMMAND AND CONSCIENCE

War is very simple, direct and ruthless. It takes a simple, direct, and ruthless man to wage war.
— George S. Patton, Jr., Diary Entry, 15 April 1943

In war the chief incalculable is the human will.
— B. H. Liddell Hart, "Strategy," (*Encyclopedia Brittanica*, 1929 ed.)

From Plato's *Crito* to William F. Buckley's recent book *Gratitude*,[1] from Thucydides' accounts of Athenian patriotism to the outburst of national fervor in the United States during the 1991 Gulf War, people generally are willing to accept the obligations of citizenship. The nature and the extent of that acceptance are the elements of the notion of civic virtue. To what extent does the citizen owe his regime loyalty? When is that loyalty forfeited by a regime because of its heinous actions or hideous beliefs? *Command* can mean *authority, control, dominion, leadership*, or *rule*. *Conscience* refers to *ethics, morals, principles, scruples*, or *standards*. The premier task of political theory is to effect harmony between the good man and the good society. The good man in Nazi Germany will be a bad citizen. The good citizen in Nazi Germany will be a bad man. Because man is a political being, as both Aristotle (politically) and the Bible (religiously) have instructed us for 2000 years, the good political order is needed for man's full contentment. One can, of course, enjoy moral liberty even if he be in chains. But we humans require material well being, physical safety and security, *and* a sense of self-worth in order to know the kind of happiness about which the classical and early Christian philosophers wrote. (*Happiness* as a concept is little understood today; it is frequently confused with the kind of reckless self-indulgence and libertinism of pop rock music. There is a difference between liberty and libido.)

One of the reasons that one finds both Aristotle and Paul discussing the need for community is their awareness of human weakness. The most heroic of us may be willing, for a time, to buck the crowd, to take the lonely stand; but all except the greatest among us will soon accept the popular mandate. "To get along," goes the popular wisdom, "you gotta go along." To excuse or rationalize cheating on exams, students sometimes will suggest that the "wise" among them "cooperate and graduate." The circumstances in which one daily finds himself contribute powerfully, if not principally, to the development of one's character. We are more than our family and our friends and our country; but precisely how much more we may be is a subject of great dispute. This chapter is not intended to deal with the nature vs. nurture debate. It is intended to suggest, with Michael Howard, that "A good community will be one whose laws a good man will wish to obey—in which he can, without offence [*sic*] to his conscience, be a law-abiding citizen."[2]

VIEWS OF THE NATION

One supposes—always a dangerous thing, such conjecture!—that most will perceive the ever present strains between command (politics, the sword) and conscience (ethics, the cross). But many perceive no such tension. On the one hand, for example, are those who see the nation or the state as the fount and origin of all values. The good life, therefore, "consists in total and selfless dedication to the service of the state, particularly in its armed conflicts with other states."[3] This view of the nation is rare today, the events of 1945—and of 1990— largely canceling it out; there is no doubt, however, that it will manifest itself again in the near future. This view of the nation exalts it to the point of jingoism; it admits of little room for conscience, except for a conscience entirely in keeping with the aims of the state.

A different kind of view of the state would be the type common on many American college campuses in the late 1960s and early 1970s in which a kind of radical nihilism became popular. From this perspective the state could make no claims on personal fealty; a kind of anarchism triumphed. (One wishes to write "ruled.") This view of the state allows for little command, instead exalting privacy, approving a kind of balkanization of interests. In the first view, there is little, if any, private concern; in the second view, there is little, if any, public concern. In the first view, all that matters is the state; in the second view, all that matters is the self. In the first view, the superpatriot triumphs; in the second, the solipsist. In neither view is there room for sword and cross; in neither view is there concern about civic virtue.

A third view of the state holds, as Michael Howard writes, "not that the state creates ethical values, but that it has itself been created by and embodies them."[4] In this view, the state becomes a kind of universal ideal, comprised of globally shared values.[5] Revolutionary France, Soviet Russia, and a sociopolitically (if not economically) imperialist America might well be subsumed under this heading. As Arthur Schlesinger, Jr. has observed, "The Anglo-American tradition, in particular, has long been addicted to the presentation of egoism in the guise of altruism."[6] Thus the state exists in the service of a cause far greater than itself. The state and its citizens identify with themselves "writ large." This extreme case of ethnocentrism is described well by the late Hans Morgenthau:

So each nation comes to know again a universal morality—that is, its own national morality—which is taken to be the one that all the other nations ought to accept as their own. The universality of an ethics to which all nations [ought to] adhere is replaced by the particularity of national ethics which claims the right to, and aspires toward, universal recognition. There are then potentially as many ethical codes claiming universality as there are politically dynamic nations.[7]

The third view of the state permits the nation and its institutions effectively to supersede any idea of a transcendent power or order, for they themselves become that power in much the same way that the fascist (in view one) might perceive the state. In the third view, the state's commitment to higher values endows the country with license to do practically what it will, for its aims have been universalized. By the same token, however, that state has deprived itself of the perspective and the balance which a sense of limitation and an awareness of divine judgment can impart. In the third view of the nation, its citizens have become religious zealots; their god themselves; their state, their church; their leaders, their priests; their national documents, their scripture; their national goals, their demands of all others—in the name, not of their country, but of their glorified national image. They sit in judgment on themselves, and they therefore have no judge; nor have they standards to appeal to or to measure themselves by, for, although they detest fascism, they have created the idol of "The People."

The fourth view of the nation is that of the early church fathers, although theirs is not an exclusive claim to this conception of the state or nation. In this view the state is a necessary means of political organization. To be sure, Augustine and Thomas Aquinas would have disputed the worth and integrity of the state, the former holding that it owes its genesis to corruption and the latter contending that it is a natural occurrence and not necessarily evil in itself. Such differences as exist between them, however, are in degree and not of kind. The state, in this view, can lay legitimate claim upon the conscience of the citizen. In promoting good order and discipline, the state can serve reasonable and practical ends and, on that account alone, has the right to command obedience until the secular fiat and the divine order, as understood through right reason and the teaching of the church, conflict. It is only with this latter view of the people (the nation) and the state (their political institutions) with which one can associate the problems and prospects of command and conscience. For it is here that the tensions between the two are sharpest.

In the third view, there is conscience consisting of private (that is, nationalistic) goals and glories projected onto the global screen; there *is* a morality and even a higher standard that would pass some of the customary ethical tests. But the higher cause has been usurped by a nationalistic universalism. The nation seeks, not after natural law, but after national law. This is not to say that such a nation is always bad, but only that it sees good only as *its* good, magnified.

In the fourth view, politics is a noble enterprise, for it consists not only in the accommodation of competing interests but also in the quest for the consummate interest, which is to say the best regime; here politics is the continuous enterprise of reconciling the "is" with the "ought"; here, too, politics and ethics and education together work to ensure that good men and good society will coincide, that justice and law will coexist. There is eternal conversation about "civic," which means secular, and "virtue," meaning sacred—and how the two can most be complementary this side of the angels.

Without a fourth view of the people and of their institutions, which is necessarily a limited view, promising no eternal redemption through political machinations, there is no problem of "command and conscience." Consequently, in views one through three, there is no politics; for, at its heart, politics is the perpetual struggle between command and conscience, a struggle illusorily concluded in views one through three.

One superbly concise statement of this is that of Jacques Maritain:

The State is not the supreme incarnation of the Idea, as Hegel believed; the State is not a kind of collective superman; the State is but an agency entitled to use power and coercion, . . . an instrument in the service of man. Putting man at the service of that instrument is political perversion. The human person as an individual is for the body politic and the body politic is for the human person as a person. But man is by no means for the State. The State is for man.[8]

Conscience, whatever it is, can be no mere reflection of either national will or of macropolitical reality. At the same time, because we have duties to the state, as to our neighbor, conscience can be no mere reflection of private convenience or personal preference. The task of reconciling private desire and public demand, of preserving personal dignities while accomplishing public duties, is of the very essence of any scheme of ordered liberty, requiring cultivation of all the virtues, both cardinal and theological—and ample grace.

CONSCIENCE

Conscience, then, must be more than mere personal choice, for if that were all the matter involved, one could "follow his conscience"— and do practically anything. Upon apprehension and trial the felon could simply say, "I was doing what my conscience instructed me; I was being sincere!" But conscience must also be more than sycophancy, more than blindly following the dictates of some leader. If that were all the matter involved, one could "follow the leader"—and do practically anything. Upon apprehension and trial the felon could simply say, "I was just following orders; I was being sincere!" Richard John Neuhaus has this explanation:

The choice, we would contend, is not between the private conscience and the public conscience expressed by the state . . . . Private conscience too is communal; it is shaped by the myriad communities from which we learn to "put the world together" in an order that is responsive to our understanding of right and wrong. As for "the public conscience," it is a categorical fallacy. It harks back to Rousseau's mythology of a "general will" of which the state is the expression. "The Public" does not have a conscience. "The People" does not have a conscience. Only persons and persons-in-community have consciences.[9]

Our conscience is formed, as Neuhaus suggests, by a plethora of communal sources. One can argue that human community builds and shapes the inchoate sense sealed into the human heart. The term *conscience* is met about thirty times in the New Testament: twenty times in Paul's Epistles, five times in the Epistle to the Hebrews, three times in the first Epistle of Peter, and twice in the Acts of the Apostles. As one scholar has concluded:

[F]or the NT authors conscience-*syneidesis* meant a consciousness of the true moral content of human life founded on faith . . . insofar as this faith is conceived as a personal engagement with God coloring man's whole outlook on reality—on God, on man, and on the cosmos itself and all that happens in it (cf. Rom. 14.1, 23; 13.5; 1 Pt. 2.19).[10]

One begins to see a pattern here. Through faith (or, as some would have it, as a function of the inherent powers of reason we are born with[11]), we engage in a dialogue of sorts with God—prayer, the sacraments, and various devotions assisting—as we nurture our conscience with good education, or with education in the Good. It is, of course, the community, the polis, the nation, the state which nurtures us. The term *socialization* has a limited sociological meaning, but I employ it here to mean the development of a social consciousness. The term *paideia* (and *arete*) might well be used; we refer to education in character. But in the same source, one reads this remarkable passage:

In the business of Christian daily living, with its infinite variety of changing situations and circumstances, *it is clearly not enough to rely on a spontaneous reaction alone as a guide. For from the very nature of things, this may be faulty* . . . . The corrective of counsel and deliberation, ordained toward fitting Christian living to all the demands of human life, is necessary. In other words, over and above conscience, practical wisdom, also called prudence or discretion in the Christian tradition, is of vital importance. Without this wisdom, which on the one side looks to the objective and divine order of things and on the other is always in the service of charity, mediating it realistically and truly into the flux of life, *conscience alone would frequently lead man astray.*[12]

Private revelation is a matter for religious speculation. The great danger with such episodes, bordering on the gnosticism of which Eric Voegelin wrote so powerfully, is that God's private epiphanies have been the sign and symbol to some of "divine mandates" most of the rest of us might well reject as sinful. When Jim Jones, for example, went off to South America, there to slaughter his followers on the strength of some inner vision, few of the rest of us were prepared to accept Jones's conscience or his claims of revelation as justification for his personal perversions. *Conscience* must square itself both with the political order and with the wellsprings of honor and of shame, of right and of wrong, alluded to so frequently in the Bible (OT, see Wisd. of Sol. 17:11). Nobody ever said being human was easy.

ON LAW

A way to understand this dilemma, perhaps the greatest in political life, is to examine briefly the idea of law itself. *Law* is defined by some as merely an "institutionalized norm," meaning that what people do over time is given force of law. One could examine here the notion of *common law* and of *stare decisis*, but such carries us too far from the present concern. St. Thomas Aquinas offers this provocative definition: Law is "an ordinance of reason for the common good, made by him who has care of the community, and promulgated" (*Summa Theologica*, XC, Art. 4). This succinct definition in fact summarizes our argument to this point: Unless one is an anarchist or a nihilist— or the most extreme solipsist—one is prepared to accept community.

Community implies leaders and laws, which give effect to the people's needs and desires and expectations. *Law* suggests that there is consensus on certain issues, although politics has led to such consensus and may, over time, remove or alter it. Leaders and laws require an ethical sense *and* a practical wisdom, deriving from our nature and our education. Laws serving solely private ends are by definition defective; laws held by the community to be irrational are, by definition, defective. Laws must be communicated, announced, and explained in order to gain widespread understanding and respect; they cannot apply privately to a few. The one who has "care of the community," failing seriously and repeatedly in that trust, has forfeited his claim to the exercise of legal power. Politics is the art of reconciling faith (which is essentially private with public consequences) and reason (which through the province of education is essentially public with private consequences).

Aquinas (1225–1274) suggests that positive, or human, laws are either just or unjust. "If they are just," he writes, "they have the power of binding in conscience, from the eternal law from which they are derived, according to Prov. 8.15: *By Me kings reign, and lawgivers decree just things*." But laws "contrary to human good" or "being opposed to the Divine good" should "in no way be observed, because, as stated in Acts 5.29, *we ought to obey God rather than men*" (*Summa Theologica*, XCVI, Art. 4). In his famous "Letter from Birmingham Jail," Martin Luther King was to employ precisely this logic in refusing to accept the power of what he regarded as unjust and discriminatory laws. Indeed, from *Antigone* through *Billy Budd*; from the *Apology* through *To Kill a Mockingbird*; from Augustine and Aristotle and Marcus Aurelius through the social contract theorists to Hannah Arendt and Niebuhr and through the plays of Ibsen and Sartre and so many others, serious thinkers have debated the power of command as opposed to the power of conscience.[13] But when law is coincidental with justice, the debate is resolved.

This is a rhetorical solution only. Perfect law and perfect justice will not prevail, short of the Parousia. Perfect justice suggests an end to conflict, save only for the most wicked. But we know that conflict accompanies human community. Thus those who deal in politics and law must deal in conflict *unless* they withdraw from civic affairs altogether (the "pereat mundus" position) or, at the other end of the spectrum, abandon their consciences entirely, consenting wholly to the judgment of the State. But to say, "Thy will be done!" (without any reservation whatever), while perhaps a religious good when said to and in the service of Almighty God, is the ultimate idolatry when said to and in the service of the almighty state. Only God can combine perfect power with perfect justice; when the state—and its mortal leaders—have perfect power we may be sure only of the antithesis of justice, which is corruption.

ON COMPROMISE

We come then to the denouement: compromise. John Silber points out that the moralist insists upon acting in accordance with his conscience, saying "Let justice be done, though the heavens fall [the *pereat mundus* position]." But the politician says, "I'll compromise my conscience and the ideal of justice to achieve as much actual justice as I can." Silber explains that "Persons who consider their consciences the final authority commit the sin of pride, since there is no guarantee of the rightness of an individual conscience." Both Bull Connor and Martin Luther King, Jr., he suggests, were sincere, but we can reject Sheriff Connor (of Birmingham) and his views about segregation, for they are rooted in a debased moral insight. "In humility, we must test the promptings of our conscience against those of others who may be more knowledgeable, wiser, and better than ourselves." We must, he contends, reject the "arrogant purists, who deify their own personal consciences, and the cynical opportunists, who sell out their ideals for political expedience."[14]

A brilliant and concise rendition of this problem is the recent work of Joseph S. Nye, Jr., who suggests that we can talk about the ethics of virtue (focusing on the person doing something) and the ethics of consequence (focusing on the results of the act).[15] Nye asks, much as Silber did, "At some point does not integrity become the ultimate egoism of fastidious self-righteousness in which the purity of the self is more important than the lives of countless others?" Almost plaintively, he asks "Is it not better to follow a consequentialist approach, admit remorse or regret over the immoral means, but justify the action by the consequences?" At the same time, Nye hesitates: "Once the ends justify the means, the dangers of slipping into a morality of convenience greatly increase." If a utilitarian is prepared to judge every act regardless of rules which, in the view of some might well apply to that act, the peril is a shallowness that corrupts moral judgment. Moreover, he points out, "when it becomes known that integrity plays no role and you will always choose the lesser of evils as between immediate consequences, you open yourself to blackmail by those who play dirty games."[16]

But this seems antiseptic, clinical. What is its actual application to politics? Almost thirty years ago, Dean Acheson, Truman's Secretary of State, made a little-known speech. He died a few years later (1971) and the speech was largely forgotten. Although Nye makes no mention of it, Acheson's speech is strikingly similar to Nye's analysis. "The righteous," Acheson said, "who seek to deduce foreign policy from ethical or moral principles are as misleading and misled as the modern Machiavellis who would conduct our foreign relations without regard to them." Moral maxims, Acheson contends, have little relevance to the affairs of state; it is necessary, he argues, to employ criteria that are "hard-headed in the extreme." His peroration merits quotation at length:

Is it moral to deny ourselves the use of force in all circumstances, when our adversaries employ it, under handy excuses, whenever it seems useful to tip the scales of power against every value we think of as moral and as making life worth living? It seems to me not only a bad bargain, but a stupid one. I would almost say an immoral one.

Was the United States right to develop a thermonuclear weapon?

A respected colleague advised me that it would be better that our whole nation and people should perish rather than be a party to a course so evil as producing that weapon. I told him that on the Day of Judgment his view might be confirmed and that he was free to go forth and preach the necessity for salvation. It was not, however, a view which I could entertain as a public servant.

Is that not saying merely that the ends justify the means, a crass consequentialism? "If you object that is no different from saying that the end justifies the means, I must answer that in foreign affairs only the end can justify the means; that this is not to say that the end justifies any means, or that some ends can justify anything."[17]

Professor Nye suggests what he terms "three-dimensional ethics" as a way of discerning the right and prudent path to choose in the jungle of world politics. One must understand motives and means and consequences. Nye introduces a table showing the possible trade-offs among these three considerations; the specifics of Nye's argument need not detain us here. His point, however, is critical. He asks for a strong presumption in favor of rules (deontology or "virtue") placing a heavy burden on those wishing to depart from the rules in certain cases (leaning toward consequentialism). "Moral praise would be for the person or a society disposed toward careful moral reasoning that was respectful of all three dimensions," Nye says.[18]

There is, as novelist Edwin O'Connor might have put it, "an edge of sadness" to all of this. Here is Guenter Lewy arguing about the command decision of American leaders as they intervened in Vietnam. Did their decisions violate the dictates of conscience?

Just as the success of a policy [consequentialism] does not prove that it was the only possible successful course of action, a policy can be correct even if for a variety of reasons it fails. The commitment to aid South Vietnam was made by intelligent and reasonable men who tackled an intractable problem in the face of great uncertainties . . . . The fact that some of their judgments . . . [were] flawed and that the outcome has been a fiasco does not make them villains or fools. If Hitler in 1940 had succeeded in conquering Britain, this would not have proven wrong Churchill's belief in the possibility and moral worth of resistance to the Nazis. Policy-makers always have to act on uncertain assumptions and inadequate information, and some of the noblest decisions in history have involved great risks. As long as there exists a reasonable expectation of success, the statesman who fails can perhaps be pitied, but he should not be condemned.[19]

Morgenthau for years told the sad story of Neville Chamberlain, a good man faced with Hitler. His good motives *may* have helped produce World War II. "Good motives," Morgenthau writes, "give assurance against deliberately bad policies; they do not guarantee the moral goodness and political success of the policies they inspire."[20] The statesman has to act, in the words of Michael Howard (although it could as easily be Acheson) "not as his own values would dictate, but as the policy of his government requires." He continues: "The best that a 'moral' statesman involved in such a dilemma can do is to realise that it *is* a dilemma; that he is an actor in the familiar tragedy brought about by a conflict of values; and that though nothing can be gained by renouncing his role, that role is a tragic one."[21] Thus did another analyst say that "The best solution rarely is without its costs . . . . And one mark of moral maturity is an appreciation of the inevitability of untoward and often malignant effects of benign moral choices.[22] Howard, incidentally, does not want the statesman pitied; he wants him to be remembered in prayers.

Nye's "three-dimensional ethics" *is* a useful paradigm. But we need to keep prominently in mind that statesmen politically and morally *must* choose as prudentially as possible. But they can prophesy *neither* means *nor* ends. When George Bush began the war against Iraq in 1991, he could not augur exactly how U.S. weaponry would be employed (proportionality and discrimination); nor could he predict with certainty the outcome of the conflict. Lewy's point, then, is well taken. The outcome of a conflict should not be the sole criterion by which to judge a statesman's sword or cross. How, for example, would Lincoln be seen today if the North had lost the Civil War? Morgenthau points out that statesmen bear a continuous moral responsibility for "the unforeseen and unforeseeable consequences of their actions." He points out as well that Roman law suggested that nobody is obligated beyond his capacity (*ultra vires nemo obligatur*). That is worth keeping in mind when we hold statesmen responsible for "unforeseeable" things![23]

In the same way that we must compromise the ethic of virtue with the ethic of responsibility, so must we compromise between holding the statesman responsible for catastrophes and, at the same time, pitying him or praying for him, if not fully pardoning him. Before he was made Henry VIII's Lord Chancellor, Sir Thomas More had considered whether moral philosophy had any place "in the council of princes." He concluded that it did, but in a subtle way. "You must strive to guide policy indirectly, so that you make the best of things, and what you cannot turn to good, you can at least make less bad. For it is impossible to do all things well unless all men are good, and this I do not expect to see for a long time."[24]

Some reject the ambiguity of statesmanship, choosing wholly either the sword or the cross. They are the great simplifiers, the fundamentalists, to whom humane uncertainty[25] is anathema. They fail to appreciate that such ambiguity endows us with the opportunity to choose as we ought to and thus to discover and to preserve our humanity by employing finite reason in the service of the infinite ideal of faith.

ON THE SOLDIER'S FAITH

Oliver Wendell Holmes, Jr., who served in the Civil War, claimed that "the faith is true and adorable which leads a soldier to throw away his life in obedience to a blindly accepted duty, in a cause which he little understands, in a plan of campaign of which he has no notion, under tactics of which he does not see the use."[26] Such extreme abnegation of conscience is both immoral and, as will be pointed out below, illegal. But it is a common theme. Fred Downs was an infantry lieutenant and platoon leader in Vietnam. His argument is as extreme as that of Holmes, if rather less elegant:

In the jungle we never took prisoners if we could help it. Every day we spent in the jungle eroded a little more of our humanity away. Prisoners could escape to become our enemy again. Hence, no prisoners.

The philosophical arguments in favor of man's ability to resist the slide into barbarism sound noble and rational in a classroom or at a cocktail party. But when the enemy is bearing down, bent on taking your life away from you, it's not his country against your country, not his army against your army, not his philosophy against your philosophy—it's the fact that that son-of-a-bitch is trying to kill you and you'd better kill him first.[27]

Still another variety of this extreme view—this one from the top—is mentioned by General Matthew Ridgway in his book *Soldier*: "At a staff meeting before a big attack [in World War I] some fire-eating division commander tapped at a little dot on the map . . . and said: 'I'd give ten thousand men to take that hill.' There was a moment of silence, and then from the back of the room, . . . there came an ironic voice: 'Generous son-of-a-bitch, isn't he?'" At Gallipoli in 1915, Major General Hunter-Weston is supposed to have said, "Casualties? What do I care about casualties?"

A very different point of view was that of a young Marine in 1990, who refused to board a military transport plane for deployment to Saudi Arabia as the Gulf War was beginning. He claimed that he could not allow himself to be "an accomplice of the military-industrial complex," even though he had volunteered for the Marine Corps.[28] Many other examples might be cited, but the case of Air Force Lieutenant John VanderMolen is worth a note. That Air Force officer decided he could not push a button sending off nuclear missiles; the Air Force removed him from the service for "substandard performances of duty."[29] As there can be people with no scruples, so can there be, as one writer put it, "moralitymongers," who see ethical issues everywhere: "In staff meetings, regardless of whether the problem under discussion is animal, vegetable or mineral, the Moralitymonger manages to frame it in ethical terms, thus putting the other staffers on the defensive while elevating his own soul—but rarely coming up with a practical solution."[30]

Many military problems are, at heart, leadership issues.[31] General John J. Pershing is supposed to have said, "All a soldier needs to know is how to shoot and salute." Precisely that kind of attitude led George Bernard Shaw to observe, "I never expect a soldier to think." But if they are to be ethical—and to obey both the natural (and, if you will, divine) law *and* the positive law of nations, soldiers *must* think. How do they resolve the possibly terrible (if relatively rare) contradictions between accomplishment of the mission and the welfare of the men? Military autobiographies—one thinks of General Curtis Lemay's—are filled with reflections about the traumas of getting their jobs done at the expense of men's lives.[32] But a soldier thrown into paroxysms of "moralitymongering" to the point of ethical paralysis will do no good for anyone. While the remark attributed to Pershing is surely outrageous, the soldier is and must be expected to obey so that the mission can be accomplished. As Samuel Huntington has written:

[L]oyalty and obedience are the highest military virtues . . . . When the military man receives a *legal* order [my emphasis] from an authorized superior, he does not argue, he does not hesitate, he does not substitute his own views; he obeys instantly. He is judged not by the policies he implements, but rather by the promptness and efficiency with which he carries them out. His goal is to perfect an instrument of obedience; the uses to which that instrument is put are beyond his responsibility . . . . Like Shakespeare's soldier in *Henry V*, he believes that the justice of the cause is more than he should "know" or "seek after." For if the king's "cause be wrong, our obedience to the King wipes the crime of it out of us."[33]

Such unthinking loyalty to the command and to the mission, while appearing commendable, runs the risk of political stupidity and of ethical peril. In Tokyo, in 1925, a dog named Hachiko used to wait every day at the train station for his master until, one day, the master died while away. The dog remained there, fed by the public, for ten years until he died. A statue was erected in memory of Hachiko and his loyalty. As Sidney Axinn points out, "A human who behaved like Hachiko, whose knowledge of the facts of the world was as limited, would be classified as retarded."[34] International law is designed to prevent "political Hachikos" from exercising unrestrained power.

The American Uniform Code of Military Justice is very clear that it is a court-martial offense for any soldier to disobey a lawful command, order, or regulation (Articles 90–92). At the same time, "the King's cause" is not enough to excuse vicious or wanton behavior. The International Law Commission stipulates that "the fact that a person acted on the orders of his Government or of a superior officer does not relieve him from responsibility under international law, *provided a moral choice was in fact open to him.*"[35] The notion of *Respondeat Superior*—let the higher commander answer—was struck down at the post-World War II war crimes trials. As a U.S. Army field manual carefully explains:

The fact that the law of war has been violated pursuant to an order of a superior authority, whether military or civil, does not deprive the act in question of its character of a war crime, nor does it constitute a defense in the trial of an accused individual, unless he did not know and could not reasonably have been expected to know that the act ordered was unlawful.

The same manual states that "The fact that domestic law does not impose a penalty for an act which constitutes a crime under international law does not relieve the person who committed the act from responsibility under international law."[36]

Because the Declaration of Independence justified the birth of the American nation as an entitlement of the "Laws of Nature and of Nature's God"; because American coins and currency proclaim that "In God We Trust"; and because, since 1954, the American pledge to the flag assumes "one nation under God"—the American nation and its command can hardly do other than to recognize the soldier's conscience as complementary to, and not necessarily destructive of, military discipline. The American soldier, for his part, is urged by his Code of Conduct to "trust in [his] God and in the United States of America." Should circumstances require him to choose between the two, honor obliges him to be "responsible for [his] actions" and to accept willingly and manfully the consequences of that choice.

ON THE SOLDIER'S FATE

In *The Ghost of Napoleon*, Basil H. Liddell Hart observed that "The nature of armies is determined by the nature of the civilization in which they exist." If the command is morally and politically sound, the consciences of the subordinates will rarely have to be troubled. Still, there clearly can be stupid commanders; gifted and wildly ambitious commanders incapable of admitting mistakes or misjudgments, and intent upon self-promotion; and institutional or bureaucratic tyranny, which holds the lives of individuals in contempt compared with the advancement of the group—all these situations lead, or may lead, to the kind of ethical and political command defects requiring decisions of conscience by soldiers (or by subordinates in any field).[37] J. Glenn Gray, a World War II soldier, contended that "survival without integrity of conscience is worse than perishing outright," and, in support of that position, he tells the story of a German soldier, a member of an execution squad, who, when ordered to shoot innocent hostages, refused to participate. Charged with treason, the soldier was then placed with the hostages and promptly executed by his comrades.[38] Josiah Bunting, a former U.S. Army officer, wrote that military bureaucrats are fascinated "by power, fame, station and place to the extent that their consciences, individually, rarely can inoculate them against such claims." His solution: "Therefore we must inoculate the system itself by encouraging men to follow the dictates of conscience and to ignore the worldly rewards of bureaucratic success."[39] That is the spirit of the biblical counsel: "Do not conform yourself to this age but be transformed by the renewal of your mind, that you may discern what is the will of God, what is good and pleasing and perfect" (Rom. 12:2).

The problem, of course, is that merely encouraging soldiers to follow their conscience (whatever that may be) or to ask of men that they not conform themselves "to this age" is unlikely to settle or to solve the fate of the soldier. For the soldier suffers the same fate, experiences the same conundrum, as do we all: living in the world, we frequently make our way (and our living) from working in and for a bureaucracy; we have civic duties. Aspiring to the next world and abiding by its adjurations, we owe loyalty to the dominion of justice; we have duties, as well, under the rubric of virtue. The fate of the soldier is the destiny of his human race: to do the very best he can. To aid him, he has the notions of strategy, the stipulations of the just war, the concepts of Nye's "three-dimensional ethics." But the profoundly unhappy truth of the matter is that none of us ever knows perfectly well where the right lies. We cannot predict consequences, for we are not clairvoyant; we cannot determine in advance in what direction our means may lead us, for "the fog of battle" clouds our finite vision. We are left, as William Safire tells us, with the idea of honest intention, however unsatisfactory that may be, for "the protection of acting in good faith, with no malicious intent, is what makes decision-making possible. It applies to all of us . . . . The doctor who undertakes a risky operation, the lawyer who gambles on an unorthodox defense to save his client, the businessman who bets the company on a new product." As Professor Nye points out, "While such an argument can be abused if good motives are treated as an automatic one-dimensional exculpation, it can be used by broad consequentialists as a grounds for including evaluation of motives in the overall judgment of an act."[40]

A particularly compelling insight into this critical point is one provided by Abraham Lincoln:

In great contests each party claims to act in accordance with the will of God. Both *may* be, and one *must* be wrong. God can not be *for*, and *against* the same thing at the same time . . . .

I am approached with the most opposite opinions and advice, and that by religious men, who are equally certain that they represent the Divine will. I am sure that either the one or the other class is mistaken in that belief, and perhaps in some respects both. I hope it will not be irreverent for me to say that if it is probable that God would reveal his will to others, on a point so concerned with my duty, it might be supposed that he would reveal it directly to me; for, unless I am more deceived in myself than I often am, it is my earnest desire to know the will of Providence in this matter. *And if I can learn what it is I will do!* These are not, however, the days of miracles, and I suppose it will be granted that I am not to expect a direct revelation. I must study the plain physical facts of the case, ascertain what is possible and learn what appears to be wise and right.[41]

Lincoln's powerful passage moves us, in part, *because it is Lincoln.* But listen to Machiavelli in a passage from *The Prince*, written in 1513: "In the nature of things, you can never try to escape one danger without encountering another; but prudence consists in knowing how to recognize the nature of the different dangers and in accepting the least bad as good" (Chapter 21). In this Lincolnesque and Machiavellian mode, Reinhold Niebuhr wrote about the idealists who have too many illusions and the realists who have too little conscience. Thus the commander, whether civilian or military, must resist, on the one hand, the Scylla of perfectionism and the Charybdis of cynicism. As John Coleman Bennett says in his book *Foreign Policy in Christian Perspective*, "We may say that Christian faith and ethics offer ultimate perspectives, broad criteria, motives, inspirations, sensitivities, warning, moral limits rather than directives for policies and decisions."[42] These are not the days of miracles.

CONCLUSION

In a famous passage in the *Critique of Pure Reason* (1781), Immanuel Kant wrote: "Two things fill my mind with ever new and increasing awe . . . the starry heavens above me and the moral law within me." As John Silber says,

Kant identifies in this one short statement the fundamental conditions on which moral action—whether in personal or public life—depends. One must with good intentions follow the moral law. But to apply the moral law effectively, the person of goodwill must take account of external reality, to which Kant refers as "the starry heavens above." This dual task is difficult: The pursuit of fairness can take unexpected turns. Glib maxims and obvious answers rarely succeed. Fairness is to be found only at the end of an arduous and painful process of analysis tested against experience—a process that requires all our intelligence, all our judgment, and all our goodwill.[43]

The statesman who seeks to lead and the soldier planning to do battle are both in command; both are responsible to their national traditions and for their national interest; both have—or ought to have—a developed conscience, in which reason wells up, prepared to examine the "plain physical facts of the case." One does the best one can. That simple sentence is no guarantee of success; it is, regrettably, not even a guarantee of integrity, of honor, of reverence. The perpetual labor of harmonizing command and conscience is truly Sisyphean. But with Albert Camus, we may learn that "The struggle itself toward the heights is enough to fill a man's heart. One must imagine Sisyphus happy."[44]

NOTES

1. William F. Buckley, *Gratitude: Reflections on What We Owe to Our Country* (New York: Random House, 1990).

2. Michael Howard, *Studies in War & Peace* (New York: Viking, 1970), p. 235.

3. Howard (above, n. 2), p. 245.

4. Ibid.

5. See Ben Wattenberg, *The First Universal Nation* (New York: The Free Press, 1991).

6. Arthur Schlesinger, Jr., "The Necessary Amorality of Foreign Affairs," *Harper's*, August 1971: 75.

7. Hans J. Morgenthau and Kenneth W. Thompson, *Politics Among Nations* 6th ed. (New York: Knopf, 1985).

8. Jacques Maritain, *Man and the State* (Chicago, IL: University of Chicago Press, 1951), p. 13.

9. Richard John Neuhaus, *The Naked Public Square* (Grand Rapids, MI: Eerdmans, 1984), p. 92.

10. *New Catholic Encyclopedia*, 1967, s.v. "Conscience": 199–200.

11. There are unfortunately the mentally retarded and the insane; the argument is generally intended.

12. *New Catholic Encyclopedia* (above, n. 10): 202. Emphasis supplied.

13. Herman Wouk, *The Caine Mutiny* (Garden City, NY: Doubleday, 1951) is a classic example.

14. John Silber, *Straight Shooting* (New York: Harper & Row, 1989), pp. 188–89.

15. Because this is not an ethics textbook, I must refrain from extended explanation of terms (or references to Max Weber's notions of ethics, to which Nye's concepts are very similar). Briefly, we may understand ethics as deontological or teleological. The latter refers to the results of actions (such as utilitarianism); the former refers to rules or standards which should not be broken, regardless of

consequences. Utilitarians may be act-based or rule-based; similarly, deontologists may be divided into different schools. For details see, e.g., William K. Frankena, *Ethics*, 2d ed. (Englewood Cliffs, NJ: Prentice-Hall, 1973).

16. Joseph S. Nye, Jr., *Nuclear Ethics* (New York: The Free Press, 1986), ch. 2.

17. Dean Acheson, "Ethics in International Relations Today," *Vital Speeches of the Day 31* (1 February 1965): 226–28.

18. Nye (above, n. 16), pp. 21–23. He says that "Moral integrity is a disposition toward: 1. Standards of clarity, logic and consistency. 2. Impartiality (i.e., respect for the interests of others). 3. Initial presumption in favor of rules and rights. 4. Procedures for protecting impartiality. 5. Prudence in calculating consequences" (p. 22).

19. Guenter Lewy, *America in Vietnam* (New York: Oxford University Press, 1978), pp. 440–41.

20. Morgenthau (above, n. 7), p. 6.

21. Howard, (above, n. 2), p. 247.

22. Stephen K. Bailey, "Ethics and the Public Service," in *Public Administration*, ed. Roscoe C. Martin (Syracuse, NY: Syracuse University Press, 1965), p. 298.

23. Morgenthau (above, n. 7), p. 277. See, for example, the rather sad interview with former Secretary of Defense Robert McNamara, in *Time*, 11 February 1991: 70–72.

24. Thomas More, *Utopia*, ed. H. V. Ogden (Arlington Heights, IL: AHM Publishing Corp., 1965), p. 23. Beheaded in 1535, More was canonized in 1935.

25. The term is Glenn Tinder's in his book *Political Thinking: The Perennial Questions,* 3d ed. (Boston, MA: Little, Brown, 1979), p. 193.

26. Quoted in William Pfaff, "Reflections," *The New Yorker*, 10 November 1986: 131.

27. Frederick Downs, *The Killing Zone* (New York: Norton, 1978), p. 149. See also pp. 214–15. Downs's charge to the cadets at West Point makes for interesting reading. See *The Washington Post*, 16 August 1987: D1–D2 or the reprint in *Parameters* 17 (December 1987): 91–95.

28. *Manchester Guardian*, 11 October 1990: 20. An Air Force major (Harold Hering) was retired by the Air Force in 1975 because of his desire to be sure that any order he received for a nuclear missile launching be valid, precluding an unlawful launch. Major Hering was not a conscientious objector, but when he was unable to satisfy himself about an adequate back-up to the "Fail-Safe System," he requested reassignment on grounds of conscience—leading to his forced retirement. *The New York Times*, 13 January 1975: 16. See also Ron Rosenbaum, "The Subterranean World of the Bomb," *Harper's*, March 1978: 85–105.

29. VanderMolen returned to duty after a court ordered the Air Force to reinstate him, largely on legal procedural grounds (*San Francisco Chronicle*, 18 November 1977). That newspaper quoted a dissenting judge, who said, "the Air Force was entitled to discharge an officer who might refuse to obey a legal order." Observed the editor: "That's certainly sound reasoning. The least a military group, whose basic business is waging war, may expect is general obedience to its orders. And we are not talking here about a specific, extraordinary situation (such as the My Lai massacre), where an individual may be forced beyond the bounds of moral conscience, and should, indeed, refuse."

30. Lloyd J. Matthews, "Resignation in Protest," *Army*, January 1990: 18.

31. Two books, of many, might be recommended here. The first is by "David Donovan" [pseudonym for Terry Turner], *Once a Warrior King: Memories of an Officer in Vietnam* (New York: McGraw-Hill, 1985), a superb reminiscence and commentary. The other is Robert L. Taylor and William E. Rosenbach, eds., *Military Leadership: In Pursuit of Excellence* (Boulder, CO: Westview Press, 1984), an extraordinary collection of essays.

32. Curtis E. LeMay with MacKinlay Kantor, *Mission With LeMay: My Storm* (Garden City, NY: Doubleday, 1965). Observed LeMay: "I used to be tormented in losing my airmen . . . . But to worry about the *morality* of what we were doing—Nuts. A soldier has to fight. We fought."

33. Samuel Huntington, *The Soldier and the State* (Cambridge, MA: Belknap Press, 1957), p. 73.

34. Sidney Axinn, *A Moral Military* (Philadelphia, PA: Temple University Press, 1989), pp. 60–61. "Suppose that someone served one and only one master for all or most of his or her life? Would that behavior be beautiful, or would it be doglike? Slavelike?" We think it would be, of course. But then what do we think of the minister, the priest, the rabbi? Does it matter what or whom they serve?

35. Quoted in Sir James Glover, "A Soldier and His Conscience," *Parameters* 13 (September 1983): 54. He writes: "In essence, then, the soldier when answering to his conscience must remember that he not only has the right, but he also has the duty, to disobey an unlawful order."

36. U.S. Department of the Army, *The Law of Land Warfare*, Field Manual 27-10 (Washington, DC: Government Printing Office, 1956), pp. 182–83.

37. Josiah Bunting, "The Conscience of a Soldier," *Worldview*, December 1973, p. 7.

38. J. Glenn Gray, *The Warriors* (New York: Harper & Row, 1959), pp. 185–86, 193. He observes: "Were it not for the revelation of nobility in mankind, which again and again appears in time of war, we could scarcely endure reading the literature of combat." One feels a similar emotion in watching the powerful 1990 film *Glory*, the story of the first black regiment to see combat in the Civil War and of its commander, Colonel Robert Gould Shaw of Massachusetts.

39. Bunting (above, n. 37), p. 11. See also his excellent war novel about the dangers of careerism: *The Lionheads* (New York: Braziller, 1972).

40. Nye (above, n. 16), p. 26.

41. Quoted in Morgenthau (above, n. 7), p. 278.

42. Quoted in Schlesinger (above, n. 6), p. 75. The book was published by Scribner in 1966.

43. Silber (above n. 14), p. 196.

44. Albert Camus, *The Myth of Sisyphus and Other Essays*, trans. Justin O'Brien (New York: Knopf, 1961), p. 123.

6 THE POLITICAL CHRIST OF THE SYNOPTIC GOSPELS

Shame on you! you who call evil good and good evil, who turn darkness into light and light into darkness, who make bitter sweet and sweet bitter.

—Isaiah 5:20

If we claim to be sinless, we are self-deceived and strangers to the truth.
—1 John 1:8

Unless one is either teaching or taking a course in "Christian political theory," one only rarely finds substantial exploration of Christology in most undergraduate-level "political ideas" courses. The thought of raising such notions is simply too controversial. But if this book has suggested a single theme, it would be that faith and reason together form the basis for the apothegms which pass for wisdom in statecraft. Indeed, the very heart of strategy itself (concern for the national interest); the just war theory; the concept of a "three-dimensional ethics" and of careful combined consideration of deontological and consequentialist and situationalist imperatives— all these things add one more layer to the sword (which is reason) and the cross (which is faith). If we must study the "plain physical facts of the case," as indeed we must, we are not thereby released from choosing a course of action which seems to us, after our best pruden-

tial judgment, to be the most ethically and politically defensible which
our poor powers allow us to descry. The good man tries. In the end,
man fails. And dies. He is not a lamp unto himself. His quest for
political adequacy melds with his religious pilgrimage, the purpose of
which is the discovery of Truth and of Redemption. The political
quest seeks the order of law and the justice of man; the pilgrimage
seeks the Order of the Cosmos and the Justice of the Divine. The one
is politics; the other, theology. One is concerned with balance and
limitation of human power; the other, with submission to and unquestioning acceptance of divine authority.

But the division is not absolute. Politics is not theology, nor
theology politics. When the two are confused, a Hitler or a Stalin or
a Mao will appear, claiming to be the "great leader of the people."
But when the two are wholly segregated, we lack the standards to
judge those self-anointed great leaders. There must be something of
the sacred in the profane, if not of the profane in the sacred. If that
sentence troubles, think that, to Christians, the very embodiment of
the sacred took profane form in the magnificent mystery of the
Incarnation. So Christianity is political. Here is Johann Baptist Metz:

Christianity is in its very being, as messianic praxis of discipleship, political.
It is mystical and political at the same time, and it leads us into a responsibility, not only for what we do or fail to do but also for what we allow to
happen to others in our presence, before our eyes.[1]

We know that politics will conclude with the second coming of
Christ, the Parousia. As Reinhold Niebuhr wrote sixty years ago,
"Politics will, to the end of history, be an area where conscience and
power meet, where the ethical and coercive factors of human life will
interpenetrate and work out their tentative and uneasy compro-
mises."[2]

Referring to the Pauline statement that the church, as cleansed by
Christ, is to be without spot or wrinkle (Eph. 5:27), Saint Thomas
remarks: "This will be true only in our eternal home, not on the way
of [*sic*] it, for now we would deceive ourselves if we were to say that
we have no sin, as 1 John 1:8 points out."[3] That may be the point and
purpose of this admonition: "See to it that no one deceives you
through any empty, seductive philosophy that follows mere human
traditions, a philosophy based on cosmic powers rather than on
Christ" (Col. 2:8).

THE GOSPELS

The Latin word commonly used for Gospel is *evangelium*, a term derived, in turn, from Greek. In the New Testament, it means the glad news or the good news of salvation, news delivered, as it were, by the one that Christians regard as the Son of God and, later, by word of mouth by the Apostles. Some time around the end of the first century or the beginning of the second, this word *gospel* was applied to the book containing the glad tidings and, of course, the authors were called evangelists.

The gospels (from the Anglo-Saxon *godspel* or good tidings) are not biographies either in the modern or in the ancient sense. Only four are regarded by most Christian churches as inspired, or canonical, works. They are the accounts according to Matthew (written about A.D. 80 to show Jesus as the messiah of the Jews), Mark (written about A.D. 70 for the Romans), Luke (written about A.D. 85 for the Greeks), and John (written sometime between A.D. 90 and 110 for all Christians). There are, of course, differences in the gospels, but the differences are largely, but not exclusively, stylistic. Matthew is symbolized by man, for that gospel is significantly concerned with Christ's earthly ancestry and his human and divine kingship. Mark is symbolized by *lion*, for his account begins with reference to John the Baptist, "crying in the desert." Luke is symbolized by the *ox*, the animal of sacrifice, because his account begins with the history of Zachariah, the priest who offered sacrifice to God. John's account is symbolized by the *eagle*, for his account fairly soars above the earthly and dwells on the divinity of Jesus.

It is beyond the scope of this book to explore even a few of the most critical themes to be found in Christian political theory. Although distinct in many ways, the man, the lion, and the ox show striking resemblance in content and form and thus are referred to as "Synoptists" (and their writings as the "Synoptic Gospels") because whenever they are placed in parallel columns, they provide the same general view of Jesus' life. The eagle has a somewhat different focus. The "Synoptic Problem"[4] need not detain us here. Similarly, questions about the "Q Source"—(*Q* from *Quelle*, the German word for "source"), never found but deduced, containing about 240 verses which Mark does not include but which Matthew and Luke seem to have had, in addition to the Marcan source (regarded, as mentioned above, as the first of the four canonical gospels)—cannot concern us here.

Our sole concern here is what might be called political kerygma. (*Kerygma* refers to the proclamation of God's revelation in Christ, especially as preached by the Gospels.) The political Christ of the Synoptic Gospels has been viewed and accepted as the Savior of the World—as well as rejected for that role. Some would hold that Jesus was, at best, a mountebank. The judgment of who Jesus was is ultimately a personal matter, and we are not concerned here with proving or disproving the divinity of Jesus. Rather, we are concerned here only with viewing Jesus as a political figure on the basis of his portrayal in the three Gospels.

Jesus, as seen in the texts of those Gospels, appears to be a rather protean, amorphous figure, subject to various interpretations and exegeses. That may be the point of the warning of Peter: [Paul's epistles] "contain some obscure passages, which the ignorant and unstable misinterpret to their own ruin, as they do the other scriptures" (2 Peter 3:16). Unlike the Constitution of the United States, which is subject to a (somewhat) definitive exegesis by the U.S. Supreme Court—Chief Justice John Marshall decreed in *Marbury v. Madison* (1803) that "It is emphatically the province and duty of the Judicial Department to say what the law is"—the Bible is not universally interpreted by any court. Some faiths, notably Catholicism, have an ecclesial interpretive power of Scripture (what Catholics call the Magisterium) but, due largely to the multiplicity of sects, there is no universally accepted and ultimate exegetical authority.

Thus many interpretations of the same scriptural passage are possible, even to commonly believing people. In a religiously pluralistic world, one must doubt whether a given interpretation of a text is empirically or demonstrably possible. That is not to say, however, that all interpretations of Christian scripture are either equal or equally plausible. For example, one could cite Jesus' curse of the fig tree as incontrovertible evidence that he was an irascible and short-tempered man. The judgment, however, seems unsound—given the preponderant weight of New Testament evidence. Thus there may well be a contextual integrity which the tendentious reading of an isolated passage may violate. A rather similar problem exists, of course, with respect to what is called *original intent*, which seeks to understand the purpose of the U.S. Constitution's framers with regard to certain issues.[5] Original intent appears, on its surface, to be wholly impracticable. Yet one might ask whether the contextual integrity of the Constitution—its overarching ideas and purposes—

may help shape contemporary politics even if the long-dead founding fathers can offer no specific advice about the particularities of the 1990s.

Christ—whoever he was or is—remains perhaps the most political of all the great figures in history, despite his assertion that "My Kingdom is not of this World" (Jn. 18:36). Throughout the ages countless thousands have been imprisoned or executed, have suffered and died, in his name; countless more thousands of "Grand Inquisitors" have caused suffering, imprisonment, or have killed or executed in his name. For 2,000 years, his adherents might say, the cruelest mockery of Christ crucified has been what has been sanctified in his name and for his cause.

The political Christ of the Synoptic Gospels is a mosaic assembled according to the principles and beliefs, the prejudices and bigotries, of those who find him there. Those who read the scripture may easily be able to find there precisely the kind of Christ they seek—a kind of kerygma by cognitive dissonance. Rather than attempting to emulate him, they demand, in essence, that he suit them; theirs is not the duty to be like him, but his the duty to be like them. If that is merely a kind of warped selective perception, it is also what Shakespeare observed in *The Merchant of Venice*: "The devil can cite Scripture for his purpose." The Synoptic Gospels, then, are a political and religious kaleidoscope, and the shards of holy glass found there may be assembled by the viewer-reader with a mere flick of the fingers of his imagination. The believer, of course, will say that there is a transcendent Christ, risen far beyond our human tastes and predispositions; that may well be true. Marx is reputed to have said, toward the end of his life, that "I am not a Marxist"—so upset was he with some of the revisions of his doctrines. What might Jesus say of Jim Jones in Guyana or the legion of Jesus' "followers," not only centuries ago, but in the television studios of today? These people, after all, sell us a version of Christ and of his truth. They tell us not only whom to pray for, but whom to support financially and whom to vote for. They are the political apostles of a politicized Christ. Their scandal may be, not that they know not what they do, but that they know exactly what they do. About twenty-five years ago, a stir was created by Joe McGinniss when he described *The Selling of the President, 1968*. But that pales by comparison with the selling of Christ by those who, for their own purposes, portray the scriptural Jesus precisely as they wish him to be.

THE GREAT QUESTION

One could argue that any political question, carried to its *ultima Thule*, would become a theological inquiry. To the extent that is true, political questions are not the superstructure of a religious edifice. This is not to say that one must *be* religious; it is, however, to suggest that one must be sensitive to the religious. It is precisely in that sense, then, that one must answer personally, and comprehend others' answers to, the Great Question of Jesus to his disciples, "But you— who do you say that I am?" (Lk. 9:20; Mt. 16:15). In the absence of an answer of one kind or another to that question, one cannot reasonably develop a spirit of command—or a sense of conscience; failure to respond to that question dulls the sword and trivializes the cross.

For on the answer to that question[6] turn the fates of countless peoples, ideologies, and states. Was the principal mission of Jesus to save people from their sins (cf. Mt. 1:21), or to inspire the Jews of the day to overcome their Roman oppressors? Even the name *Christ* (usually rendered as "the anointed one") can thus be controversial. Jesus' use of the title *Son of Man* (Mt. 8:20; Mk. 8:31) thus becomes troublesome both politically and theologically.

From the beginning of Jesus' public life until his crucifixion, questions abounded about him. Thus John the Baptist himself addressed Jesus with the question, "Are you 'He Who is to come' or do we look for another?" (Mt. 11:3; Lk. 7:20). Pilate, of course, demanded to know whether Jesus was the king of the Jews (Mt. 27:11). The crowds at the crucifixion similarly wanted proof—the empirical test—that Jesus was divine: He was to remove himself from the cross (Mt. 27:40; Mk. 15:32). Even Peter, who had known Jesus so well, denied him (Lk. 22:54–62).

The existence of God and the nature of his being may be considered the greatest problem of philosophy (as well as, of course, theology). The existence of a benevolent deity endows human history with a teleology which it would otherwise lack. Should there be no benevolent deity, such Providence as exists would emanate only from the human psyche, and divine worship would be the height of folly and futility. As Russell Kirk put it:

Is there not a power independent of our senses, independent even of our ordinary reason, to which we may appeal against our very selves? In sober fact, do men have souls or not? Upon one's solution of this inquiry rests the basis of politics, for if men do not possess souls, if there is no higher will, then they may as well be treated as parts of a machine—indeed, they cannot be treated otherwise.[7]

Thus the ancient quarrel between Protagoras (who believed man is the measure of all things) and Plato (who believed God is the measure of all things) remains unsettled and unsolved.[8] Skeptics must say, citing "lack of evidence," that, at best, they are unable to answer the question of God's existence. Believers will say, citing the example of scripture, that by faith (the "confident assurance concerning what we hope for, and conviction about things we do not see" [Hebrews 11:1]) they know God lives.

Even if it were possible to establish whether God lives, one shrinks from the grander question: what does he care about us poor mortals? Is the God of the deists the proper portrait? Is the living God merely a clock-maker God who has created mortals for want of other things to do, or merely for his own amusement? Or, as scripture has it, can we know that "God is love" (1 Jn. 4:8), even though "No one has ever seen God"? (1 Jn. 4:5).

One must first hold, if he is to believe in the divinity of Jesus, that God exists and, second, that the living God is benevolent, which, of course, is the testimony of scripture (Jn. 3:16). But what believers sometimes fail to appreciate is that Jewish and Christian Scripture cannot and will not be accepted as unimpeachable authority by non-believers. Citing biblical chapter and verse in support of a given proposition can no more sustain and justify that position in the eyes of skeptics than, say, the Palestinians' abandoning the West Bank as forever Israeli because the Bible refers to that land as Samaria/Judea. The practice of using proof text (citing passages of scripture to prove a special doctrine or belief) is hardly convincing to those to whom the text itself is not authoritative; proof texting is merely circular reasoning in different clothing. One must doubt that agnostic baseball fans are converted to Christianity because a fan sitting in the stands behind home plate holds up a placard with, say, "John 3:5" on it!

The ultimate expression of the love of the living God is his presumed willingness to intervene in human history, taking human form (the Incarnation) and suffering and dying to make possible the redemption of a fallen race. Here, precisely, is the *fons et origo* of politics. Here lie the disputes between the Pelagians, who argued, in essence, that we can save ourselves without divine grace, and the Augustinians, who believed that original sin is the premier fact of

both theological and societal life. Here begin all the classic debates
between the liberals and the conservatives about the nature of
humankind and the best form of government to facilitate our reason
and to impede our passion. As Clinton Rossiter wrote:

Man, says the Conservative, is a composite of good and evil, a blend of
ennobling excellencies and degrading imperfections. He is not perfect; he
is not perfectible. If educated properly, placed in a favorable environment,
and held in restraint by tradition and authority, he may display innate
qualities of rationality, sociability, industry, decency, and love of liberty.
Never, no matter how he is educated or situated or restrained, will he throw
off completely his other innate qualities of irrationality, selfishness, lazi-
ness, depravity, and corruptibility. Man's nature is essentially immutable,
and the immutable strain is one of deep-seated wickedness. Although some
Conservatives find support for their skeptical view of man in recent experiments in psychology [see Chapter 2], most continue to rely on religious
teaching and the study of history. Those who are Christians, and most
Conservatives are, prefer to call the motivation for iniquitous and irrational
behavior by its proper name: Original Sin.[9]

Here start all the religious debates about Christology and the future
of the human race. Here are the roots of the pacifist question. (See
Chapter 7.) Ultimately, the question, "Who do you say that I am?"
must be answered by Jew and Gentile, capitalist and communist,
liberal and conservative, believer and skeptic. And behind it all is a
terrible realization: the normal rules of evidence, the customary
canons of scholarship, are unlikely ever to adduce a full and final
answer to the Great Question of philosophy: is there a God and, if so,
what is God's relationship to the daily problems of this planet? Thus
we are left with belief and non-belief, with conjecture and speculation, with a plethora of creeds and cults. We are left, in a word, with
politics.

POLITICAL IMPLICATIONS

Those who follow what they perceive to be the will and wishes of
God are suspended between two worlds, much as Augustine testified
centuries ago. If they attempt to implement what they understand to
be the Mandate of Heaven, they must still deal with and through
human agency. Thus the divine word finds form in leaders, in rules,
in churches, and in human precepts. Even those who are, in a way,
religious anarchists, eschewing all organized religion, still must employ

the artifacts of religion—a translated bible, for example (but which translation? and with which books to be included? and with which, if any, notes?). The reality of "human agency" means that as we attempt to find and follow the will of the divine—"Thy will be done"—we nevertheless are unable to escape from the human compulsion of "My Will be done." As Arnold Toynbee wrote,

I am convinced that man's fundamental problem is his human egocentricity. He dreams of making the universe a desirable place for himself, with plenty of free time, relaxation, security and good health, and with no hunger or poverty.

Of course, this is a forlorn hope. All except the most primitive species of living creatures die, and the fact of death is enough to doom egocentricity to ultimate failure. Human beings try to forget about it as much as they can, but any human being, at critical moments of his life, is aware of the irony of his egocentricity, and the futility of it confronts him and distresses him.

"All the great historic philosophies and religions," he continues, "have been concerned, first and foremost, with the overcoming of egocentricity."[10] While there can be doubt about the fundamental idea that the Christian must develop his talents as fully as he can (e.g., Mt. 24:14–30; Lk. 12:48), arrogance, hubris, or the consuming egotism of which Toynbee writes are contrary to the fulfillment of the heavenly kingdom (and, as will be discussed in Chapter 8, preclude communitarian politics). *Pride*, then, can mean a dignified self-respect or a fiery presumptuousness, the impetus to the original, and continuous, sin. As C. S. Lewis put it, pride is our constant companion:

This sin is committed daily by young children and ignorant peasants as well as by sophisticated persons, by solitaries no less than by those who live in society: it is the fall in every individual life, and in each day of each individual life, the basic sin behind all particular sins: at this very moment you and I are either committing it, or about to commit it, or repenting it.[11]

Pride and egotism must be limited if any organization or collectivity is to be effected. Aristotle suggested that, because we are gregarious as well as self-centered people, we form naturally into groups, poleis, and nations. He did not say churches, but he might have. Of course, such bodies may be only the self "writ large," but the ego must be limited or controlled in some manner in order to design and develop the larger order. The larger order is thus the product and the policeman of individual ego. But the larger order cannot always accommodate our private desires—hence, the existence of coalitions, interest groups, political parties, alliances. We band together with others of like mind to advance our personal and particular agendas. If, as in Madisonian politics, faction is inevitable, so in ecclesiastical politics is faction the apparent norm. In that regard, Jesus himself testified: "Do not suppose that my mission on earth is to spread peace. I have come to set a man at odds with his father, a daughter with her mother, a daughter-in-law with her mother-in-law" (Mt. 10:34–35). Indeed, even while Jesus lived among them, the disciples themselves quarreled about who was the greatest among them (Lk. 22:24–26). Is it any wonder, therefore, that the consequence has been centuries of internecine religious warfare and bloodshed?

To Christians, the "infidel" in human history has been, at various times, not only the Jew or the Moslem, the agnostic or the atheist, but the Christian who interprets a word or phrase or clause just somewhat differently from his brother, or who disputes him about who deserves the greater ecclesial deference, or whose sense of ritual varies by degrees from the orthodox. "You," as Jesus said, "will be delivered up even by your parents, brothers, relatives and friends, and some of you will be put to death" (Lk. 21:16). The observation of the late Bishop Fulton Sheen is pertinent: "Unless souls are saved, nothing is saved; there can be no world peace unless there is soul peace. World wars are only projections of the conflicts waged inside the souls of modern men, for nothing happens in the external world that has not first happened within a soul."[12]

The definitions of politics referred to earlier in this book now take on particular importance. Lasswell's definition (that politics is "who gets what, when, how") and Easton's definition (politics is the "authoritative allocation of values") share in Lenin's perspective of politics. (The Soviet leader is supposed to have defined politics as Who/Whom?—meaning who will control whom?) In religion, too, the matter of authority is central. How are we to know who is the "Authority"? Scripture testifies that Jesus gave his disciples and, presumably, their successors "power to tread on snakes and scorpions and all the forces of the enemy, and nothing shall ever injure you" (Lk. 10:19). Such authorities, we read, "will be able to handle serpents; they will be able to drink deadly poison without harm" (Mk. 16:18). But here, of course, enters in the question of exegesis: Are these passages intended to be taken literally? In some places and parts of the country, they are indeed taken quite literally. Most

Christian authorities, however, are rather less intent upon such strict fundamentalism, and the test of leadership is something other than the consumption of poisons.

But who, then, is the Authority who decides the winners and the losers in the politics of religious cases and controversies? We know from Jesus that "any man who is not against you is on your side" (Lk. 9:50), but we are also instructed that "He who is not with me is against me, and he who does not gather with me scatters" (11:23). Not only, apparently, was there intramural squabbling among the disciples about the place of honor, but the beginnings of inter-church rivalry: "False messiahs and false prophets will appear performing signs and wonders to mislead, if it were possible, even the chosen" (Mk. 13:22). One is led to the lugubrious conclusion that argument about honor, about authority, about the allocation of values is not only the stuff of secular politics but as well of "sacred politics." The consequences of all this rapacious quarreling is most evident in the pages of the contemporary daily press with its reports about television evangelists gone wrong, about the endless horror (much of it clearly religiously motivated) in Lebanon, in Ireland, in India-Pakistan, and elsewhere. Even those who doubt the legitimacy of scripture[13] have cause for belief in Jesus' admonition that "Brother will hand over brother for execution and likewise the father his child; children will turn against their parents and have them put to death" (Mk. 13:12).

Religion is often thought of in terms of peace and harmony. Too often is forgotten the admonition of Jesus: "Do you think I have come to establish peace on the earth? I assure you, the contrary is true; I have come for division" (Lk. 12:51). And so, by practically any test, it has been. The struggle for power and domination—the desire to be the authority deferred to in the allocation of values—is apparently not assuaged by religious precept and practice. Frequently mis-placed, too, in the politico-religious quest for power is the normative ideal of the early philosophers in Athens and Jerusalem, for they held that politics without ethics was a corrupt endeavor. The unspeakable carnage at Jonestown, Guyana, suggests that religious authority can be evil incarnate and that very few "authorities" can "drink deadly poison without harm." Thus one is left with the ancient maxim *Quis custodiet ipsos custodes?* (Who will guard those who are themselves the guardians?)[14] Religion, then, does not solve the ancient problem of command and conscience, of sword and cross. The biblical charge ("Obey your leaders and defer to them, for they will keep watch over you" [Hebrews 13:17]) leaves us frustrated: *When* do we obey? *When* do we defer? *What* does "keep watch" mean? *Who* are the leaders to be? *How* do we choose them?[15] When Jesus tells us to pay Caesar what is due to Caesar and to pay to God what is due to God (Mt. 22:21), one wishes to ask for more instruction. But the command is left to our conscience. We cannot know perfectly what to do; we cannot see perfectly the divine will. We are left to do the best we can.[16]

ON LIBERATION THEOLOGY

Two themes characteristic of much of Christian thought are the love of Jesus toward the poor and the pacific (or, alternatively, the pacifistic). There is, in the Gospel of Luke, what is known as the Sermon on the Plain (6:20–49), a distinctive verse of which is this: "Blest are you poor; the reign of God is yours . . . . But woe to you rich, for your consolation is now" (6:20, 24). One reputable source offers this commentary on the Sermon on the Plain:

The Lucan Sermon on the Plain characterizes the Christian as distinctive for his poverty (20–23), cautious against the dangers of wealth (24f), loving toward his enemy (27–38), critical of himself (39–45), and obedient to the teachings of Jesus (46–49). It is reasonable to assume that this Lucan arrangement of Jesus's teaching was addressed to the economically deprived and politically threatened Christian communities of Asia Minor and Greece. It thus possesses special poignancy, born of Luke's faith in the inevitable victory of the Christian message in a hostile environment, provided Christians accept their poverty in the spirit of Christ and endeavor to conquer their persecutors by the love they show them.[17]

As Jesus said, "[I]t is easier for a camel to pass through a needle's eye than for a rich man to enter the kingdom of God" (Mt. 19:24; Mk. 10:23). The famous beatitudes recorded in the fifth chapter of Matthew announce religious joy for the *anawim*—those who have few, if any, material goods and stand in need of the spiritual blessings promised by God.[18] Jesus is repeatedly clear in instructions of this sort: "Go and sell what you have and give [it] to the poor; you will then have treasure in heaven" (Mk. 10:21). Indeed, when Jesus entered Jerusalem as king of peace, he rode, not the horse (symbol of the conqueror), but the ass, the work beast of the poor (Mt. 21:5). Jesus' reaction to those who sought to make money in God's temple is well known (Mt. 21:12), for "You cannot give yourself to God and money" (Lk. 16:13; cf. 12:16–21).

The power of this Christian message of love of and for the poor suffuses the Gospels. It has also proved to be something of an embarrassment for Christians in the wake of the typical Marxist vitriol that the Christian can offer nothing to the poor of this world except vague promises of joy in the next. What, then, the Marxist asks the Christian, of love of neighbor?

In the past thirty or so years, a number of Christian thinkers have suggested that political, even revolutionary, action—rather than the humility and "passivity" of prayer—is required to redress the grievances of the poor. Juan Luis Segundo, *Liberation of Theology*; Enrique Dussel, *A History of the Church in Latin America*; Leonardo Boff, *Jesus Christ Liberator*; and Gustavo Gutierrez, *A Theology of Liberation*—these, and others, suggest that the church (particularly the Catholic Church) must increasingly take its place in secular politics in order to improve the temporal order.[19] Not all liberation theologians view Jesus as a guerrilla warrior, but many would not reject that image. (Some to the left of the spectrum may see Jesus as an urban street-fighter; some to the right of the spectrum may see Jesus as a U.S. Army Green Beret.) We continue to hang Christ onto the cross that we design for him.

There can be no doubt that perusal of scripture supports the case for liberation theology—up to a point. Still, the political Christ of the Synoptic Gospels can be seen as unclear here as well. "The poor," he says, "you will always have with you" (Mt. 26:11). And "[t]o those who have, more will be given; from those who have not, what little they have will be taken away" (Mk. 4:25); or "whoever has will be given more, but the one who has not will lose the little he has" (Lk. 19:26). This last quotation is taken from the fascinating parable of the "Sums of Money," or "pounds," or "talents." Although one can read this as encouraging us to develop our powers and to employ them well, one must admit that this passage could be cited with approval by those people intent upon multiplying money, rather than loaves and fishes. A classic book in this regard is *The Man Nobody Knows* (1925) by Bruce Barton, in which Jesus is presented "as a back-slapping good guy, a go-getter and regular rotarian."[20] It is, therefore, not just the televangelists who may contend that God favors the wealthy. John Calvin (1509–1564) did likewise, leading, in the judgment of some, to the so-called "Protestant ethic."

It is a sobering thought that, at the same time liberation theologians may be calling for Christians to aid in the implementation of political revolution, other Christian preachers call for the multiplication of wealth for reasons that have little indeed to do with the squalor and poverty of the Third World. Both camps, however, make their appeals and justify their causes in the name of Jesus; still, such attempts at justification do not necessarily validate either the avarice of greedy preachers or the insurrectionist rhetoric or political revolution of the liberation theologians. Noted Protestant theologian Carl F. H. Henry offers this astute assessment of liberation theology:

Christianity is not a utopian religion: it takes seriously original sin and human selfishness. But it is a religion of ideal justice and continuing compassion nurtured by the transcendent gift and grace of God. In these respects it towers head and shoulders above the liberation theology that readily confuses the real meaning of biblical salvation. The Bible calls for a striking alternative to the social status quo and its colossal injustices. It promises a final victory of justice and peace—whether rebellious human beings want it or not. It publishes the assurance of Jesus of Nazareth that no one need reconcile himself or herself to the crush of evil forces as finally determinative of human existence. The New Testament announces a Gospel of total victory over injustice and oppression. It is thus doubly tragic that liberation theology, with its imperative call to social justice, should so sadly have missed the biblical way.[21]

On 11 November 1984, the National Conference of Catholic Bishops produced their first draft of a "Pastoral Letter on Catholic Social Teaching and the U.S. Economy." That document led to a number of questions and concerns about the bishops' involvement in economic and financial theory, as well as worry that the bishops were leaning toward an inchoate socialistic thinking held, by some, to be inimical to the prospect of genuine wealth development in the Third World. As Michael Novak observed:

The Pope has called attention to the right moral issue—yes, we must help the poor nations—but he hasn't said how to do that. In my view, the overwhelming evidence is that you do that by helping them develop the kind of ideas and institutions that do engender wealth.[22]

"If a rich person sees his brother in need, yet closes his heart against his brother, how can he claim that he loves God?" (1 Jn. 3:17). But "[w]hoever refuses to work is not allowed to eat" (2 Thess. 3:10). The reconciliation of these passages demands faith and reason, which is to say civic virtue, wise politics. Wise politics comprehends both feasibility and fairness.

The liberation theologians, morally outraged by the extremes of sybaritic luxury and mind-numbing poverty sometimes in adjacent neighborhoods in most countries of the world, have leaned too far, many would contend, in the direction of "fairness" at the expense of "feasibility." Are they too concerned with things of the flesh and not enough with things of the spirit? But what is the Christian to do in the face of hunger, illiteracy, disease, and widespread destitution? The Church has held that *balance* is a key, that the Christian must not expect eschatological peace and justice on earth as gifts of revised politics or economics. But that should not imply an obsequious acceptance of evil; one does the best one can, balancing what ought to be with what is, and remembering that the final victory is God's. Asked once if she did not get discouraged by the seemingly endless poverty and hunger and misery in the cities of India where she labors, Mother Teresa responded, "Oh, my job is not to succeed, but to be faithful to my mission." The Church ministers as best it can to the minds and the bodies of all its children, for it must live the Beatitudes; it ministers always to the immortal souls of all its children, for that is its primary responsibility and it must be "faithful to [its] mission."

In what is sometimes called the parable of the "crafty steward" (Lk. 16:1–8), a manager about to be fired is anxious to insure that he will be subsequently well received, so he reduces the indebtedness of people who owe his boss. The *Jerusalem Bible* concludes the parable with this translation: "The master praised the dishonest steward for his astuteness. For the children of this world are more astute with their own kind than are the children of light." Confronted with the intractable questions of politics (abortion laws,[23] capital punishment, divorce, economic justice, homosexuality, war/peace issues,[24] and similar troubling problems), the Church does what it can to bring into reasonable harmony the political imperatives of command and the moral sanctions of conscience. It does not expect to complete its task, only to be faithful to it. The Church waits for the "days of miracles."[25]

ON HUMAN NATURE

In a marginal comment on Matthew (6:1–6), the *New American Bible* suggests that "To be of value in the eyes of God, religious duties, public and private, must be performed for the single-hearted purpose of serving God, and not for human esteem."[26] A recurring Biblical theme—among its most powerful, in fact—is the weakness of human nature. Some theologians would hold that the central message of the Hebrew Bible (or Old Testament) is God's quest for humanity, despite our infidelity. The Matthaean text, in fact (after presenting the genealogy of Jesus), describes the human emotion of jealousy or envy. Informed of a recently born king greater than he, Herod sends out his troops to slaughter the innocents, hoping that the child-king (Jesus) will thus be eliminated (2:1–18). In the garden, before his crucifixion, Jesus, who had asked Peter to watch with him for a time, discovers that Peter cannot remain awake: "The spirit is willing but nature is weak" (Mt. 26:41). Shortly afterwards, of course, Peter denies Jesus three times, exactly as Jesus had prophesied. One understands, then, why value is to be derived from serving God, and not primarily humans.

Jesus appears concerned about human attachment to human things, rather than to things above, at a number of points in the Synoptic Gospels. By way of example, Jesus accuses the Pharisees of hypocrisy, quoting from Isaiah: "This people pays me lip service but their heart is far from me. They do me empty reverence, making dogmas out of human precepts" (Mt. 15:8–9). In the Marcan text is added this sentence: "You disregard God's commandment and cling to what is human tradition" (7:8). Jesus similarly chastises Peter at one point, telling him, "You [Peter] are not judging by God's standards but by man's" (Mt. 16:23; Mk. 8:33).

In a religious sense, one comprehends the sense of Jesus's adjurations and admonitions. But one returns to the dangers of false prophets in wondering how, in all cases, one may be able to descry the will of God. Two parables will help to make this point. The famous parable of the prodigal son (Lk. 15:11–32) demonstrates love and even, perhaps, a divine perspective as represented by the father who welcomes his returning son with open arms. Seen from the perspective of the loyal son, however, the parable is not so easily understood. Similarly, the parable of the workers in the vineyard can be troublesome (Mt. 20:1–16). The vineyard owner hires workers from dawn to dusk, rewarding them, finally, equally at day's end. Those who had begun working at dawn are upset that their pay is the same as those who were hired at day's end. One sympathizes! To be sure, one understands, religiously, the point of the two parables but, at the same time, one asks about fundamental fairness here. Can it be that, in demanding that we judge by God's standards, the Gospel is asking more than it reasonably and effectively can? In establishing a counsel of perfection, can it be that the Gospel injunctions enervate the simpler canons of human justice and the sense of equity that impart meaning to them? Is there, in fact, an understated danger to be guarded against in rather *too* enthusiastically attempting to judge things by what we perceive to be God's standards? (One thinks of the Scopes trial and the issue of teaching biology in the public schools.[27]) Henry Kissinger points out that "Those who grab for everything, who forget that politics is the art of the possible, in the end may lose all."[28] It was Talleyrand who is supposed to have said that the key to diplomacy was: "Above all else, not too much zeal."

This dilemma between the counsels of perfection and the realities of an imperfect world can be seen, as well, in what can be called the anti-intellectualism of the Gospels. In the Old Testament book of Sirach, one reads: "What is too sublime for you, seek not[;] into things beyond your strength search not" (3:20; cf. Job 38). A similar sense obtains in the New Testament. Thus does Jesus say, "Trust me when I tell you that whoever does not accept the kingdom of God as a child will not enter into it" (Lk. 18:17; Mk. 10:14–15). In prayer at one point, Jesus says to the Father, "[W]hat you have hidden from the learned and clever you have revealed to the merest children" (Lk. 10:21). In fact, what appears to be an anti-intellectualism may be more of a counsel of humility, from which point genuine intellectual activity originates. One must be leery of "expedient exegesis"![29]

Although it is true that children were the symbol Jesus used for the *anawim*, the poor in spirit or the lonely within the Christian community, and that the apostles whom Jesus chose were not scholars, one can see a danger here. It is one thing to be humble and meek of heart; it may be quite another to be credulous. The people who followed Jim Jones to Guyana may or may not have been humble; but the spectacular catastrophe of Jonestown seems inextricably linked to a child-like, naive willingness to accept, without the slightest question, the corrupted authority of the "Master."

In one of his books, the French scholar J. F. Revel writes of the "Totalitarian Temptation." Odd as it may seem, it is precisely that temptation of which one must be cognizant in reading the pages of the Synoptic Gospels and in worrying about the political implementation of the scriptures.

The Great Commandment is the Shema (Deut. 6:4 and Mk. 12:29–30): "You shall love the Lord your God with all your heart, with all your soul, with all your mind, and with all your strength." Believers are to "[s]eek out his kingship over you, and the rest will follow in turn" (Lk. 12:31; Mt. 6:33). Indeed, we are told that "In a word, you must be perfect as your heavenly father is perfect" (Mt. 5:48). This leads, as we have seen, to counsels of perfection which, in an imperfect world, may well lead to an all-or-nothing mentality—precisely the stuff of totalitarianism. To those who question the feasibility of his ideas, Jesus offers this consolation: "For man it is impossible but not for God. With God all things are possible" (Mk. 10:27; Lk. 18:27, 1:37). Critically important, however, is the understanding that this is a reference to purifying the individual human soul, not the political devices created for the management and administration of earthly resources.

Jesus' followers are told that their devotion to his cause must be complete: "If a man wishes to come after me, he must deny his very self, take up his cross, and follow in my steps. Whoever would preserve his life will lose it, but whoever loses his life for my sake and the gospel's will preserve it" (Mk. 8:34–35). The promise is that "From now on you will be catching men" (Lk. 5:10; Mk. 1:17). In that connection the Gospels are clear that Jesus himself was an effective leader: "The people were spellbound by his teaching because he taught with authority" (Mk. 1:22; Lk. 4:32). Those who challenged Jesus were warned that their egotism was the stumbling block to holiness: "Whoever exalts himself shall be humbled, but whoever humbles himself will be exalted" (Mt. 23:13); indeed, the followers had to remain loyal to the teachings at all times and in all places: "If a man is ashamed of me and my doctrine, the Son of Man will be ashamed of him when he comes in his glory and that of his Father and his holy angels" (Lk. 9:26, 12:9). The great Christian prayer says to "Our Father": "thy will be done on earth as it is in heaven." The Pharisees and the scribes were not doing the will of the Father, we read, and Jesus castigated them severely: "Woe to you scribes and Pharisees, you frauds! You are like white-washed tombs, beautiful to look at on the outside but inside full of filth and dead men's bones" (Mt. 23:27).

The Christian perspective insists that we need have no fear of Jesus, who died for us, and who is the Savior. God, who is love, is unsullied by total power. A sinful humanity, however, not only aspires to influence and to control the instruments of domination, but is virtually certain to abuse their power, once achieving it. Montesquieu, for example, suggests in his master work about the law that "Every man who has power is impelled to abuse it." Lord Acton's dictum bears repetition: "Power tends to corrupt; absolute power corrupts absolutely." Madison's idea of power checking power derives from his perspective on human nature itself.

But a theocracy, practically by definition, is not self-controlling. One suspects that the principles of separation of powers and checks and balances do not operate in heaven—any more than that a policy of balance of power or deterrence must be effected by heaven's foreign minister in his dealings with other "celestial powers." It is exactly the theocratic tendency toward absolute power which fascinates Dostoevsky in his brilliant piece "The Grand Inquisitor" (from *The Brothers Karamazov*). One wonders, in pensive moments, how many of those who have obtained prominent Christian command positions would receive the full benediction of Jesus, whose strict instruction to his apostles is sometimes—perhaps too often—forgotten: "Anyone among you who aspires to greatness must serve the rest; whoever wants to rank first must serve the needs of all" (Mk. 10:43–44). One fears that, like Pilate, too many leaders (many of whom would claim the title Christian) have been prepared to wash their hands (Mt. 27:24) of any consequences of their employment of the trust of power. The temptations endured in the desert by Jesus—and written about so strikingly by Dostoevsky—can be resisted by Jesus, but the meretricious lure of glory and power (Mt. 4:1–11; Lk. 4:1–13) seem irresistible to many human leaders, reinforcing the wisdom, one concludes, of a political structure of limited governmental powers. Such a structure is an institutional realization of the conviction that the conscience, even of the political commander, ought to be compared with, and perhaps restrained by, the community conscience.[30]

CONCLUSION

Because Christianity promises life eternal, redemption, and meaning in (and for) life, it is a totalitarian creed—not necessarily a pejorative notion. Yet its dangers are legion. One looks for an analogy. Is fire the servant of humankind? Can fire be a destroyer? Is water required for life? Can water kill? Do we understand the beneficial uses of the atom or of electricity? Can both maim and mutilate?

A principal danger of religion in general and of Christianity in particular is that they demand the surrender of self. Christianity demands that we conform our will to the greater, the eternal, will. In requiring all this, it offers no evidence to sustain itself; its believers have only faith. Because we cannot on this earth possess the transcendent God, we are left in a state of uncertainty and anxiety. The tensions and strains of this uncertainty lead, from time to time, to ideologies, to movements, to leaders promising to resolve the human tension of life in a mundane world and to ameliorate the human condition.[31] A tendency exists—and will always exist—for people to see in political movements religious truth and to see in religious truth political opportunity.

A full solution to the quintessential human dilemma of uncertainty is not ours, short of grace. To invest daily life or political ideology with eternal significance is to create a false god, a Leviathan. This Moloch, whether the Third Reich or Stalinism or Maoism, will promise a heaven but deliver a hell, for it admits of no self-limitation and accepts no superior conscience. The very core of the distinction between the secular and the sacred is that the latter is unlimited whereas the former is necessarily and self-evidently limited. To confuse the two spheres is to court disaster in either or in both.

The lot of humankind was perceptively explained by Augustine, who wrote that we are citizens of two worlds, the eternal and the temporal. Maintaining that dual citizenship can help the statesman inject the serum of ethics into the body politic in the hope of warding off political disease and decay. But maintaining that dual citizenship is a constant reminder that human life is essentially tragic. The political Christ of the Synoptic Gospels presents many images, but that is not to say that an objective reality—apprehended in millions of ways by millions of people—may not, in fact, exist. In the city of God, love is the highest virtue (cf. 1 Cor. 13:13); but in the city of man, prudence (cf. Mt. 25:9) is the highest virtue because "It is characteristic of all politics [wrote Hans Morgenthau], domestic as well as international, that frequently its basic manifestations do not appear as what they actually are—manifestations of a struggle for power."[32] To believers, the bridge between the sacred and the profane is Jesus, man-God and God-man, the only power ultimately capable of delivering us, finally, from evil.

NOTES

1. Johann Baptist Metz, *The Emergent Church* (New York: Crossroad, 1981), p. 27. See also H. Mark Roelofs, "Hebraic-Biblical Political Thinking," *Polity* 20 (Summer 1988): 572–97.

2. Reinhold Niebuhr, *Moral Man and Immoral Society* (New York: Charles Scribner's Sons, 1932), p. 4.

3. Quoted in Avery Dulles, *A Church to Believe In* (New York: Crossroad, 1982), p. 151.

4. This is the presence of two series of contradictory literary phenomena in the three gospels. A concise study of this, along with the "Synoptic Fact," is available in the *New Catholic Encyclopedia* (1967).

5. On "original intent," see Robert H. Bork, *The Tempting of America* (New York: Free Press, 1990).

6. Jesus' question, "Who do you say that I am?" (Mk. 8:29); Pilate's question, "What is truth?" (Jn. 19:38—answered for Christians in Jn. 14:6); and Peter's question, "Lord [if not to you], to whom would we go?" (Jn. 6:68) are the great questions of the New Testament.

7. Russell Kirk, *Decadence and Renewal in the Higher Learning* (South Bend, IN: Gateway, 1978) is a discerning study of the importance in education of the ideas of wisdom and virtue.

8. See A.J. Beitzinger, *A History of American Political Thought* (New York: Dodd, Mead & Co., 1972), p. 503.

9. Clinton Rossiter, *Conservatism in America* (New York: Knopf, 1955), p. 21.

10. Arnold Toynbee, "Is Religion Superfluous?" *Intellectual Digest*, December 1971: 59. See also Alfred G. Killilea, *The Politics of Being Mortal* (Lexington, KY: University Press of Kentucky, 1988).

11. C.S. Lewis, *The Problem of Pain* (New York: Macmillan, 1948), p. 63.

12. Fulton J. Sheen, *Peace of Soul* (New York: Whittlesey House, 1949), p. 1.

13. For example, Michael Arnheim, *Is Christianity True?* (London: Prometheus, 1984).

14. Jacques Maritain wrote that we must consider "the immense burden of animality, of egoism, and of latent barbarism that men bear within themselves and which keeps social life from achieving its truest and most elevated aims. Let us realize . . . that the part of instinct and irrational forces is even greater in communal existence than in individual existence . . ." in *Christianity and Democracy*, trans. Doris Anson (New York: Charles Scribner's Sons, 1950), pp. 60–61.

15. Hobbes's use of the Leviathan ("that twisting sea-serpent, that writhing serpent" [Isa. 27:1]) is fascinating, for the text cited promises that in time the Lord will punish Leviathan with his "mighty and powerful sword."

16. But the promise is made that, in our struggles, we are not alone (Mt. 28:20).

17. *The New American Bible* (New York: P. J. Kenedy [sic] & Sons, 1970), New Testament, p. 89n.

18. Ibid., p. 8n.

19. A useful short discussion may be found in Roy C. Macridis, *Contemporary Political Ideologies*, 4th ed. (Glenview, IL: Scott, Foresman, 1989), Ch. 13. See also James T. Burtchaell, "How Authentically Christian Is Liberation Theology?" *Review of Politics* 50 (Spring 1988): 264–81.

20. Samuel Eliot Morison, *The Oxford History of the American People* (New York: Oxford University Press, 1965), p. 892.

21. Carl F. H. Henry, "An Evangelical Appraisal of Liberation Theology," *This World* (1985) No. 15: 107.

22. Michael Novak, "A Catholic's Reply to Bishops: Poor Nations Can Learn form U.S.," *U.S. News and World Report*, 26 November 1984: 62. A useful summary of the Bishops' Pastoral Letter appears in *Time*, 26 November 1984: 80–82.

23. Of interest in this connection is Mario M. Cuomo, "The Confessions of a Public Man," *Notre Dame Magazine*, Autumn 1984: 21–30, where Cuomo gives his views on abortion.

24. Although the issue of pacifism will be taken up in the next chapter, of interest in this connection are two interesting books: Richard McSorley, *New Testament Basis of Peace-Making,* 3d ed., revised (Scottsdale, PA: Herald Press, 1985) and Peter C. Craigie, *The Problem of War in the Old Testament* (Grand Rapids, MI: Eerdmans, 1978).

25. "The world will make you suffer. But be brave! I have defeated the world," Jesus promised (Jn. 16:33). The Church waits and watches and prays, drawing inspiration from Revelation 22:20–21.

26. *The New American Bible* (above, n. 17), p. 10n.

27. The moving story of Abraham and Isaac (Gen. 22) is meant, certainly, to testify to power and faith. Read as a parable, it is a majestic, even stirring, tribute to God's love and Abraham's response. Read at a political level, however, the story is horrifying. Abraham, who deeply loves his son Isaac, responds (in love? in fear?) to a God, commanding him to murder his son. Abraham's reaction is shocking. Isaac prepares for the sacrifice, not knowing what the offering will be: "Here are the fire and wood, but where is the young beast for the sacrifice?" asks Isaac. "God will provide himself with a young beast for the sacrifice, my son," Abraham responds. At the last moment, God stays the hand of the would-be murderer, Abraham, whose response to God is total and absolute and unquestioning. Read at a political level, the story is macabre. What better passage for any totalitarian to cite than this? In a sinful world, where rulers covet power (as do we all), we need to understand the beautiful message of Genesis 22, which is about faith; should anyone read these passages literally, however, we create a political peril that threatens the very integrity of the source (the Bible) from which it derives.

28. Henry A. Kissinger, *White House Years* (Boston, MA: Little, Brown, 1979), p. 1293.

29. Bible exegesis is not the subject of this book. But I would argue that faith and reason are, in fact, complementary in reading scripture as in making ethical choices. The educated reader should be able to distinguish between literal and figurative text and to be able to comprehend the meaning of a certain verse within the context of the larger document, constitution, or Bible. We know Jesus' parables do not concern actual people but are meant to teach by example. By extension, certain biblical verses are best understood, not for their isolated literal meaning, but as propaedeutic devices. That in no way diminishes their inspired character; it is only to recognize that that which is infinite in substance (God's Truth) is difficult to compress into that which is finite in structure (human language).

30. This does not preclude leadership, which, at its best, is the elevation of the community conscience. But leadership and followership take place within the confines of national traditions, values, and norms. See Chapters 3 and 8 for discussion.

31. See Eric Voegelin, *The New Science of Politics* (Chicago, IL: University of Chicago Press). His magnum opus is the four volumes of *Order and History* (Baton

Rouge, LA: Louisiana State University Press, various dates). See also his book *From Enlightenment to Revolution*, ed. John H. Hallowell (Durham, NC: Duke University Press, 1975). Excellent background is in Ellis Sandoz, *The Voegelinian Revolution* (Baton Rouge, LA: LSU Press, 1981). A useful collection of Voegelin's writings appears in his book *Anamnesis*, ed. Gerhart Niemeyer (Notre Dame, IN: University of Notre Dame Press, 1978).

32. Hans Morgenthau and Kenneth W. Thompson, *Politics Among Nations*, 6th ed. (New York: Knopf, 1985), p. 101.

7 ON PACIFISM

"Peace, peace!" they say, though there is no peace.[1]

—Jeremiah 8:11

"When a strong man fully armed guards his courtyard, his possessions go undisturbed."

—Luke 11:21

"It may well be that, morally speaking, the United States ship of state is today comparable to the *Titanic* just before it hit the iceberg," admonished William Sloane Coffin, who, at the time, was chaplain of Yale University.[2] One would have little difficulty in reciting a lengthy list of scholars and clergymen who would strongly agree with Pastor Coffin about the bellicose nature of American foreign and military policy. As Catholic Archbishop Raymond Hunthausen contended, "[O]ne obvious meaning of the cross is unilateral disarmament."[3] The Reverend Richard McSorley, a Jesuit priest, agreed: "It's a sin," he said, "to build a nuclear weapon."[4] There appears to be no doubt that pacifist scholars and clergymen can, if they wish, corroborate their judgments by appeal to often-quoted biblical sources. We are told that the peacemakers are blessed (Mt. 5:9), that "[t]hose who use the sword are sooner or later destroyed by it" (Mt. 26:52), and that we "shall not kill" (Ex. 20:13).

Scholar and Christian Michael Novak wishes, however, "that all persons were of good will and that all would receive into their hearts the message of peace. But that is not the world we live in."[5] As St. Augustine put it in *The City of God*: "War and conquest are a sad necessity in the eyes of men of principle, yet it would be still more unfortunate if wrongdoers should dominate just men" (Book IV). The notion of a Christian bellicism, however, seems slightly absurd—a kind of impossible oxymoron. Although the Reverend Pat Robertson has contended that "Pacifism is not biblical,"[6] and the French Catholic bishops have pointed out that "[i]n a world where one man still preys upon another, to change oneself into a lamb could be to provoke the wolf,"[7] the idea that pacifism is quintessentially Christian permeates the thinking of many contemporary analysts.[8] The contrast between the commands of Jesus and those of General George S. Patton[9] is clear.

But the point to be made here is that the counsels of Christian realism can and, indeed, must permit the judicious and ethical use of violence—that, in a manifestly imperfect world, to abandon the employment of raw power to the most brutal is itself an act of barbarism. The abolition of war is, finally, the abolition of sin—a work never to be completed through the ken and competence of mortals. In asking questions of violence, therefore, we are asking about the nature of man and the nature of the cosmos. Although we have already explored the idea of the "just war," we return here to an unexamined assumption of Chapter 4: are we ourselves just in assuming that the Christian conscience permits the soldier to accept military commands?

Reinhold Niebuhr, in contending that "most modern forms of Christian pacifism are heretical,"[10] may well be correct.[11] Throughout this book runs the theme of effort, of trying as hard as one reasonably can, given the "plain physical facts of the case," to decide as one ought to decide. As discussed in the preceding chapter, Christ is seen in many ways by many people. Sincerity, alone, is insufficient to assure judicious judgments; but sincerity of effort is necessary. Father Robert Griffin of Notre Dame:

It is a difficult century. A priest does the best he can, like a doctor in an epidemic. Such is the ambiguity of good and evil, that each of us is called to be decent in separate ways. Love and duty will wear a thousand faces. One man's light will be another man's blindness.

It will never again be as simple as handing out daisies to the flower children. One might be more responsible handing out coffee and cigarettes in a USO.[12]

It may well be true that we are "called to be decent in separate ways." Moreover, we are instructed: "Do not judge, and you will not be judged" (Lk. 6:37; Mt. 7:1). The pacifist inveighs, as he justifiably can, against remorseless violence; the Christian realist inveighs, as he too reasonably can, against *remorseless peace*, contending that the application of violence may, at times, be ethically preferable to an absolute, and consequently a possibly pitiless, pacifism. *Heresy* is a particularly vitriolic word; to call a pacifist a heretic may contravene the admonitions of the Gospel. But the argument of this book is that our twin duties, sacred and secular, *must* be merged into a civic virtue, enabling us to know how we should act for the common interest as well as for our own. The pacifist's unremitting refusal to use violence has social consequences.[13] Even as pacifists commendably call us always and carefully to examine our consciences when we think about the employment of military power, we who subscribe to the idea that one can be a soldier call upon our pacifist brethren, even as Cromwell wrote to the Church of Scotland in 1650: "I beseech you, in the bowels of Christ, think it possible you may be mistaken." The purpose of this chapter is to explain why pacifism may well be mistaken.

MUSINGS OF A FICTIONAL PONTIFF

In Walter Murphy's powerful novel *The Vicar of Christ*, Declan Walsh serves as a Marine Corps officer in Korea, as a law school dean, as Chief Justice of the Supreme Court, and (finally, if improbably) as Pope. Curiously, the novel works and is, to some extent, credible. After his election as Pope, Walsh chooses the name Francis I, and he determines that a number of changes are needed in the Catholic Church, among them the adoption of pacifism.[14] As "Pope Francis" says:

The error came in the early Church when its fathers made a false peace with Rome and allowed Christians to serve in the legions. The only way not to have war is not to have armed forces. The Quakers have been right all along on this. The Church must make pacifism an integral part of its moral teaching.

Warming to his subject, the fictional Catholic pontiff contends that

Human life is sacred. How can it be moral for mass armies to kill each other as well as innocent civilians? Or for Christians to join those armies? Christ was a pacifist. He preached pacifism, and he preached it in the Garden of Gethsemane and on Calvary. There is simply no way you can love your neighbor and then go about preparing to murder him.[15]

Thus the Pope intends "not only [to] condemn war but categorically [to] forbid all Catholics—yes, all humans—to participate."[16] This ethical and religious dilemma—can the man of conscience serve both God and country?—is hardly new.[17] One can mention Dietrich Bonhoeffer (1906–1945), the well-known Protestant clergyman, who was hanged on 9 April 1945 for having participated in the plot to kill Hitler. One can also cite the case of Franz Jagerstatter, who was beheaded on 9 August 1943 for refusing to serve in Hitler's army.[18] Bonhoeffer the Protestant and Jagerstatter the Catholic were convinced that Hitler and the Nazis were evil and that to serve their cause was therefore evil. Some pacifists would contend that such a feeling should be universalized—that men of good will must learn that they may not cthically scrvc thcir country in the uniform of the armed services (either as a combatant or as a uniformed non-combatant).

In a very real sense, then, the issue of whether a Christian can be a soldier is a genuine military problem—at least in the armed forces of the United States, whose Code of Conduct tells soldiers that they are to trust in their God and in the United States of America, the perfect example of a suggested blend of cross and sword. American soldiers, similarly, are instructed that they must disobey unlawful orders and that they must seek to prevent and certainly to report war crimes. Indeed, we place the inscription "In God We Trust" on our coins, and our president (the commander-in-chief of our military forces) takes his oath of office with his left hand on a Bible. From the beginning of his time in office, then, the President of the United States serves as our principal "ethical leader," much as Solomon once suggested that he needed "an understanding heart to judge your people and to distinguish right from wrong" (1 Kgs. 3:9). Could our president reach the conclusion that his two roles—leader of "Command" *and* leader of "Conscience"—conflict absolutely? Practically all our presidents have professed adherence to Christianity. What would happen if our current president or his successor were to convert to the views of "Pope Francis I"?

Much thought—and even spiritual agony—went into the Catholic Bishops' pastoral letter, now a decade old,[19] about the morality of nuclear war and deterrence. The issue, plainly, is not confined to the Catholic Church. Concerned people of practically every religious and ethical persuasion have discussed and debated the merits and morality of warfare.[20] Many of the arguments about the use of military power are based upon tendentious exegetics; it may well be that the kind of hermeneutical histrionics one can read from pro- and anti-military exponents is merely another manifestation of the five-hundred-year-old rending of Christendom. It does appear clear, however, that "Pope Francis" was mistaken, for the real Church tradition is clear:

Certainly, war has not been rooted out of human affairs. As long as the danger of war remains and there is no competent and sufficiently powerful authority at the international level, governments cannot be denied the right to legitimate defense once every means of peaceful settlement has been exhausted. Therefore, government authorities and others who share public responsibility have the duty to protect the welfare of the people entrusted to their care and to conduct such grave matters soberly.

But it is one thing to undertake military action for the just defense of the people, and something else again to seek the subjugation of other nations. Nor does the possession of war potential make every military or political use of it lawful. Neither does the mere fact that war has unhappily begun mean that all is fair between the warring parties.[21]

The American President, moreover, responding to "Francis's" notions of pacifism would have to square the remarks of Pope John Paul II, who has said: "We are not pacifists. We don't want peace at any price." The Pope was adamant that "Peace is always the work of justice."[22] While no scriptural reference can hope to be more than heuristic, for we are not released from the need to form our consciences by revelation and reason, the references following are the core of any argument, pro or con, about pacifism.

AN ARGUMENT FROM TEXT

Can it be reasonably argued on the strength of this Lukan passage that Jesus understood (and implicitly approved?) what might today be called "balance of power"?

Or if a king is about to march on another king to do battle with him, will he not sit down first and consider whether, with ten thousand men, he can withstand an enemy coming against him with twenty thousand? If he cannot, he will send a delegation while the enemy is still at a distance, asking for terms of peace (14:31–32).

One recognizes, as mentioned earlier in this volume, that, as Shakespeare put it, "The devil can cite Scripture for his purpose." Indeed, one can cite Marx's animadversion that "The social principles of Christianity have justified ancient slavery, glorified medieval serfdom, and they now recognize the need for approving the oppression of the proletariat—with, of course, a slightly contrite air."[23]

One must guard, then, against being too tendentious or histrionic in citing texts; such can be the fallacy of card-stacking or special pleading. One must consider the totality of the evidence (as was argued in the preceding chapter), not isolated elements of it. Still, those who employ scripture in order to press their case for pacifism should be able to marshal persuasive biblical evidence. In the Sermon on the Mount, for example, Jesus says, "Blest too are the peacemakers; for they shall be called sons of God" (Mt. 5:9), and Jesus gives us a new law of return, to replace the *lex talionis*, referred to in the Old Testament: "You have heard the commandment, 'An eye for an eye, a tooth for a tooth' [Ex. 21:24]. But what I say to you is: offer no resistance to injury. When a person strikes you on the right cheek, turn and offer him the other" (Mt. 5:38–39). Similarly, we are instructed by Jesus to "love your enemies" (Mt. 5:44; Lk. 6:29). In reading these scriptures, one must ask whether, given the totality of biblical testimony, soldiers can be peacemakers. In short, is Christian bellicism plainly at odds with biblical imperatives? One must ask, for instance, whether the command of Jesus to turn the other cheek is directed both at individuals and at nation-states. One must ask, too, whether one could fight, and even kill, an enemy while still loving him. This may not be as paradoxical as it appears, provided one accepts the idea that the Christian must value the principle above the person. One must love the sinner while hating the sin; it appears equally possible that one can fight an enemy in the interest of justice while still loving that enemy in the sense conveyed by the just war tradition previously discussed.

W. L. LaCroix, a Jesuit, offers this trenchant observation:

Every advocacy by Jesus of non-violence was relative to context. It was a valid option to be a Messiah of force. Jesus decided against it. That is why he got so angry with Peter. But he used force to expel the traders from the temple. Even the injunction (Mt. 5.38–39) not to resist evil was in distinction to the *lex talionis*, that is, it was to exclude doing exactly equivalent violence in revenge for injury done. This had nothing to do with the use of force in defense or in helping others.[24]

As another example of the contextual argument, one may cite Paul's letter to the Romans, in which he tells us "Never [to] repay injury with injury . . . . If possible, live peaceably with everyone" (12:17–18). There may be occasions, as Father LaCroix suggests, when peace may be suspended, as Jesus clearly shows in driving the money-changers from the temple with a whip of cords (Jn. 2:13–17). Clearly, there is a difference between driving people out of a temple and killing them, but Jesus plainly states that principle, above peace, is his mission: "Do not suppose that my mission on earth is to spread peace. My mission is to spread, not peace, but division" (Mt. 10:34). It may, therefore, be at least arguable that those who believe in the fighting of a truly just or principled war can be on solid scriptural ground.

The translation of the scripture just cited appears this way in the King James Bible: "Think not that I am come to send peace on earth: I came not to send peace, but a sword." *Sword* can mean many things; students of biblical languages can detail its meaning within context. But there appears to be little debate possible over the verse in which Jesus tells his followers that "Those who use the sword are sooner or later destroyed by it" (Mt. 26:52). Curiously, however, Jesus tells his followers that "the man without a sword must sell his coat and buy one" (Lk. 22:36). Nowhere does Jesus tell his followers that they may never do military service; that they must disarm; that the profession of a soldier is ignoble or evil.[25] One supposes therefore, that what is meant by the verse which tells us that those who take the sword may perish by the sword is either of two ideas: first, there is danger in wielding the sword, either individually or militarily; and, second, those whose lives—whose sole and sheer interest—become the sword spiritually die that way, for "where your treasure is, there is your heart also" (Mt. 6:21). St. Thomas Aquinas, moreover, distinguished between seizing the sword, as in a duel, as a private person and seizing it as a public person "through a zeal for justice" which "is not to take the sword, but to use it as commissioned by another, wherefore it does not deserve punishment."[26]

As stated, it is, of course, possible for serious and sincere people to read the gospels and learn apparently different lessons from them. But it seems that Jesus does not advocate, necessarily, strict asceticism. Jesus was no hermit, and he lived according to Jewish law and custom under Roman rule. For example, Jesus paid the temple tax expected of him (Mt. 17:27), and he offered this much-quoted, if rather vague, advice: "give to Caesar what is Caesar's, but give to God what is God's" (Mt. 22:21; Mk. 12:17; Lk. 20:25). As one scholar puts it, "All four Gospels are rather insistent on the fact that Jesus was not executed for any political offense; this insistence reflects the image which the apostolic Church wished to project."[27]

Thus Jesus says to Pilate that "My Kingdom does not belong to this world" (Jn. 18:36). Those who ask, "Can you imagine Jesus as a soldier!" certainly expect a reply in the negative. But one cannot be at all sure of that. Jesus normally followed the Jewish laws, and there are no recorded instances of his ever having violated Roman law; and, at the time, Jewish men were not being conscripted. One can only speculate whether Jesus would have allowed himself to be drafted. (When Socrates had to choose whether to serve, he entered the Athenian army and served bravely.) But when Jesus tells Pilate that "You would have no power over me whatever unless it were given you from above" (Jn. 19:11), one has a basis for suggesting that Jesus accepted Roman law and political rule and would likely have followed their requirements (conceivably even military duty) unless and until they violated the higher law. (The Socratic analogy is still valid in this regard.) As the scholar F. J. Sheed says, "we hear from the words of the Man who was God that Caesar has *rights*. Whatever the civil authority requires for the proper conduct of society, to that it has a right—Christ says so; in the truest sense, therefore, it is a divine right."[28]

Perhaps this is the sense of Paul's letter to Titus, in which we read: "Remind people to be loyally subject to the government and its officials, to obey the laws, to be ready to take on any honest employment" (3:1). In 1 Peter 2:13–15, we are told this: "Because of the Lord, be obedient to every human institution, whether to the emperor as sovereign or to the governors he commissions for the punishment of criminals and the recognition of the upright. Such obedience is the will of God."

Similarly, we are instructed that we should pray, in particular, "for kings and those in authority" (1 Tim. 2:2). Certainly the most powerful example of this adjuration to Christians to be good citizens appears in Paul's letter to the Romans, which bears lengthy quotation here:

Let everyone obey the authorities that are over him, for there is no authority except from God, and all authority that exists is established by God. As a consequence, the man who opposes authority rebels against the ordinance of God; those who resist thus shall draw condemnation down upon themselves. Rulers cause no fear when a man does what is right but only when his conduct is evil. Do you wish to be free from the fear of authority? Do what is right and you will gain its approval, for the ruler is God's servant to work for your good. Only if you do wrong ought you to be afraid. *It is not without purpose that the ruler carries the sword; he is God's servant to inflict his avenging wrath upon the wrongdoer.* You must obey, then, not only to escape punishment but also for conscience' sake. You pay taxes for the same reason, magistrates being God's ministers who devote themselves to his service with unremitting care. Pay each one his due: taxes to whom taxes are due; toll to whom toll is due; respect and honor to everyone who deserves them [13:1–7, emphasis supplied].

One can say that Paul was trying to tell the Romans only what they wanted to hear; but to those for whom the Bible is inspired text (and who spiritually consult it in the hope of effecting a reliable conscience with regard to the issue of armed service), such thought is anathema. The ruler's use of the sword is thus approved, provided it is wielded against a wrongdoer. Some have gone too far with this text from Romans and have used it to support the view, certainly a mistaken one, that whatever the secular ruler desires is therefore right. But Paul is clear that respect and honor are due to "everyone who deserves them"—a text which could be read even to justify civil disobedience in the case of unjust laws or unjust wars. This passage should be read in the context of Peter and the apostles' statement: "Better for us to obey God than men" (Acts 5:29). In other words, we are citizens with profane duties which we must discharge—until those secular duties clash with our sacred duties or with our spiritual imperatives.

THE PERSISTENCE OF WAR

War, in one form or another, will continue until the final days. "You will hear of wars and rumors of wars. Do not be alarmed. Such things are bound to happen, but that is not yet the end" (Mt. 24:6; Mk. 13:7). In the face of this knowledge, what is the Christian to do? We are told by Jesus that "'Peace' is my farewell to you, my peace is my gift to you; I do not give it to you as the world gives peace" (Jn. 14:27).

The Christian peace is an interior peace—a peace of mind "which is beyond all understanding" (Phil. 4:7). This is the meaning of the Lukan phrase, "peace on earth to those on whom his favor rests" (2:14). One supposes that political peace is rather irrelevant here. The Christian finds peace in knowing, loving, and serving God. A full, final political peace is not to be expected through the devices of politics or economics. And the mission of the Church's ministers and priests is not primarily political reform but the care of souls.

To be sure, it is difficult to define war, but in Chapter 2, *war* was defined as "the limited application of force—customarily by states—toward the achievement of reasonable and ethical political goals"; it may be harder still to define *peace*. Simply saying that peace is a state of grace, although theologically useful perhaps, is plainly inadequate politically. As Father LaCroix has noted: "[I]f by peace one means that condition wherein there is a significant order in the human values and human relationships that we include under the name of liberty and justice, then the peace of some governments does not count as peace."[29] Pope John Paul II made a vital point in that regard:

Peace requires justice, an attitude which recognizes the dignity and equality of all men and women, and a firm commitment to strive and *protect* the basic human rights of all. Where there is no justice there can be no peace. Peace is possible only where there is a just order that *ensures* the rights of everyone. World peace is possible only where the international order is just.[30]

A sense of Christian realism depends upon, and derives from, what is often referred to as the "human condition." To a very considerable extent, the Bible may be understood as a record of man's sinful nature and of God's infinite mercy, manifesting itself, as Christians believe, in God's entrance into human history in the Incarnation (1 Jn. 2:1–2). If a central truth of Christianity is our weak and sinful nature (e.g, Mt. 26:41; 1 Jn. 1:18), we are in profound error in expecting that, of our own devices, we can establish full and final peace on earth. Thus does the Old Testament refer to "whitewashers": "those prophets of Israel who prophesied to Jerusalem and saw for it visions of peace when there was no peace" (Ez. 13:15–16; and epigraph and note 1 to this chapter). Elizabeth Anscombe discusses "the dry truthfulness about human beings that so characterizes the Old Testament,"[31] underscoring the basic question of this chapter and the previous one: Is there a fundamental context in which all the discrete biblical citations can be examined, there to be seen in their full perspective? One perspective adduced here is that the Bible is, in its most general format, a record of God's fidelity and human infidelity and, again, God's enduring quest for us poor humans. In that connection, of course, the New Testament complements and supplements—it does not supplant—the Old.

One writer expressed that perspective this way:

In the Old Testament, God *ordered* the Israelites to put to the sword some of their (and His) enemies, not even sparing women, children, and livestock. This is the same God Whom the Old Testament records as wiping out Sodom and Gomorrah with fire and brimstone. To assert that Jesus objected to these actions of his Father is not merely contrary to Catholic doctrine, it is blasphemy.[32]

If it is correct to think that one must judge pacifism by the pattern rather than by the strand, the comments of Father LaCroix are especially telling: Pacifists, he says, tend to absolutize verses such as Exodus 20:13, the commandment against killing, but ignore such passages as Exodus 32:26–29, which recounts how Moses and the Levites killed some 3000 Israelites in one day but do not, thus, violate the commandment. They ignore Deuteronomy 13:6–11, which interprets the commandment against killing by saying, in essence, that the infidel *must* be killed, and that "Your hand shall be the first raised to slay him; the rest of the people shall join in with you" (13:10). They also ignore, Father LaCroix points out, passages such as Numbers 31, in which Moses was instructed to kill his enemies.[33] Although this can be seen as macabre, one must again seek out the context, pattern, or perspective. Perhaps the backdrop for all this is to be found in the repeated Biblical notion that justice will bring about peace (Is. 32:17; but cf. James 3:18). Thus does Elizabeth Anscombe observe:

The truth about Christianity is that it is a severe and practicable religion, not a beautifully ideal but impracticable one. Its moral precepts (except for the stricter laws about marriage that Christ enacted, abrogating some of the permissions of the Old Law) are those of the Old Testament; and its God is the God of Israel.[34]

Jesus said, "Do not think that I have come to abolish the law and the prophets. I have come, not to abolish them, but to fulfill them" (Mt. 5:17; see also Rom. 3:31). If we judge individualized Biblical quotations within the scriptural panorama and within the context of salvation history, we must conclude that mankind is not politically perfectible and that history will not be self-redeeming.

THE MILLENNIAL ELEMENT OF PACIFISM

Pacifism has a strong millennial element. The ultimate pacifist argument is not that it does not matter that pacifists may be imprisoned, or even slaughtered, by aggressors; the view shared by many, if not most, pacifists is that the shining beneficence of their example will finally humanize any aggressors.[35] Religious pacifists thus share, to some extent, in the vision of the eschatological peace prophesied, for example, by Micah: "He shall judge between many peoples and impose terms on strong and distant nations; they shall beat their swords into plowshares, and their spears into pruning hooks; one nation shall not raise the sword against another, nor shall they train for war again [4:3]." There may be reason, however, for doing the opposite. Another kind of "beating" appears in Joel: "Declare this among the nations: proclaim a war, rouse the warriors to arms! Let all the soldiers report and march! Beat your plowshares into swords, and your pruning hooks into spears; let the weak man say, 'I am a warrior!' [4:9–10]."

The apparent contradiction between these two passages may be resolved by either of two approaches, the first of which is clearly least theologically sound. "Contrary to the Christian belief which stresses the salvation of individual man," wrote Thomas Molnar, "utopians believe in the salvation of mankind as a collectivity. Nobody may be left out, since God is really 'all mankind' . . . ."[36] In this approach, pacifism may be part of a radicalism which envisages a perfectible tomorrow—a kind of political Parousia, with which the Left of the spectrum in general and "liberation theology" in particular can be identified.[37] As Paul Johnson has observed, "History shows us the truly amazing extent to which intelligent, well-informed and resolute men, in the pursuit of economy or in an altruistic passion for disarmament, will delude themselves about realities."[38] One may view this as a resurgence of Jacobinism, itself "a Christian heresy [said Walter Lippmann]—perhaps the most influential since the Arian."[39] We are arrived thus at a much-maligned term, "secular humanism"; but that is precisely what Jacobinism is, albeit recast for the twenty-first century.[40] Micah, certainly, was not prophesying the ultimate victory of profane man—creating his own sacerdotal polity with himself as god. Some genuinely religious people, however, unknowingly subscribe to a political theology which would redeem the spirit of man by investing transforming power in the Person of the *Vozhd*, who will "make all things new," and, of course, abolish war. But the quotation is from Revelation (21:5), and the end of war is not on the horizon. Micah's true prophecy is not political, but religious; the "Alpha and the Omega" promising redemption (Rev. 21:6) is God, not a man-god known as "Number One," the "Fuhrer," the "Duce," or "El Caudillo."

The second way to resolve the tension between Micah and Joel is to suggest that "There is an appointed time for everything . . . A time to love, and a time to hate; a time of war and a time of peace" (Eccles. 3:1,8). This approach, emphasizing the human situation, suggests that, as Augustine wrote, in this vale of tears it may at times be necessary to resort to force in order to prevent the commission of greater evil. For the Christian, this problem is thrown into sharp relief by this question: What would the Good Samaritan (Lk. 10:25–36) have done had he arrived at the robbery as it was taking place, rather than after? Because this world is neither perfect nor perfectible (through human agency alone), we have arrived again at the need for sagacious national leadership and at the Niebuhrian charge of heresy against pacifism.

One finds a good, brief explanation of this in a recent novel by Andrew Greeley:

Paul Tillich called it "idolatry"—the confusion of temporal and contingent political goals, however laudable, with the transcendent and the absolute in religious revelation. G. K. Chesterton called it "heresy"—the confusion of part of revelation, however important, with all of it. Msgr. Ronald Knox called it "enthusiasm"—the confusion of emotional fervor, however necessary, with religious conviction. This temptation is as seductive to the right as to the left, to the traditionalist as to the modernist, to the conservative as to the liberal.[41]

This pacifist tendency to be "enthusiastic," to refuse to bear arms to prevent or to redress great wrong can be, as Ashley Tellis has explained, immoral:

[I]f the pacifist knows . . . that the oppressor is . . . devoid of residual moral sentiments, committed to executing gross and very punitive forms of exploitation over a subjugated people, then pacifist nonviolence—if it entails the death of the pacifist and others—cannot be subject to the traditional benefits of double effect, and, *hence, may be even judged immoral.*[42]

From Pelagius to Teilhard, some have sought for a progress culminating in perfection. Whether the source of that perfection is the ostensible absence of "original sin," an irrepressible linear movement to some dynamic destiny in immanent time, or a recrudescence of what Eric Voegelin called gnosticism, Christian realism forbids us from confusing spiritual and political redemption.[43] In a world of sin, we are well advised to remain prepared to beat our plowshares into swords. Consider, finally, this advice from the Old Testament book of Sirach: "Never trust your enemy, for his wickedness is like corrosion in bronze. Even though he acts humbly and peacefully toward you, take care to be on your guard against him. Rub him as one polishes a brazen mirror, and you will find that there is still corrosion [12:10–11]."

ON CHRISTIAN PRUDENCE

At one point in the New Testament, a soldier asks Jesus to cure his serving boy, who is at home in bed, paralyzed and suffering. The soldier perceives that Jesus can heal the boy, and Jesus offers to go to the soldier's home. In words which are now in essence a part of the Roman Catholic mass, the soldier says, "I am not worthy to have you under my roof. Just give an order and my boy will get better" (Mt. 8:8). Jesus says, "I assure you, I have never found this much faith in Israel" (8:10). The boy is healed. Jesus does not tell the soldier that he must renounce his military calling; he does not say, "Go, and sin no more"; he does not tell the soldier to lay down his arms. Yet Jesus nowhere else ignores sin or evil. Can we suppose, therefore, that the soldier was an honorable man in an honorable profession? (Of course, we know that all professions have their failures, and there have been many evil soldiers. But that does not make the profession of arms evil any more than Judas Iscariot makes evil the priesthood or the ministry!) In fact, one of the few people in the Gospels publicly to say that Jesus is the Son of God was the soldier (Mt. 27:54).

Peter clearly preaches the need for peace (1 Pt. 3:8–12), but he baptizes a soldier named Cornelius without any mention of his profession or without requiring the soldier in any way to renounce the bearing of arms (Acts 10:47). Is it unfair to suggest that if the military profession were itself evil, Peter would not have baptized the soldier without extracting a promise from him that he would have a "firm purpose of amendment" never again to bear arms? John the Baptist himself tells soldiers not to bully anyone, not to denounce anyone, but to be content with their pay (Lk. 3:14). There is not a word to the soldiers that they sin by being soldiers. John the Baptist was hardly obsequious in the face of authority (Mt. 14:4), and one suspects that, if soldiering were evil, John would have told the soldiers that without pause. Indeed, in considering these cases, Elizabeth Anscombe contends that Christ's praise of the soldier—to a pacifist—must be "much as if a madam in a brothel had said: 'I know what authority is, I tell the girl to do it, and she does it' and Christ had commended her faith."[44] Thus can we understand St. Augustine, who wrote: "Do not think it is impossible to please God while engaged in military service . . . . Let necessity, therefore, and not your will, slay the enemy who fights against you."[45]

On the strength of the evidence adduced, therefore, one can reasonably conclude that it is not heresy for one to be a soldier. Even "You shall not kill" (Ex. 20:13) is rendered as "Do not commit murder" in the *Good News Bible*, which may clarify some of the apparent contradictions previously outlined. Father LaCroix disposes, finally, of the argument that scripture condemns soldiery:

There is a problem with the interpretation of Scriptural passages (e.g., the Sermon on the Mount) that are cited as requiring a pacifist stance. This appears to involve a double standard when the "no revenge" command is extrapolated into a justification for not contributing to the defense of one's country, but the "judge not" command is not turned into a justification for not testifying in court or serving on juries. Why are some passages held to be literally applicable in contemporary times, but others held to be only symbolic? For example, "Let the dead bury their dead" is cited by some scriptural scholars to be just as radical as turn to [*sic*] the other cheek," yet few pacifists call for foregoing burial ceremonies. Double standards usually indicate that some hidden principle other than those expressed is operative.[46]

There is an old story, probably apocryphal, which concerns Henri Philippe Petain (1856–1951), who, after the Allies freed France in 1944–1945, was tried for treason. He is supposed to have said that his intentions were good. His judge is supposed to have replied, "Only God can judge intentions; men must judge by consequences." And so it is with pacifists, the purity of whose intentions may be judged by an omniscient Creator. The rest of us must lead lives rooted in prudence.

When Reinhold Niebuhr contended that pacifism preaches a perfectionism inconsistent with historical experience, he was arguing against "Enthusiasm." The way, the truth, and the life are not political; the notion that progress (and the implicit notion of an end to violence) can come from peace rallies rather than from The Christ is, at its heart, heretical. L. L. McReavy has thus addressed Catholics:

Catholics are certainly free to form their own opinion whether the conditions required for justification are likely to be fulfilled in any future war, but the authentic Catholic position is that a war of self-defense can still be justified, in practice as well as principle. The immense evils liable to result from it are not demonstrably greater than those that would afflict mankind if force could no longer be used to repel the armed aggression even of a godless tyranny.[47]

Religiously and politically, we must distinguish between the false peace of the prophets (or Munich-bound statesmen) and the sobering realities of world politics. Even the Lord God, for instance, was angered by "enthusiasts." As one reads in Jeremiah:

Ah! Lord God, I replied, it is the prophets who say to them "You shall not see the sword; famine shall not befall you. Indeed, I will give you lasting peace in this place."
Lies these prophets utter in my name, the Lord said to me. I did not send them; I gave them no command nor did I speak to them. Lying visions, foolish divination, dreams of their own imagination, they prophesy to you [14:13–14].

The idea of prudence (cf. Mt. 25:1–13) is both a cardinal and Christian virtue. Christian pacifists invariably suggest that all we need do is to trust in God and all will be well. Something of this is found in the temptations of Jesus, when Satan tells Jesus to hurl himself down from a high peak and then quotes the Psalms (91:11–12) to "assure" Jesus that angels will save him. Jesus answers by quoting Deuteronomy: "You shall not put the Lord your God to the test" (6:16). There appears, certainly, to be ample biblical support for the idea that we can and must trust the Lord; but one of the messages of the Bible also seems to be that we must work hard and help ourselves (Gn. 3:17–19). In the desert, for example, God gave the Israelites manna, but they were to gather it (Ex. 16:26), not expect to be fed with no effort on their part. In the New Testament, too, Paul says that, "anyone who would not work should not eat" (2 Thes. 3:10). Is it therefore wrong to think that we should not only pray for peace but work diligently toward it ourselves? And, concomitantly, is it unfair or unreasonable to think that among the blessed peacemakers may stand the prudent and just Christian soldier, whose politics will be established, not just by possible intentions but as well by probable consequences?

CONCLUSION: POLITICAL CONSIDERATIONS

In judging pacifism—if not pacifists—one should note, as Father LaCroix points out, that

[N]o one who has been both canonized as a saint and named a doctor of the Catholic church has ever defended pacifism as a social ethic. Many saints and doctors, such as Augustine, Bernard, Thomas, and Bellarmine, have defended justified war and the duty of all citizens to participate.[48]

If a given liberal society has a large number of pacifists, C. S. Lewis has explained, the state may thus be handed over to its tyrannical neighbor, which tolerates no pacifists. Thus pacifism, Lewis concludes, is self-defeating.[49] Pacifism holds in essence that the highest value is life itself, much as Jonathan Schell wrote in his book *The Fate of the Earth*. Biological existence is all that truly matters.[50] No Christian can agree to that: Jesus himself was prepared to sacrifice his human life that humankind might be redeemed. Sidney Hook had a similar view: "Those who say that life is worth living at any cost have already written for themselves an epitaph of infamy, for there is no cause and no person they will not betray to stay alive."[51]

In the end, as Kenneth Thompson has observed, "Politics is the arena where power and conscience meet, and will be meeting until the end of time."[52] It may very well be that the mantle of righteousness with which pacifists have so often sought to cover themselves may fail both to hide them from the power realities of the world and, simultaneously, be more vicious than virtuous. Aquinas wrote that appealing to the principle of nonresistance to evil when the evil is happening to another is more a moral viciousness than a moral virtue.[53] Conscience may impel us to employ power to effect the safety of our neighbors, whom we are instructed to love (and, inferentially, to protect).

Thus did Father John Courtney Murray write:

A defensive war against unjust aggression is morally admissible both in principle and in fact.

In its abstractness this principle has always formed part of Catholic doctrine; by its assertion the Church finds a sure way between the *false extremes of pacifism and bellicism.*[54]

Pacifism, as Anscombe points out, teaches people "to make no distinction between the shedding of innocent blood and the shedding of any human blood."[55] Pacifism thus leaves us in a state of ethical and political abulia; by not being able to choose, we choose: we thus abet aggressors. The alternative to failing to find just and limited ways of using nuclear weapons, Joseph Martino has written,

is to concede the use of nuclear weapons to only those who recognize no morality. By doing that we would abandon all that is decent in the world to the dubious mercies of the Hitlers, the Pol Pots, the Idi Amins of history. That would be immoral in itself. It would fly in the face of the consistent teachings of the Church from Augustine to John Paul.[56]

In a preceding chapter, we explored Nye's test of motives, means, and consequences. The late Father Murray said that the Church had a triple test to impose of war issues: (1) to condemn war as evil; (2) to limit the evils it entails; and (3) to humanize its conduct insofar as possible.[57]

When on 9 February 1933, the Oxford Union of Students at Oxford University voted 275 to 153 "not to fight for King or Country," Joseph Stalin was murdering millions in Soviet Russia. In 1935, in a comment to Pierre Laval during conversations in Moscow, Stalin, asked about morality in world affairs, replied, "The Pope! How many divisions has *he* got?" Pacifism is at odds with the reason of the sword—and with the faith of the cross. As George Kennan has written:

In approaching the individual conflicts between governments which make up so much of international relations, we must beware of pouring Christian enthusiasm into unsuitable vessels which were at best designed to contain the earthly calculations of the practical politicians.[58]

"Pacifists have every right to avoid the moral dilemmas posed by the world of statesmanship and statecraft and [to] seek individual salvation through ethical absolutism and purity," writes Guenter Lewy, "but they have no right to sacrifice others for the attainment of this vocation."[59] Of course Lewy is, in a sense, wrong. Adopting a stance of "moral purity" and looking away when injustice is done is not a right; it is failure of honor and of duty. It is a political evil; it is a religious sin.

The Christian, then, trusts not in the siren-song of a violence-free utopia, never to be ours on earth (see Mt. 24:4–14). Even Christ suggests (Lk. 12:51) that he came, not to give peace, but division. To expect that the renunciation of military power will lead to progress or to perfected politics is tantamount to the apotheosis of mankind, the sin condemned as blasphemous in both the Old and the New Testaments (Ex. 20:3; Mt. 16:23). Pacifism is not merely dangerous politics; it is desecrated religion. Winston Churchill offered this consolation: "The day may dawn when fair play, love for one's fellow man, respect for justice and freedom, will enable tormented generations to march forth serene and triumphant from the hideous epoch in which we have to dwell. Meanwhile, never flinch, never weary, never despair."[60]

NOTES

1. One may also see the idea of a "false peace" reflected in the Old Testament book of Judith.

2. "The Morality of War," *Time*, 20 January 1967: 40.

3. Quoted in Joseph S. Nye, Jr., *Nuclear Ethics* (New York: The Free Press, 1986), p. 43.

4. Quoted in Joseph P. Martino, *A Fighting Chance: The Moral Use of Nuclear Weapons* (San Francisco, CA: Ignatius Press, 1988), p. 33.

5. Michael Novak, "And Now a Few Words from the Real World," *Notre Dame Magazine*, February 1982: 21.

6. "Standing Tall for Moral Principles," *Time*, 17 February 1986, p. 66.

7. Quoted in Martino (above, n. 4), p. 44.

8. For discussion, see Judith Dwyer, ed., *The Catholic Bishops and Nuclear War* (Washington, DC: Georgetown University Press, 1984); Philip J. Murnion, ed., *Catholics and Nuclear War* (New York: Crossroad, 1983); and "The Christian Soldier: A Symposium," in *Catholicism in Crisis* 2 (March 1984): 1–48.

9. "War is killing business. You've got to spill their blood or they'll spill yours. Rip 'em up the belly, or shoot 'em in the guts."

10. Niebuhr is quoted in Albert Marrin, ed., *War and the Christian Conscience* (Chicago, IL: Henry Regnery, 1971), p. 134. See also James F. Childress, "Reinhold Niebuhr's Critique of Pacifism," *Review of Politics* 36 (October 1974): 467–91.

11. Another useful background reading is John W. Coffey, "The American Bishops on War and Peace," *Parameters* 13 (December 1983): 30–38.

12. Robert Griffin, "Blowin' in the Wind," *Sunday Magazine*, February 1983: 9.

13. It is important to stipulate that many pacifists would not share in this idea of their refusal to use military power to protect what they regard as valuable. Indeed, some pacifists will argue that they will, indeed, resist very strongly the force of evil—albeit by nonviolent means. But pacifism generally means opposition to war or to

violence as a means of settling disputes. Here we understand pacifism generically as the conviction which holds that force, violence, and war are invariably wrong and that refusal to wage war is invariably right. The Just War criteria we have reviewed (Chapter 4) make it clear that war is to be a last resort. Pacifists contend that the presumption must always be against the use of force—surely a fair presumption. Christian realists respond, however, that, when the criteria of the Just War are fulfilled, the presumption must always be that force is an acceptable alternative.

14. In reality, Bishop John J. O'Connor has pointed out, popes have not explicitly supported conscientious objection. See *In Defense of Life* (Boston, MA: Daughters of St. Paul, 1981), p. 85. On pp. 46–47, he quotes Pius XII, who, on Christmas Eve 1948 said that "A people threatened with an unjust aggression, or already its victim, may not remain passively indifferent, if it would think and act as befits a Christian." Pope Paul VI said that "as long as people remain weak, changeable, and even wicked as they often show themselves to be, defensive arms will, unfortunately, be necessary." (Quoted in W. L. LaCroix, *War and International Ethics: Tradition and Today* [New York: University Press of America, 1988], p. 18). Text also available in the Bishops' Pastoral Letter on War and Peace (below, n. 19), p. 24. Pope John Paul II has said that "peoples have a right and even a duty to protect their existence and freedom by a proportionate means against an unjust aggressor." (Quoted in Martino [above, n. 4], p. 202n.).

15. Walter F. Murphy, *The Vicar of Christ* (New York: Ballantine, 1979), p. 688.

16. Ibid., p. 689.

17. For example, see "Reverberations!" in *The World Tomorrow*, June 1931: 192–93, wherein Army Chief of Staff Douglas MacArthur responds to a poll of clergymen, most of whom, in strongly opposing war, were, in MacArthur's judgment, "proclaim[ing] their willingness to see this nation perish rather than participate in its defense." An interesting novel, whose author shares MacArthur's outlook, is *A Country Such as This* (New York: Bantam, 1983). The author, James Webb, is a former Marine and past Secretary of the Navy.

18. See Gordon Zahn, *In Solitary Witness: The Life and Death of Franz Jagerstatter* (Boston, MA: Beacon Press, 1964).

19. *The Challenge of Peace: God's Promise and Our Response* (Washington, DC: United States Catholic Conference, 1983).

20. See Donald L. Davidson, *Nuclear Weapons and the American Churches: Ethical Positions on Modern Warfare* (Boulder, CO: Westview Press, 1983).

21. Ibid., p. 23.

22. *The Montgomery Advertiser*, 18 February 1991: 6A. *The Catholic Week* (official weekly publication of the Archdiocese of Mobile), 22 February 1991: 1.

23. Shakespeare's comment is in *The Merchant of Venice*, Act I, Scene 3. Marx is quoted in John A. Hardin, S.J., *The Catholic Catechism* (Garden City, NY: Doubleday, 1975), p. 290.

24. LaCroix, (above, n. 14), p. 43.

25. Ernest L. Fortin, in "St. Augustine," in Leo Strauss and Joseph Cropsey, eds., *History of Political Philosophy*, 2d ed. (Chicago, IL: Rand McNally, 1972), expresses a similar judgment:

"Finally, it is unfair to assert without further qualification that Christianity breeds contempt for military valor. The New Testament does not order soldiers to surrender their arms but rather commends them for their righteousness and virtue.

The injunction to requite evil with good concerns not so much external actions as the inward disposition with which these actions are to be performed. It seeks to insure that war, if it must be waged, will be carried out with a benevolent design and without due harshness. Men are compelled at times to do what is most likely to benefit their fellow men. In some instances, peace and the correction of wrongdoers are more readily and more perfectly achieved by forgiveness than by castigation; whereas in other instances, one would only confirm the wicked in their evil ways by giving free reign to injustice and allowing crimes to go unpunished. What Christianity reproves is not war, but the evils of war, such as the love of violence, revengeful cruelty, fierce and implacable hatreds, wild resistance, and the lust for power. By yielding to these evils, men lose a good that is far more precious than any of the earthly goods an enemy could take from them. Instead of increasing the number of the good, they merely add themselves to the number of the wicked. Just wars are therefore permissible, but they must be undertaken only out of necessity and for the sake of peace. The decision to wage such a war rests with the monarch or ruler, to whom is entrusted the welfare of the community as a whole" (pp. 176–77).

Because the soldier possesses armed might and therefore has inordinate power to coerce, it may be particularly true of him that his profession of arms is ethically valid precisely to the point that his actions are in keeping with moral canons. One may argue, then, not only that the religious person may be a soldier but that the soldier must be a "religious" person.

26. Quoted in LaCroix (above, n. 14), p. 70.

27. John L. McKenzie, *The Power and the Glory* (Garden City, NY: Doubleday, 1965), p. 257. Cf. the views of the fictionally radicalized nun "Sister Catherine" in Andrew Greeley's novel *Virgin and Martyr* (New York: Warner Books, 1985): "The Latin American theologians [see Chapter 6 in this book, section "On Liberation Theology"] have done wonderful work on the theme of liberation in the Gospels. Jesus was a man of the poor. He organized them. He marched on Jerusalem with them. He challenged the corrupt power structures of his day and demanded freedom and justice for his followers. And he was arrested on the charge of sedition and executed because he was a revolutionary leader" (p. 325). It is difficult, to be sure, to square that image of Jesus' earthly task with this one: "Jesus' mission is not to represent our interests before the Father, but to disclose his relentless love to us. Mediation is downwards. It is we, not God, who are hard to reach." James T. Burtchaell, "An Ancient Gift, a Thing of Joy," *Notre Dame Magazine* (Winter 1985/86): 22.

28. J. Sheed, *To Know Christ Jesus* (New York: Sheed and Ward, 1962), p. 312. See also the arguments of "Brother William" in the fascinating novel by Umberto Eco, *The Name of the Rose*, trans. William Weaver (New York: Harcourt Brace Jovanovich, 1980), pp. 351–57.

29. LaCroix (above, n. 14), p. 101.

30. Quoted in Martino (above, n. 4), p. 169.

31. Elizabeth Anscombe, "War and Murder," in *War, Morality, and the Military Profession*, ed. Malham M. Wakin (Boulder, CO: Westview Press, 1979), p. 294.

32. Martino (above, n. 4), p. 276.

33. See LaCroix (above, n. 14), pp. 47–48.

34. Anscombe (above, n. 31), p. 292.

35. A useful book is Michael Walzer, *Obligations: Essays on Disobedience, War,*

and Citizenship (New York: Simon & Schuster Clarion Book, 1970). For information on pacifism and pacifist resistance, see Joan V. Bondurant, *Conquest of Violence: The Gandhian Philosophy of Conflict* (Princeton, NJ: Princeton University Press, 1958); Anders Boserup and Andrew Mack, *War Without Weapons: Non-Violence in National Defense* (New York: Shocken, 1974); Kenneth Boulding, *Conflict and Defense* (New York; Harper & Brothers, 1962); Duane L. Cady, *From Warism to Pacifism* (Philadelphia, PA: Temple University Press, 1989); Gene Sharp, *Civilian-Based Defense* (Princeton, NJ: Princeton University Press, 1990); and Sharp's earlier work *The Politics of Nonviolent Action* (Boston, MA: Porter Sargent, 1973); and Gordon Zahn's pamphlet "An Alternative to War" (New York: The Council on Religion and International Affairs, 1974). Invariably, the notion of nonviolent resistance assumes an underlying goodness in the minds and hearts and souls of oppressors. Confronted with the virtuous stoicism of the nonviolent resisters, the evil oppressor will be transformed. One fervently wishes. One also knows better. The books above might well be read in the context of a single reference (although scores of others could be suggested): See Robert Conquest, *The Harvest of Sorrow: Soviet Collectivization and the Terror-Famine* (New York: Oxford University Press, 1986).

36. Thomas Molnar, *Utopia: The Perennial Heresy* (London: Tom Stacey, 1971), p. 159.

37. Anscombe (above, n. 31) argues that pacifism has led, paradoxically, "to a universal forgetfulness of the law against killing the innocent" (p. 294). Secular chiliasm seems invariably to lead to totalitarianism, and pacifism is, in its essence, a chiliastic doctrine, whether religiously or politically inspired.

38. Paul Johnson, *Modern Times* (New York: Harper & Row, 1983), p. 175.

39. Walter Lippmann, *Essays in The Public Philosophy* (New York: Mentor, 1955), p. 60.

40. The late Professor Eric Voegelin has explored this theme in a number of his works. See, for example, *The New Science of Politics* (Chicago, IL: University of Chicago Press, 1952) Also of interest would be the writings (and life) of Joachim of Fiore (1130/35–1201/02), the Italian mystic, theologian, and philosopher of history—a heretic to some, orthodox to others. Voegelin offers analysis in the book cited. See also chapter 8 of Karl Lowith's *Meaning in History* (Chicago, IL: University of Chicago Press, 1949) for details.

41. Prefatory note to Greeley's novel (above, n. 27).

42. Ashley J. Tellis, "Nuclear Arms, Moral Questions, and Religious Issues," *Armed Forces and Society* 13 (Summer 1987): 607.

43. Pelagianism was practiced by a fifth century heretical sect that derived its name from a monk and theologian named Pelagius (who lived about 355–425). He argued that a child is born innocent—without original sin—and therefore need not be baptized. His argument was essentially that grace was natural and available to all, thus challenging the function of the Church and its sacraments. Augustine vigorously contested this notion, and Pelagianism was condemned at the Council of Ephesus in 431. See Teilhard de Chardin, *The Divine Milieu* (New York: Harper Torchbooks, 1965) and Philip Hefner, *The Promise of Teilhard* (Philadelphia, PA: J. B. Lippincott, 1970).

44. Anscombe (above, n. 31), p. 293.

45. Quoted in Martino (above, n. 4), p. 137.

46. LaCroix (above, n. 14), p. 93.

47. L. L. McReavy, "Pacifism," *New Catholic Encyclopedia*, 1967, Vol. 10, p. 856.

48. LaCroix (above, n. 14), p. 52; see also p. 93. Paul specifically uses the analogy of a soldier to tell us how we should act: "Bear hardship along with me as a good soldier of Jesus." About the profession of arms, Paul says simply that "no soldier becomes entangled in the affairs of civilian life; he avoids this in order to please his commanding officer" (2 Tim. 2:3–4).

49. Quoted in Michael Novak, *Moral Clarity in the Nuclear Age* (Nashville, TN: Thomas Nelson Publishers, 1983), pp. 37–38.

50. See Charles Krauthammer, "On Nuclear Morality," *Commentary*, October 1983, p. 49 for comment. See also Richard John Neuhaus, "A Crisis of Faith," in *Ethics and Nuclear Arms*, ed. Raymond English (Washington, DC: Ethics and Public Policy Center, 1985): 61.

51. Sidney Hook, *Marxism and Beyond* (Totowa, NJ: Rowman & Littlefield, 1983), p. 207.

52. Kenneth W. Thompson, "Ethics and International Relations: The Problem" in *Ethics and International Relations*, K. W. Thompson, ed. (New Brunswick, NJ: Transaction Books, 1985), p. 17.

53. Quoted in LaCroix (above, n. 14), p. 96.

54. John Courtney Murray, "Morality and Modern War," *The Moral Dilemma of Nuclear Weapons*, W. Clancy, ed. (New York: Council on Religion and International Affairs, 1961), p. 11. Emphasis supplied.

55. Anscombe (above, n. 31), p. 294.

56. Martino (above, n. 4), pp. 281–82.

57. Murray (above, n. 54), p. 14. Father Murray says that "[the] use [of force] in extreme circumstances may be morally obligatory *ad repellandem iniuriam*. The facts assert that today this *ultima ratio* takes the form of nuclear force." "Do not be afraid of those who kill the body and can do no more," said Jesus (Lk. 12:4). Modern tyrannies are spirit killers, as Solzhenitsyn and James Bond Stockdale have testified. Thus, in resisting them, we help save the soul as well as the body.

58. George Kennan, "Foreign Policy and Christian Conscience," *Atlantic*, May 1959, p. 49.

59. Guenter Lewy, *Peace & Revolution: The Moral Crisis of American Pacifism* (Grand Rapids, MI: Eerdmans, 1988), p. 242.

60. From a Churchill address of 1 March 1955, in *Parliamentary Debates*, 5th Series, Vol. 537, col. 1905.

8 THE SWORD AND THE CROSS

Nothing that man is and does is quite without political significance.[1]
—Hans J. Morgenthau

But the root dilemma of our time is that if the quest for peace turns into the *sole* objective of policy, the fear of war becomes a weapon in the hands of the most ruthless; it produces moral disarmament.[2]
—Henry A. Kissinger

What doth the Lord require of thee, but to do justly, and to love mercy, and to walk humbly with thy God?
—Micah 6:8

The tragedy of human existence, simply put, is that we need one another—in families, in groups, in nations. Perhaps, one day, even a global government will be feasible, although that will not solve the problem of conflict. As Glenn Tinder wrote, "the project of uniting all human beings, and even all creation, is compelling and inextinguishable . . . . [and] giving up all hope of community must mean a fall into despair." It is, he writes, "impossible to describe a particular human being except in terms of relationships—occupation, social status, interests, and so forth."[3] Tinder merely repeats the views of

Aristotle in this regard. But in our desperate need for society, we bind ourselves inexorably to the problems relationships are sure to produce: who will be the leaders; who will be the led? who will make the rules; who will be ruled by them? under what conditions must the rulers forfeit their power? what are the purposes of the society? under what or whose superior judgment is the society ordered? Once create a bonding (be it even of two people in marriage, let alone in a modern society) and one simultaneously invents the reason for its dissolution. There are at work, at any given time in social (or familial) history, two competing and powerful drives: a centripetal force, urging ever greater community and consensus; and a centrifugal force, urging disruption and dismemberment. Wise politics comprehends the cross pressures at work in society.

THE END OF PUBLIC EDUCATION

This book has argued that conflict begins in human nature, for we are unfulfilled creatures, locked in space and time, seeking eternity. If our political structures seek after community but repeatedly find only revolution and violence and combat, those institutions, as Plato observed, are merely man "writ large." There will be no perfect order, Aristotle said, until kings are philosophers and philosophers, kings—yet not even then. We call out for world government; yet we witness the frenzied cries for nationalism among the "Soviet" peoples, among the Kurds, among the Basques, among the Serbians. When we say that there will be no peace of command until there is peace of conscience; when we say that war proceeds from the first and repeated sin; when we say that politics and ethics must be integrated if we are to deal wisely with statecraft and with soulcraft—we invite the cynicism of the age.

"For I know," wrote Paul, "that good does not dwell in me . . . . For I do not do the good I want, but I do the evil I do not want" (Rom. 7:18–19). Writes Ashley Montagu:

It is this sort of thinking, so damaging, so pessimistic, so fettering of the human spirit, that is so dangerous because it diverts the focus of attention from the real causes of "sin," of aggression, and encourages a Jansenist view of the nature of the human condition. The evidence of scientific inquiry does not support this dismal view of human nature, still less does it provide any support for the idea of "innate depravity," whatever form that doctrine may take.[4]

But it is with such moral conjecture with which "scientific inquiry" cannot be at home; the suggestion that "science" finds ethical and theological judgments suspect is itself invalid and ultra vires. Paul's notion of sin must be understood in terms of his conception of human community: we are all sinners (Rom. 3:23) and we all have access, through reason, to the power of God's law (Rom. 2:14–15). There is a goodness, a holiness, an ultimate virtue in which all can share. There is, in short, an image of the Good offered to us all. Because we sin— to sin is to choose the selfish and wrong in full knowledge of another alternative, which is to choose the divine and right—we so often forfeit the fruits of genuine peace. The profound evidence of theology, of politics, of history, of ethics sadly but substantially supports Paul's dismal view of human nature; to look away from it in vain expectation of deliverance from evil by science is to court disaster.

If "command" and "conscience" must be brought into balance, so must "science" and "humanities." *Balance*, we have argued in these pages, is the key to politics, both international and intranational. In education, as well, *balance* is critical. Mindless efforts to drive science out of the classroom result in superstition, not education. But scientific pharisees who wish to drive moral philosophy from the classroom create a soulless and ethically arid instruction.

How is it possible for us to have wise leaders unless they are soundly educated, unless they have an image of the Good? "[M]en and women are biological facts, but . . . ladies and gentlemen fit for self-government are social artifacts, creations of the law."[5] Good and proper education inculcates wisdom and virtue. But how can we inculcate that of which we can no longer conceive? As MacIntyre has written, we must think of formal academic education "not primarily as a preparation for something else, a life of work, which terminates when that life of work begins, but rather as itself the beginning of, and the providing of skills, virtues and resources for, a lifelong education directed toward and informed by the achievement of the good."[6] In dismissing sin, as Montagu does (under the rubric of "science"), must we also dismiss its opposite, which is grace? Of course we must. We are left with a kind of ethical autism, in which we are deprived of any sense of direction about where we should go, bereft of any sense of purpose about what we should do, lacking in any sense of duty to God or to neighbor; there is, in that state, no sense of sin, for neither is there any sense of justice. The first and elemental questions of politics can hardly be asked. There is no community, for no bonding is possible. That terrible *I* (the ego) of Ayn Rand has at last been achieved—all in the name of a science which denatures education and precludes politics. For wise politics incorporates ethics; and wise ethics incorporates politics. And both must know the sense of limitation which derives from understanding the difference between good and evil, the very question science cannot and will not ask.

As Alasdair MacIntyre has observed, "The privatization of the good thus ensures not only that we are deprived of adequately determinate shared moral rules, but that central areas of moral concern cannot become the subject of anything like adequate public shared systematic discourse or inquiry."[7] Pastor Neuhaus, similarly, has suggested that "In a thoroughly secular society notions of what is morally excellent or morally base are not publicly admissible . . . as moral judgment: they have public status only as they reflect the 'interests' of those who hold them."[8] Elsewhere, he has written that "Moral philosophy has become simply the ethics of personal preference. Therefore we do not talk about the truth, because we do not believe that anybody possesses or can possess the truth."[9] Still, we persist in the delusion that we are a nation with powerful centripetal forces; in fact, dangers and difficulties swirl about us, for we inhabit, says MacIntyre, "a political and economic system in which a rhetoric of moral consensus masks fundamental dissensus and moral impoverishment."[10] We see the problem clearly in education, which, instead of creating "ladies and gentlemen," is viewed as a political arena in which each interest group must have its agenda upheld and promulgated with precious little concern for the common good—or for the inculcation of wisdom and virtue. A "multicultural curriculum," one that is regarded as "politically correct," becomes increasingly *de rigueur*. "Afrocentrism," for example, emphasizes the heritage and accomplishments of blacks. No reasonable person can object to (belated) objective treatment of blacks (or whites or yellows or women or men, etc.). But when Afrocentrism insists that most philosophy and civilization originated in Africa, one must call a halt. Arthur Schlesinger, Jr. has contended that "Afrocentrism in the schools is a symptom of a growing fragmentation that is threatening to divide our society."[11]

Living in a society which increasingly seeks to substitute, say, *Star Wars* (the movie) or M*A*S*H (the TV show) for the Bible and Shakespeare we deprive students of "civilizing models of virtue and vice . . . which make possible a unifying common bond of communication."[12] To be sure, even Madison made reference to faction, which he defined as "a number of citizens . . . actuated by some common impulse of passion, or of interest, adverse to the rights of other citizens, or to the permanent and aggregate interests of the community" (in *Federalist* No. 10). If Paul is right, pace Montagu's "science," our inveterate egotism turns us from the common good to the private vice—precisely what MacIntyre and Neuhaus and Schlesinger mention. "All government," wrote political scientist Maurice Duverger more than forty years ago, "is by nature oligarchic"[13] Even before that, in 1915, Robert Michels offered his classic "iron law of oligarchy," much as Duverger discussed.[14] Milovan Djilas argued along roughly similar lines in his striking work, *The New Class*.[15] If our loyalty is only to our private interests (or to our "class"), then the public interest and *public education* have no point (and no advocates). In the Lincoln-Douglas debates in 1858, Lincoln contended, rightly, that "There are limits to the sway of self-interest."[16] But modern education and modern entertainment will not tell us where those limits may be.

REBUILDING THE COMMUNITY

"[O]ur most pressing moral and political project," writes Michael Sandel, "is to revitalize those civic republican possibilities implicit in our tradition but fading in our time." He argues that the totalitarian impulse springs principally from "the confusion of atomized, dislocated, frustrated selves, at sea in a world where common meanings have lost their force."[17] One does not build a society by establishing structures, however important they may be; were that the case, to have global government we would need only to design a world constitution (as some groups, myopically, have urged for years). But, as Glenn Tinder tells us, "spirit is prior to structure and spiritual renewal prior to political action. Good institutional arrangements are not equivalent to a good society, and sometimes, before acting, we must wait."[18] Until we know who we are, where we come from, and why we exist, we cannot effectively rebuild our balkanized national society. We must recreate a moral, as well as physical, community. We cannot blend sword with cross until we understand again the idea of the responsibilities of command and the obligations of conscience. But both demand images of the Good, which we forsake. Neuhaus puts it this way:

From Aristotle through Jefferson, and up to the very recent past, politics was thought of as that process of persuading and being persuaded; a process engaged in by a community brought into being by its shared acknowledgment of the existence of truth beyond its certain grasp.[19]

There can be no sense made of the origins of war; of war and politics; of the just war tradition; of problems of command and conscience; and, certainly, of Christ's meaning or of the moral beauty or squalor of pacifism—until we rebuild sufficient philosophical perspective from which to see these matters. We have no moral vista from which to see wisely and well. We have no image of virtue, for we define virtue as the advancement of private interests; and we have no understanding of civic, or common, good, for the concept escapes us; hence, we can hardly converse rationally about the problems alluded to here.[20] The discussion of virtue and practical sense (i.e., prudence in the classical connection) is the essence of education in political science; yet those notions are of no concern to a people given to self-exaltation, to pride. As Tinder suggests, "Only in modern times has it come to be taken for granted that politics is entirely secular. The inevitable result is the demoralization of politics. Politics loses its moral structure and purpose, and turns into an affair of group interest and personal ambition."[21]

We can—we must—debate the meaning of Christ and God and religion; but there must be (as C.S. Lewis tried to tell us in *The Abolition of Man*) some fundamental agreement on what Walter Lippmann called "the Public Philosophy." "If we turn away from transcendence, from God, what will deliver us," asks Tinder, "from a politically fatal fear and faintheartedness?"[22] God, Providence, natural law, the idea of civic virtue—all these things suggest standards to which we can appeal in order, at least to some considerable extent, to reconcile the clash of competing interests. Without such higher standards, there is no sense of sin and, consequently, no sense of virtue. *Time's* David Aikman had it exactly right in a report about the atrocities in Cambodia in the late 1970s:

In the West today, there is a pervasive consent to the notion of moral relativism, a reluctance to admit that absolute evil can and does exist . . . . [The Cambodian atrocities are] the deadly logical consequence of an atheistic, man-centered system of values, enforced by fallible human beings with total power, who believe, with Marx, that morality is whatever the powerful define it to be and, with Mao, that power grows from gun barrels.[23]

"[I]f I were called upon to identify briefly the principal trait of the *entire* twentieth century, here too I would be unable to find anything more precise and pithy than to repeat once again: 'Men have forgotten God.'"[24] This observation of Solzhenitsyn is in keeping with that of Will Herberg that the peculiar crisis of our time is not in the widespread violation of accepted moral standards, "but in the repudiation of those very moral standards themselves."[25] Dostoevsky once wrote that if God does not exist, then everything is permitted. If by "God" we understand either the supreme personal Being believed in by Jews, Moslems, and Christians or the idea of transcendent moral powers and standards available to right reason, we have the basis of what is desperately needed if we are to restore any idea of genuine civic virtue today.

Herberg concludes his article in this way:

The humanity of man—our wisdom and our suffering ought to have taught us—is ultimately grounded in that which is *above* and *beyond* man, or the pride and power of man . . . . We have lost, we are losing, the tradition—the tradition of the higher law and the higher reality—and are therefore also losing our standards. Is it ever really possible simply to regain what has once been lost? We do not know. That is our problem, our plight, and our task.[26]

Thirteen years after Herberg's article appeared, the sepulchral voice of Alasdair MacIntyre expressed the hope that "new forms of community [might be constructed] within which the moral life could be sustained so that both morality and civility might survive the coming ages of barbarism and darkness . . . . We are waiting not for a Godot, but for another—doubtless very different—St. Benedict."[27]

THE PERSISTENCE OF EVIL

More than sixty years ago Carl Becker offered a brilliant analysis of the Enlightenment, which suggested that

The essential articles of the religion of the Enlightenment may be stated thus: (1) man is not natively depraved; (2) the end of life is life itself, the good life on earth instead of the beatific life after death; (3) man is capable, guided solely by the light of reason and experience, of perfecting the good life on earth; and (4) the first and essential condition of the good life on earth is the freeing of men's minds from the bonds of ignorance and superstition, and of their bodies from the arbitrary oppression of the constituted social authorities.[28]

Thus St. Paul may correctly be dismissed as a crank; there is, as Pelagius told us, no original sin; progress, as Joachim told us, is illimitable; there is no God; there are no standards, save our own skins. If no evil exists (except for that something which a given interest finds in opposition to its own desires), then there is no virtue; if no virtue exists, then no idea of civic virtue or natural law makes sense. All is *sauve qui peut*; and politics is merely the long shadow of solipsism.

But we know that evil exists (*even though* Paul said so!). As Henry Fairlie wrote, "We will recognize that the inclination to evil is in our natures, that its existence in us presents us with moral choices, and that it is in making those choices that we form our characters."[29] In thinking about the evil of slavery, Jefferson once wrote that "I tremble for my country when I reflect that God is just." That language seems archaic, the sentiment of a Pro-Life rally. In 1986, a man named Sherrill gunned down fifteen people (including himself) at a post office in Oklahoma. Social theorists labored long and hard to explain the savagery. John Podhoretz did so in a paragraph:

There is evil in the world, and when we come face-to-face with it, we cannot run and hide behind theories designed to make the inexplicable comprehensible. Sherrill represented the darkest side of human nature, the nihilistic side that will not go away despite the drugs we invent and the theories we propose. The world is not a nice place where evil is the exception. More often than not, evil is the rule. And the more we deny this, the more our sense of good and evil will atrophy.[30]

Our liberal, value-neutral state, however, in seeing no evil privatizes the good. It sees value in little, or in nothing at all. Alistair Cooke lectured once about a placard he saw at Princeton University, which carried the slogan: "There is nothing worth dying for." Cooke's response: "That seems to me to be the witless end of Know-Nothingism. If enough Americans felt that way, this nation would long ago have succumbed to dictatorship." Cooke tells the story of Governor Calvin Coolidge of Massachusetts who, in 1919, ended a police strike by declaring, "There is no right to strike against the public safety by anybody, anywhere, any time." Today, says Cooke, he would be censured for his assertion. "In Coolidge's time, society had the positive restraints of institutional religion, and the negative restraints of the general unthinkability of many forms of outrageous behavior."[31] As an example of a standard clearly transcending personal interests, one might cite elementary decency. Does a protestor today, for example, have the right to shout any epithets, however outrageous, to make his point? (Cooke's contention is that in Coolidge's time the protestor would have known better.) Archibald Cox asks, "Does the guaranty of freedom of speech leave any scope for legislation designed to protect the moral, aesthetic, or patriotic sensibilities of the community, or to preserve the tone of public discourse?"[32]

No evil; no virtue; nothing worth dying for; nothing worth living for—these are the products of an Enlightenment which apotheosized Man, which told us that earth would be heaven, that all that mattered was the preservation of our own lives (for there was nothing beyond), that politics must therefore be supreme, that there was no transcendence, that self-indulgence was the only virtue. If all this be true, the idea of the sword and of command (the preservation of the national interest and of the common good) is absurd. If all this be true, the idea of the cross and of conscience (acting in accordance with divine and natural law and working to square that tradition with the positive law, thus effecting civic virtue) is pointless. If all this be true, war is always the exaltation of might rather than the vindication of right; war and politics serve always and only the interests of the dominant; the just war tradition is jejune; problems of command and conscience are parlor games; the gospels are feckless and flighty; pacifism prevails, for life itself is all that matters; and questions of the "sword and cross" are nugatory or medieval and irrelevant to modern man. But it is not true. There is evil. There is virtue. Some things are worth dying for; and many things are worth living for, just one of which is our duty to tell our benighted fellow humans that there is a point and a purpose to it all. And then to live that way.

A COMMON DEFENSE?

As one writer put it, "those who serve the nation in a military capacity no longer can assume any dominant moral consensus in the United States."[33] The absence of overarching ethical values, imparting national meaning and purpose to policy, results in a cacophony of competing interests. It remains the premier task of prudent national leadership to identify those courses of political, diplomatic, and military action most in keeping with the country's values and needs and most consonant with ethical standards (pace those relativists who hold that no such norms obtain). The imperatives of the cross and the obligations of the sword meet in the minds and souls of those who lead. If there are no transcendent standards (or if, in our hubris, we have obliterated them), then one finds it difficult to argue that there can be any *integrity* (if all is merely hedonist calculus). If there is no personal integrity, then leaders acquire power merely for the purpose of self-aggrandizement; political activity is merely indulgence of the ego on the grand scale. And so, much too frequently, it has been. But not always. There are those leaders touched by grace, the truly charismatic leaders, who lead by inspiration and in whose authority command and conscience are linked.

In seeking and advocating true national interest, however, and in providing for the common defense, such leaders pay a fearful price. "He who acts is always unjust; nobody is just but the one who reflects," remarked Goethe. Hans Morgenthau agreed, writing: "The very act of acting destroys our moral integrity. Whoever wants to retain his moral innocence must forsake action altogether and, following Hamlet's advice to Ophelia, 'go . . . to a nunnery.' "[34] In the very act of composing a kind of symphony of national purpose from the dissonance of contentious parochial interests, the statesman offends and outrages some of his constituencies. The corrupt and venal politician will cater to the lowest (or loudest) horde, accepting evil; the sacrosanct or reclusive politician will hear or see or speak no evil, lest he soil himself. But the leader whose policies are sealed with the glue of civic virtue spends himself in the effort to ensure planned coincidence, insofar as practicable, between what ought to be done and what can be done. He knows that, in choosing and in acting, he will alienate some people and sacrifice some rights; but he must not give in to the meretricious charms of insouciance, believing that his purity constitutes wise statecraft. The wise leader does not choose the evil course willingly or selfishly; but the wise leader may have to choose a less evil course with genuine reluctance and with judicious concern for the national interest and for ethical imperatives. (War, as discussed earlier, is always wrong; but it is not always the greatest wrong.)

John Silber has a succinct explanation of this when he writes that "moralistic postures and purist expectations are particularly dangerous and inappropriate in foreign policy." He continues:

We must not fall into the moral trap of opposing the better in anticipation of an unattainable best. . . .

We would all be happier if we lived in a world where there were always clear alternatives between good and evil, right and wrong, innocence and guilt. The determination of foreign policy in the real world cannot be made on such distinctions. Unfortunately, we live in a world that far too often imposes on us choices that are inherently tragic.[35]

Max Weber, in his well-known discussion of an "ethic of ultimate ends" and "an ethic of responsibility," means that the saint (observing the first "ethic") cannot be confused with the national leader (observing the second). Weber would not have mixed the two ethics. In fact, to achieve civic virtue and genuine Christian realism, the two ethics must be judiciously blended, lest, on the one hand, power be absolutized or, on the other, purity be exalted (regardless of results). German Catholic theologian Karl Rahner said: "it is impossible to make our existence a paroxysm of nonviolence. [The Christian] should always first opt for the path of love; yet as long as the world exists, a rational, hard, even violent striving for justice may well be the secular personification of love."[36] Is it too late to learn from E. H. Carr that "it is as fatal in politics to ignore power as it is to ignore morality"?[37]

In political ethics, then, we must guard against the twin evils of perfectionism and of despair, even as, in politics, we guard against concentrations of power—even our own power (which we tend to see always as righteous power). "Moralism in foreign policy," Arthur Schlesinger, Jr., has written, "ends up in fanaticism, and the fanatic, as Mr. Dooley put it, 'does what he thinks th' Lord wud do if He only knew th' facts in th' case.'"[38] Edmund Burke (1729–1797) had it right in saying that "among precautions against ambition, it may not be amiss to take one precaution against our *own*. I must fairly say, I dread our *own* power and our *own* ambition; I dread our being too much dreaded."[39] But unless the statesman has the power of dimension afforded by his perception of the Good, he has no means of judging the prudence of his policies. The statesman's task, as Christian realism has long counseled, is to augment his nation's power— *but* in the service of ideals not fit, as if by Procrustes, into that one nation's bed. "Even the best-intentioned men," wrote Otto Friedrich, "once they enter the jungle of power politics, have to confront the necessity of directing actions that they would, in normal circumstances, be inclined to call immoral." Even Lincoln revoked the writ of habeas corpus, he points out. He offers these examples in addition:

Foreign affairs seem particularly apt to bring out a presidential capacity for hypocrisy. Kindly William McKinley, who used U.S. troops to suppress the fledgling Philippine republic in 1898, said he had prayerfully searched his soul before deciding it was his duty to "civilize and Christianize" the Filipinos. Theodore Roosevelt, who encouraged an insurrection in the Colombian province of Panama so that he could build a canal through it, liked to consult with Attorney General Philander Knox about the legality of his various aggressions, but Knox was not the sternest of critics. "Ah, Mr. President," he asked on one occasion, "Why have such a beautiful action marred by any taint of legality?" When Roosevelt yearned to seize the Hawaiian Islands, Admiral Alfred Mahan was equally encouraging: "Do nothing unrighteous, but take the islands first and solve afterward."[40]

The *common defense* is exactly that: the protection and preservation of vital national interests. In a brilliant essay more than thirty years ago, Arnold Wolfers pointed out that "In every case the interpretation of what constitutes a vital national interest and how much value should be attached to it is a moral question. It cannot be answered by reference to alleged amoral necessities inherent in international politics; it rests on value judgments." Wolfers added that "Even national survival itself . . . is a morally compelling necessity only as long as people attach supreme value to it."[41] So often academic international relations is taught in an ethical vacuum; so often academic international relations is thus in default of its obligation to pursue issues, metonymically, of cross as well as of sword.

When Professor Wolfers argues that in international politics, statesmen hold so much power that there is room for many abuses for which the "necessity of state" doctrine can serve "as a convenient cloak," he speaks to the core issue of this chapter. Statesmen, he writes, may believe that their country's "vital" interests direct a certain policy, but "judged by nonnationalistic standards of ethics they may be placing undue value on certain interests of their people or underestimating the value of things not pertaining to their nation which their policy would sacrifice."[42]

Certainly Michael Howard is correct in calling to task Joseph Cropsey, who, in the early 1960s, wrote that "The teaching of morality may be reduced to this: we must do everything that needs to be done to insure the survival of ourselves, our friends, and our free principles . . . ."[43] But what does *everything* mean? Can it mean *anything*? To be sure, we can judge others according to our desires; but how do we take the measure of our own interests unless it be in the context, not merely of what we *can* do, but also of what we *should* do? But that requires a normative ethics, a sense of honor and of shame; a sense of virtue and of vice—a perception of the cross and of the sword. Ignoring the exigencies of the sword, the languid statesman will quiver and cower, uncertain which direction to take in a world dominated by power; ignoring the counsels of the cross, the truculent statesman will bully and bluster, dubious about which direction to take in a world desperate for justice.

UNION OF POWER AND PRINCIPLE

Noting the need for practical concern as well as for ethical awareness in the statesman, Michael Howard has observed that "The political actor, be he statesman or soldier, needs to grow in moral awareness and responsibility as he grows in power."[44] Political action, he holds, needs to be *diagonal*, a blend of ethics and power. As Alberto Coll has commented, "Renunciation or reduction of power for the sake of maintaining inner moral purity overlooks the reality of sin and corruption in the midst of weakness, while it leaves one dangerously exposed to the ravages of adversaries." Thus "[w]hile power may tend to corrupt, weakness by itself does not necessarily purify."[45] Prudence is thought of as a political quality; in fact, it is as well a Christian property. In the Old Testament books of Proverbs and Ecclesiastes, in Jesus' distinction between his Father's Kingdom and this world (in which the full Kingdom was not to be found), and in Paul's epistles, prudence assumes its rightful place at the heart of Christian realism and, consequently, at the center of civic virtue. Augustine, of course, recognized the significance of prudence, as did medieval theologians, Luther and Calvin, and the Catholic Church in the just war tradition.[46]

Aristotle wrote that "without virtue or excellence this eye of the soul [intelligence] does not acquire the characteristic [of practical wisdom]." Alberto Coll is correct in observing that "Unless virtue is its end, prudence is little more than knavery, shallow cleverness." According to Aristotle, "a man fulfills his proper function only by way of practical wisdom and moral excellence or virtue: virtue makes us aim at the right target, and practical wisdom makes us use the right means."[47]

We have reached a political and ethical impasse. The great and fundamental task of command is to embrace wise conscience that we might understand the awful contest between man's insatiable lust for power and his critical need for justice. These conflicting drives constitute the human anxiety afflicting all God's creation after (and because of) the Fall. "Yet, where the occasion calls for the comprehension of one of the great tragic antinomies of human existence," writes Morgenthau plaintively, "the age has nothing better to offer than a narrow and distorted formulation of the problem and a sentimental and irrelevant solution in the spirit of political reform."[48] At a time when education is called upon to review and renew inquiry into the moral law, into civic virtue, its otiose offerings amount to little more than bows in the direction of a pantheon of "multi-cultural" masters.

However urgent may be the rejuvenation of the idea of natural law—with its promise of helping us understand those points upon which rational and decent men have agreed through the centuries as the *fons et origo* of politics and as a standard to which we might appeal our cases of sword or cross—there is little prospect of such revivification.[49] Unless we reestablish the link between the sacred and the secular order, we will drift (or perhaps proceed "full speed ahead") into the shoals of desultory politics, desecrated ethics, rampant narcissism. MacIntyre, as mentioned, believes we stand today on those shoals of shame. It is all right, however, with many, perhaps most of us, for we no longer recognize the ancient notion of *shame*. Who would be so bold, as the twenty-first century draws nigh, to brand anything "shameful"?

It is a principle, writes Paul Johnson, that "when legitimacy yields to force, and moral absolutes to relativism, a great darkness descends and angels become indistinguishable from devils."[50] But is that not precisely the case today? "Were the mythical Man from Mars to watch television news and read the prestige press for many months," says Richard J. Neuhaus, "he would likely be quite oblivious to the role of religion in this society."[51] In the schools, however, the children still pledge allegiance to the flag "and to the Republic for which it stands, one nation, under God, indivisible, with liberty and justice for all." But that is, of course, the whole point: That we are a nation under God; that our policies are subject to inspection by powers both mortal and divine; that our national needs and our eternal responsibilities are and must be ineffably linked; that our politics and our ethics are mutually informed. It is no small task for the statesman to bring into harmony the elements of political success and the standards of ultimate right and wrong. Such an effort requires that the statesman have what Athens classically called "character" and what Jerusalem knew as "grace." Without those two desiderata of statecraft and of public life, there will be no merger of cross and sword; there will be no symbiosis of command and conscience; there will be no light. We will confuse the angels with the devils.

CONCLUSION

Paul's argument is that we sin because we are selfish and ignore the Law of God. Political selfishness defeats community and encourages, not genuine politics, but ideology (which, at its root, is a substitution for transcendent reality). In the absence of community—when virtue is privatized—one cannot reasonably discuss war and politics, for they are about common interests and the common defense. Nor can one fathom any cause of war except class struggle, for war can hardly be about anything except selfish advancement. There is no just war, for there is no justice, and we return, limping, to the debate between John Rawls and Robert Nozick. Conscience is a product of environment and is informed by no treasury of established, reasonable principles or deposit of faith. Pacifism becomes an argument without purpose, for life itself becomes an experience without purpose, save what we ourselves "authentically" create in the despair of self-apotheosis. God becomes the fairly affable object of occasional attention at tea following agreeable-enough services with not too much theology, for such is altogether too redolent of the unpleasantries of yesteryear with all that nastiness about original sin and suffering, and about examination of conscience and repentance. It was all so thoroughly medieval. And the state becomes the object of worshipful contemplation by masses who confuse duty to the state with veneration of the cross. Or, alternatively, the state becomes an object of contempt, lampooned by the privileged and opulent, defended by the destitute, respected in measured patriotic esteem by a small fraction of the populace.

"Man," said Blaise Pascal (1623–1662), "is neither angel nor beast and his misery is that he who would act the angel acts the brute." "[I]t is only the awareness of the tragic presence of evil in all political action which at least enables man to choose the lesser evil and to be as good as he can be in an evil world," wrote Hans Morgenthau. He continues:

Neither science nor ethics nor politics can resolve the conflict between politics and ethics into harmony. We have no choice between power and the common good. To act successfully, that is, according to the rules of the political art, is political wisdom. To know with despair that the political act is inevitably evil, and to act nevertheless, is moral courage. To choose among several expedient actions the least evil one is moral judgment.

Morgenthau concludes:

In the combination of political wisdom, moral courage, and moral judgment, man reconciles his political nature with his moral destiny. That this conciliation is nothing more than a *modus vivendi*, uneasy, precarious, and even paradoxical, can disappoint only those who prefer to gloss over and to distort the tragic contradictions of human existence with the soothing logic of a specious concord.[52]

To combine the sword and the cross, command and conscience, into a politically practicable and ethically desirable tool of statecraft has always been the chief goal of dutiful statesmen. In their quest to establish the result of that merger, which is civic virtue, they had two beacon lights, the intersection of which revealed enough wisdom for them to carry on the Sisyphean tasks of statecraft. One was the beacon light of the national interest, based on the rock of national values and traditions. Imperfect as it was, it nonetheless offered far more than the rampant solipsism of today. The other was the beacon light of the divine and natural law, which offered them insights into, and was based upon, that treasury of principles agreed upon over the centuries by decent and discerning men and women of character and grace. Imperfect as it was, it nonetheless offered far more than today's contempt for standards, traditions, and integrity. To aid them in seeking to bring into balance their "political nature" and their "moral destiny," the statesmen could seek out an erudite literature and a contemplative professoriate, many—if not most—of whom had earned doctorate of *philosophy* degrees without smirking at the antediluvian reference to a common scholarly knowledge and a common scholarly passion.

But these things are past. And Morgenthau's impassioned peroration is rarely quoted, little understood, and hardly appreciated today. Its sentiment, it seems, has passed with him. To read Lincoln's inaugural addresses today is a melancholy task; despite their brilliance, they seem, at least to so many ostensibly bright undergraduates, archaic and torpid, somehow curiously nostalgic. Students too often listen to the majestic Gettysburg Address with a puzzled air as they hear references to consecrated and hallowed ground, to work nobly advanced, to honored dead, to a nation under God—a perplexity relieved by the brevity of the President's remarks. There are, of course, those who greet such statements, and such people as Lincoln, with the sense of marvel and of wonder and of reverent gratitude that there yet is hope that the best of the traditions in which we share will be rejuvenated; that the beacon lights of the national interest and of the natural law will be restored; that the inestimable and intractable problems of war, and of politics, and of justice, and of peace will be evaluated by scholars who know that the dilemmas of command and conscience are more than merely the empirical subjects of logical positivism.

One hopes, moreover, that Job's deepest conviction will again be discovered: "I know that my Redeemer liveth" (19:25). And one hopes that the Lincolnesque wisdom of the late Waldemar Gurian of the University of Notre Dame might find its path into the sometimes hardened hearts of us all: "Man is neither beast nor angel; rather he is a being faced by the task of making life as human as possible in the changing world of time and history, and, even though he belongs to some particular group, he must never forget that he participates always in the unity of mankind." In those apothegms is the unity of command and conscience, the convergence of the sword and the cross.

NOTES

1. Quoted in Greg Russell, *Hans J. Morgenthau and the Ethics of American Statecraft* (Baton Rouge, LA: Louisiana State University Press, 1990), p. 181.

2. Henry A. Kissinger, *White House Years* (Boston, MA: Little, Brown, 1979), p. 67.

3. Glenn Tinder, "Transcending Tragedy: The Idea of Civility," *American Political Science Review* 68 (June 1974): 549, 550.

4. Ashley Montagu, "Introduction," *Man and Aggression*, 2d ed., ed. Ashley Montagu (New York: Oxford University Press, 1973), xix.

5. George Will, *Statecraft as Soulcraft* (New York: Simon & Schuster, 1983), pp. 90–91.

6. Alasdair MacIntyre, "The Privatization of the Good: An Inaugural Lecture," *Review of Politics* 52 (Summer 1990): 359.

7. MacIntyre (above, n. 6), p. 353.

8. Richard John Neuhaus, *The Naked Public Square* (Grand Rapids, MI: Eerdmans, 1984), p. 111. He explains there how child pornography in New York is banned, not on moral grounds, but because it is regarded as injurious to the health of the young. "A secular polity," he observes, "requires that we profess more confidence in the 'scientific' notions of psychiatry than in our moral judgment."

9. Richard John Neuhaus, "A Crisis of Faith," *Ethics and Nuclear Arms*, ed. Raymond English (Washington, DC: Ethics and Public Policy Center, 1985), p. 62.

10. MacIntyre, (above, n. 6) p. 354.

11. See Karen J. Winkler, "Organization of American Historians Backs Teaching of Non-Western Culture and Diversity in Schools," *The Chronicle of Higher Education*, 6 February 1991: A5. Schlesinger is quoted on that page.

12. Will, (above, n. 5), p. 142. See also Allan Bloom, *The Closing of the American Mind* (New York: Simon and Schuster, 1987); and Eric D. Hirsch, *Cultural Literacy: What Every American Needs to Know* (Boston, MA: Houghton Mifflin, 1987).

13. Maurice Duverger, *Political Parties* (New York: Wiley, 1964; first published in 1951), p. 425.

14. Robert Michels, *Political Parties*, trans. Eden and Cedar Paul (Glencoe, IL: The Free Press, 1949; first published in 1915), pp. 377–92.

15. Milovan Djilas, *The New Class* (New York: Praeger, 1957). Or George Orwell, *Animal Farm*.

16. Quoted in George Will, "The Meaning of Freedom," *Parameters* 13 (June 1983): 9.

17. Michael J. Sandel, "Morality and the Liberal Ideal," *The New Republic*, 7 May 1984: 17.

18. Glenn Tinder, "Christianity and the Welfare State," *Review of Politics* 49 (Fall 1987): 568.

19. Neuhaus (above, n. 8), p. 112.

20. Neuhaus quotes from Psalm 81:11–12 ("And yet my people did not hear my voice, and Israel would not obey me. So I gave them over to the stubbornness of their hearts, to follow their own devices.") "[H]ell," he writes, "is man abandoned, man on his own." (Above, n. 8), p. 152.

21. See Glenn Tinder, "Can We Be Good Without God?" *The Atlantic*, December 1989: 69, 77.

22. Ibid., p. 85.

23. David Aikman, "Cambodia: An Experiment in Genocide," *Time*, 31 July 1978: 40. See also Paul Johnson, "The Heartless Lovers of Humankind," *The Wall Street Journal*, 5 January 1987: 16: "Beware the intellectuals . . . . For . . . [they] are in fact ultra-conformist within the circles formed by those whose approval they seek and value. This is what makes them . . . so dangerous . . . ."

24. Aleksandr Solzhenitsyn, "Men Have Forgotten God," *National Review*, 22 July 1983: 873. "When God is hated, every basis of morality is undermined," said Pope Pius XII in 1939. (Quoted in Guenter Lewy, *The Catholic Church and Nazi Germany* [New York: McGraw-Hill, 1964]—a very disturbing book for Catholics; consequently, it is one that Catholics ought to read.)

25. Will Herberg, "What Is the Moral Crisis of Our Time?" *The Intercollegiate Review* 22 (Fall 1986): 7. (Originally published in 1968.)

26. Ibid., p. 12.

27. Alasdair MacIntyre, *After Virtue*, 2d ed. (Notre Dame, IN: University of Notre Dame Press, 1984), p. 263.

28. Carl L. Becker, *The Heavenly City of the Eighteenth-Century Philosophers* (New Haven, CT: Yale University Press, 1932), pp. 102–3.

29. Henry Fairlie, *The Seven Deadly Sins Today* (Washington, DC: New Republic Books, 1978), p. 19. In many of his books, Russell Kirk has argued that

leaders must face the fact of evil if they are to lead in the direction of good. See also Genesis 6:5–6, 11–13.

30. John Podhoretz, "Psychobabble Masks an Evil Deed," *Insight*, 15 September 1986: 72. See also Chapter 4 of the present book (section entitled "The Conservative Connection"). See also the *Time* essay by Howard G. Chua-Eoan, "The Uses of Monsters," 19 August 1991: 66 and "Did They All Have to Die?" *Time*, 12 August 1991: 28. The case of Jeffrey Dahmer of Milwaukee, who has confessed to murdering and mutilating numerous people over the past dozen years, is so horrifying as to demand the adjective *evil* and to remind us of evil's terrible reality.

31. Alistair Cooke, "Freedom and the Soldier," *Parameters* 10 (September 1980): 6, 5.

32. Archibald Cox, *The Role of the Supreme Court in American Government* (New York: Oxford University Press, 1976), pp. 45–46. See also Donald P. Kommers, "Comment on MacIntyre," *Review of Politics* 52 (Summer 1990): 362–68.

33. Donald A. Zoll, "The Moral Dimension of War and the Military Ethic," *Parameters* 12 (June 1982): 14.

34. Hans J. Morgenthau, *Scientific Man vs. Power Politics* (Chicago, IL: University of Chicago Press, 1946), p. 189.

35. John Silber, *Straight Shooting* (New York: Harper & Row, 1989), p. 195.

36. Quoted in "The Morality of War," *Time*, 20 January 1967: 41.

37. E. H. Carr, *The Twenty Years' Crisis* (New York: Harper Torchbooks, 1964), p. 97. See also James H. Toner, "Peacekeeping by Wishful Thinking," *Parameters* 17 (September 1987): 68–76.

38. Arthur Schlesinger, Jr., "The Necessary Amorality of Foreign Affairs," *Harper's*, August 1971: 74.

39. Quoted in Alberto R. Coll, "Some Christian Reminders for the Statesman," *Ethics and International Affairs* 1 (1987): 111.

40. Otto Friedrich, "The Devilish Doctrine of Deniability," *Time*, 15 December 1986: 98.

41. Arnold Wolfers, *Discord and Collaboration* (Baltimore, MD: Johns Hopkins Press, 1962), p. 60.

42. Ibid., p. 61. In the text, Montesquieu (1689–1755) was quoted; his observation, from *The Spirit of the Laws*, bears repetition here: "The law of nations is naturally founded on this principle, that different nations ought in time of peace to do one another all the good they can, and in time of war as little injury as possible, without prejudicing their real interests [Bk I, 3]."

43. The rest of the quotation: "indulging neither ourselves nor others, avoiding sentimentality no less than brutality, and mindful that if we weakly hang back, we will ignominiously hang alone." Joseph Cropsey, "The Moral Basis of International Action," *America Armed*, ed. Robert A. Goldwin (Chicago, IL: Rand McNally, 1963), p. 83. Howard partially misquotes Cropsey in *Studies in War and Peace* (New York: The Viking Press, 1971), p. 246. One wonders if Cropsey would have delivered himself of the same opinion in 1973.

44. Quoted in Coll (above, n. 39), p. 101.

45. Ibid., p. 102.

46. Discussion based upon ibid., p. 103.

47. Ibid., p. 107.

48. Morgenthau (above, n. 34), p. 201.

49. A very useful view of natural law appears in chapter 4 of Larry Arnhart, *Political Questions: Political Questions from Plato to Rawls* (New York: Macmillan, 1987). Reo Christenson offers this trenchant point: "[H]uman experience [is unlikely] to produce higher social orders which discover that slavery, trial by ordeal, and the burning of witches were disapproved in the twentieth century only because of the cultural environment and stunted societal perceptions of that period. *If much is uncertain, at least some pillars are firm." Heresies Right and Left: Some Political Assumptions Reexamined* (New York: Harper & Row, 1983). Emphasis supplied. A brilliant novel examining a number of these themes is Walter Miller, Jr., *A Canticle for Leibowitz* (different publishers and dates). In *Statecraft as Soulcraft* (above, n. 5), George Will says: "But Lincoln believed that there can be closed questions in an open society. Indeed, a society that has no closed questions cannot count on remaining an open society. Citizenship is a state of mind. A completely and permanently open mind will be an empty mind—if a mind at all" (p. 50).

50. Paul Johnson, *Modern Times* (New York: Harper & Row, 1983), p. 201.

51. Neuhaus (above, n. 8), p. 98.

52. Morgenthau (above, n. 34), pp. 202–3.

SELECTED BIBLIOGRAPHY

The notes to this book contain listings of references and recommended readings. Cited below are the chief sources of this book, whether directly cited in the text or particularly helpful as informative background reading.

BOOKS

Adler, Mortimer. *Six Great Ideas*. New York: Macmillan, 1981.

Angell, Norman. *The Great Illusion*. New York: G. P. Putnam's Sons, 1933.

Arnhart, Larry. *Political Questions: Political Philosophy from Plato to Rawls*. New York: Macmillan, 1987.

Aron, Raymond. *Clausewitz: Philosopher of War*. Translated by Christine Booker and Norman Stone. Englewood Cliffs, NJ: Prentice-Hall, 1985.

Au, William A. *The Cross, the Flag, and the Bomb*. Westport, CT: Greenwood Press, 1985.

Axinn, Sidney. *A Moral Military*. Philadelphia, PA: Temple University Press, 1989.

Bailey, Sydney D. *War and Conscience in the Nuclear Age*. New York: St. Martin's Press, 1987.

Bennett, John C. and Harvey Seifert. *U.S. Foreign Policy and Christian Ethics*. Philadelphia, PA: The Westminster Press, 1977.

Berdyaev, Nicolas. *The Meaning of History*. Trans. George Reavey. London: The Centenary Press, 1945.

Blainey, Geoffrey. *The Causes of War.* New York: The Free Press, 1973.

Bloom, Allan. *The Closing of the American Mind.* New York: Simon and Schuster, 1987.

Bork, Robert H. *The Tempting of America.* New York: Free Press, 1990.

Borowski, Harry R., ed. *The Harmon Memorial Lectures in Military History.* Washington, DC: United States Air Force, Office of Air Force History, 1988.

Brodie, Bernard. *War and Politics.* New York: Macmillan, 1973.

Brown, James and Michael J. Collins, eds. *Military Ethics and Professionalism.* Washington, DC: National Defense University Press, 1981.

Bunting, Josiah. *The Lionheads.* New York: G. Braziller, 1972.

Burtchaell, James T. *A Just War No Longer Exists: The Teaching and Trial of Don Lorenzo Milan.* Ed. and Trans. J. T. Burtchaell. Notre Dame, IN: University of Notre Dame Press, 1988.

Butler, Nicholas Murray. *True and False Democracy.* New York: Macmillan, 1907.

Butterfield, Herbert. *Christianity, Diplomacy and War.* New York: Abingdon-Cokesbury Press, 1953.

Cady, Duane. *From Warism to Pacifism.* Philadelphia, PA: Temple University Press, 1989.

Carr, Edward Hallett. *The Twenty Years' Crisis.* London: Macmillan, 1951.

Cassese, Antonio. *Violence and Law in the Modern Age.* Trans. S.J.K. Greenleaves. Princeton, NJ: Princeton University Press, 1988.

Castelli, Jim. *The Bishops and the Bomb.* Garden City, NY: Image Books, 1983.

Child, James W. *Nuclear War: The Moral Dimension.* New Brunswick, NJ: Transaction Books, 1986.

Childress, James F. *Moral Responsibility in Conflicts.* Baton Rouge, LA: Louisiana State University Press, 1982.

Christenson, Reo. *Heresies Right and Left: Some Political Assumptions Reexamined.* New York: Harper & Row, 1973.

Clark, Ian. *Waging War: A Philosophical Introduction.* Oxford, England: Clarendon Press, 1988.

Claude, Inis L., Jr. *Power and International Relations.* New York: Random House, 1962.

Clausewitz, Carl von. *On War.* Ed. and trans. Michael Howard and Peter Paret. Princeton, NJ: Princeton University Press, 1976.

Cohen, Carl. *Civil Disobedience: Conscience, Tactics, and the Law.* New York: Columbia University Press, 1971.

Cohen, Sheldon M. *Arms and Judgment.* Boulder, CO: Westview Press, 1989.

Conquest, Robert. *Harvest of Sorrow.* New York: Oxford University Press, 1986.

Curry, Dean C. *Evangelicals and the Bishops' Pastoral Letter.* Grand Rapids, MI: Eerdmans, 1984.

Davidson, Donald L. *Nuclear Weapons and the American Churches.* Boulder, CO: Westview Press, 1983.

Djilas, Milovan. *The New Class.* New York: Praeger, 1957.

Donovan, David. [Terry Turner] *Once a Warrior King: Memories of an Officer in Vietnam.* New York: McGraw-Hill, 1985.

Dougherty, James E. *The Bishops and Nuclear Weapons.* Hamden, CT: Archon Books, 1984.

_____ and Robert L. Pfaltzgraff, Jr. *Contending Theories of International Relations*. 3d ed. New York: Harper & Row, 1990.

Downs, Frederick. *The Killing Zone*. New York: Norton, 1978.

Duchacek, Ivo D. *Nations and Men*. 3d ed. Hinsdale, IL: Dryden, 1975.

Duverger, Maurice. *Political Parties*. 2d ed., revised. New York: Wiley, 1964.

Eckert, Edward K., ed. *In War and Peace*. Belmont, CA: Wadsworth, 1990.

Finnis, John, Joseph Boyle, and Germain Grisez. *Nuclear Deterrence, Morality and Realism*. Oxford, England: Oxford University Press, 1987.

Fisher, David. *Morality and the Bomb*. New York: St. Martin's, 1985.

Fotion, Nicholas and G. Elfstrom. *Military Ethics*. Boston, MA: Routledge & K. Paul, 1986.

Fox, Richard W. *Reinhold Niebuhr: A Biography*. New York: Pantheon, 1985.

Frankl, Viktor E. *Man's Search for Meaning*. Boston, MA: Beacon, 1962.

Friedman, Thomas L. *From Beirut to Jerusalem*. New York: Farrar Straus Giroux, 1989.

Fromm, Erich. *Escape From Freedom*. New York: Holt, Rinehart and Winston, 1941.

Glahn, Gerhard von. *Law Among Nations*. 4th ed. New York: Macmillan, 1981.

Gray, Colin S. *The Geopolitics of Super Power*. Lexington, KY: The University Press of Kentucky, 1988.

Gray, J. Glenn. *The Warriors: Reflections on Men in Battle*. New York: Harper & Row, 1959.

Hackett, John. *The Profession of Arms*. New York: Macmillan, 1983.

Hadley, Arthur T. *The Straw Giant*. New York: Random House, 1986.

Hallowell, John H. *The Moral Foundation of Democracy*. Chicago, IL: University of Chicago Press, 1954.

Hartle, Anthony E. *Moral Issues in Military Decision Making*. Lawrence, KS: University Press of Kansas, 1989.

Hinsley, Francis Harry. *Power and the Pursuit of Peace*. Cambridge, England: Cambridge University Press, 1963.

Holmes, Robert L. *On War and Morality*. Princeton, NJ: Princeton University Press, 1989.

Hook, Sidney. *Marxism and Beyond*. Totowa, NJ: Rowman and Littlefield, 1983.

Howard, Michael. *The Causes of War and Other Essays*. Cambridge, MA: Harvard University Press, 1983.

_____. *Studies in War and Peace*. New York: Viking, 1970.

_____. *War and the Liberal Conscience*. Oxford, England: Oxford University Press, 1981.

Huntington, Samuel P. *The Soldier and the State*. Cambridge, MA: Belknap Press, 1957.

Johnson, James Turner. *Can Modern War be Just?* New Haven, CT: Yale University Press, 1984.

_____. *Ideology, Reason, and the Limitation of War*. Princeton, NJ: Princeton University Press, 1975.

_____. *Just War Tradition and the Restraint of War*. Princeton, NJ: Princeton University Press, 1981.

Johnson, Paul. *Modern Times*. New York: Harper & Row, 1983.

Jones, John D. and Marc F. Griesbach, eds. *Just War Theory in the Nuclear Age*. Lanham, MD: University Press of America, 1985.

Kavka, Gregory S. *Moral Paradoxes of Nuclear Deterrence.* Cambridge, England: Cambridge University Press, 1987.

Kegley, Charles W., Jr. and Kenneth L. Schwab, eds. *After the Cold War: Questioning the Morality of Nuclear Deterrence.* Boulder, CO: Westview Press, 1991.

Kertesz, Stephen D. and M. A. Fitzsimons, eds. *Diplomacy in a Changing World.* Notre Dame, IN: University of Notre Dame Press, 1959.

Kirk, Russell. *Decadence and Renewal in the Higher Learning.* South Bend, IN: Gateway, 1978.

Kissinger, Henry A. *White House Years.* Boston, MA: Little, Brown, 1979.

_____. *Years of Upheaval.* Boston, MA: Little, Brown, 1982.

Kornhauser, William. *The Politics of Mass Society.* Glencoe, IL: The Free Press, 1959.

Lackey, Douglas P. *The Ethics of War and Peace.* Englewood Cliffs, NJ: Prentice-Hall, 1989.

_____. *Moral Principles and Nuclear Weapons.* Totowa, NJ: Rowman and Allanheld, 1984.

LaCroix, Wilfred L. *War and International Ethics.* Lanham, MD: University Press of America, 1988.

Lawler, Philip F. *The Ultimate Weapon.* Chicago, IL: Regnery Gateway, 1984.

Lewis, C. S. *Mere Christianity.* Revised and enlarged ed. (New York: Macmillan, 1958).

_____. *Present Concerns*, Walter Hooper, ed. New York: Harcourt Brace Jovanovich, 1986.

_____. *The Problem of Pain.* New York: Macmillan, 1948.

Lewy, Guenter. *America in Vietnam.* New York: Oxford University Press, 1978.

_____. *The Catholic Church and Nazi Germany.* New York: McGraw-Hill, 1964.

_____. *Peace & Revolution: The Moral Crisis of American Pacifism.* Grand Rapids, MI: Eerdmans, 1988.

Lider, Julian. *On the Nature of War.* England: Saxon House, 1977. Distributed in the U.S. by Renouf (Brookfield, VT).

Lifton, Robert J. *Indefensible Weapons.* New York: Basic Books, 1982.

Lippmann, Walter. *Essays in The Public Philosophy.* Boston, MA: Little, Brown, 1955.

Lowith, Karl. *Meaning in History.* Chicago, IL: University of Chicago Press, 1949.

Luttwak, Edward N. *Strategy: The Logic of War and Peace.* Cambridge, MA: Belknap Press, 1987.

MacIntyre, Alasdair. *After Virtue.* Notre Dame, IN: University of Notre Dame Press, 1984.

_____. *Three Rival Versions of Moral Enquiry.* Notre Dame, IN: University of Notre Dame Press, 1990.

_____. *Whose Justice? Which Rationality?* Notre Dame, IN: University of Notre Dame Press, 1988.

Maritain, Jacques. *Christianity and Democracy.* New York: Charles Scribner's Sons, 1944.

_____. *Man and the State.* Chicago, IL: University of Chicago Press, 1951.

Marshall, Charles Burton. *The Exercise of Sovereignty*. Baltimore, MD: Johns Hopkins Press, 1965.

————. *The Limits of Foreign Policy*. New York: Holt, 1954.

Martino, Joseph P. *A Fighting Chance: The Moral Use of Nuclear Weapons*. San Francisco, CA: Ignatius Press, 1988.

Matthews, Lloyd J. and Dale E. Brown, eds. *The Parameters of Military Ethics*. Washington, DC: Pergamon-Brassey's, 1989.

McBrien, Richard P. *Caesar's Coin: Religion and Politics in America*. New York: Macmillan, 1987.

Michels, Robert. *Political Parties*. Trans. Eden and Cedar Paul. Glencoe, IL: The Free Press, 1949. (First published in 1915.)

Military Ethics: Reflections on Principles. Washington, DC: National Defense University Press, 1987.

Miller, Walter M., Jr. *A Canticle for Leibowitz*. New York: Bantam, 1976. (Reprint of 1959 edition.)

Montagu, Ashley, ed. *Man and Aggression*. New York: Oxford University Press, 1973.

Moral Obligation and the Military. Washington, DC: National Defense University Press, 1988.

Morgenthau, Hans J. *Politics Among Nations*. Revised by Kenneth W. Thompson. 6th ed. New York: Knopf, 1985.

————. *Scientific Man vs. Power Politics*. Chicago, IL: University of Chicago Press, 1946.

Murnion, Philip J., ed. *Catholics and Nuclear War*. New York: Crossroad, 1983.

Murphy, Walter F. *The Vicar of Christ*. New York: Ballantine, 1979.

Murray, John Courtney. *We Hold These Truths*. New York: Sheed and Ward, 1960.

Musto, Ronald G. *The Catholic Peace Tradition*. Maryknoll, NY: Orbis Books, 1986.

National Conference of Catholic Bishops. *The Challenge of Peace: God's Promise and Our Response*. Washington, DC: United States Catholic Conference, 1983.

Neuhaus, Richard John. *The Naked Public Square*. Grand Rapids, MI: Eerdmans, 1984.

Niebuhr, Reinhold. *The Children of Light and the Children of Darkness*. New York: Charles Scribner's Sons, 1944.

————. *Christian Realism and Political Problems*. New York: Charles Scribner's Sons, 1953.

————. *Moral Man and Immoral Society*. New York: Charles Scribner's Sons, 1932.

Novak, Michael. *Moral Clarity in the Nuclear Age*. Nashville, TN: T. Nelson, 1983.

Nye, Joseph S. *Nuclear Ethics*. New York: The Free Press, 1986.

O'Brien, William V. *The Conduct of Just and Limited War*. New York: Praeger, 1981.

———— and John Langan, eds. *The Nuclear Dilemma and The Just War Tradition*. Lexington, KY: D. C. Heath, 1986.

_____. *U.S. Military Intervention: Law and Morality.* Beverly Hills, CA: Sage, 1979.

O'Connell, Robert L. *Of Arms and Men.* New York: Oxford University Press, 1989.

Osgood, Robert E. and Robert W. Tucker. *Force, Order, and Justice.* Baltimore, MD: Johns Hopkins Press, 1967.

Paskins, Barrie and Michael Dockrill. *The Ethics of War.* Minneapolis, MN: University of Minnesota Press, 1979.

Phillips, Robert L. *War and Justice.* Norman, OK: University of Oklahoma Press, 1984.

Ramsey, Paul. *The Just War: Force and Political Responsibility.* New York: Scribner, 1968.

_____. *Speak Up for Just War or Pacifism.* University Park, PA: Pennsylvania State University Press, 1988.

_____. *War and the Christian Conscience.* Durham, NC: Duke University Press, 1961.

Reid, Charles J., Jr. *Peace in a Nuclear Age: the Bishops' Pastoral Letter in Perspective.* Washington, DC: Catholic University of America Press, 1986.

Revel, Jean-Francois. *The Totalitarian Temptation.* Trans. David Hapgood. Garden City, NY: Doubleday, 1977.

Roche, George. *A World Without Heroes.* Hillsdale, MI: Hillsdale College Press, 1987.

Rossiter, Clinton. *Conservatism in America.* New York: Knopf, 1955.

Russell, Greg. *Hans J. Morgenthau and the Ethics of American Statecraft.* Baton Rouge, LA: Louisiana State University Press, 1990.

Ryn, Claes G. *Democracy and the Ethical Life.* Baton Rouge, LA: Louisiana State University Press, 1978.

Schelling, Thomas. *Arms and Influence.* New Haven, CT: Yale University Press, 1966.

_____. *The Strategy of Conflict.* Cambridge, MA: Harvard University Press, 1980.

Schlesinger, Arthur M., Jr. *The Politics of Hope.* Boston, MA: Houghton Mifflin, 1963.

Seabury, Paul and Angelo Codevilla. *War: Ends & Means.* New York: Basic Books, 1989.

Sennett, Richard. *The Fall of Public Man.* New York: Knopf, 1977.

Sheen, Fulton J. *Peace of Soul.* New York: Whittlesey House, 1940.

Silber, John. *Straight Shooting.* New York: Harper & Row, 1989.

Simon, Yves R. M. *Philosophy of Democratic Government.* Chicago, IL: University of Chicago Press, 1951.

Sterba, James, ed. *The Ethics of War and Nuclear Deterrence.* Belmont, CA: Wadsworth, 1985.

Stoessinger, John G. *Why Nations Go to War.* 5th ed. New York: St. Martin's Press, 1990.

Strauss, Leo. *Natural Right and History.* Chicago, IL: University of Chicago Press, 1953.

Taylor, Robert L. and William E. Rosenbach, eds. *Military Leadership: In Pursuit of Excellence*. Boulder, CO: Westview Press, 1984.

Thibault, George E. *The Art and Practice of Military Strategy*. Washington, DC: National Defense University, 1984.

Tinder, Glenn E. *Political Thinking: The Perennial Questions*. 3d ed. Boston, MA: Little, Brown, 1979.

Toner, James H. *The American Military Ethic: A Meditation*. New York: Praeger, 1992.

U.S., Department of the Army. *The Law of Land Warfare: FM 27-10*. Washington, DC: Government Printing Office, 1956.

Voegelin, Eric. *The New Science of Politics*. Chicago, IL: University of Chicago Press, 1952.

Wakin, Malham, ed. *War, Morality, and the Military Profession*. Boulder, CO: Westview, 1979.

Walzer, Michael. *Just and Unjust Wars*. New York: Basic Books, 1977.

Wasserstrom, Richard A. *War and Morality*. Belmont, CA: Wadsworth, 1970.

Wattenberg, Ben J. *The First Universal Nation*. New York: Free Press, 1991.

Weigel, George. *Tranquillitas Ordinis*. New York: Oxford University Press, 1987.

Whitmore, Todd. *Ethics in the Nuclear Age*. Dallas, TX: Southern Methodist University Press, 1989.

Wilde, Norman. *The Ethical Basis of the State*. Princeton, NJ: Princeton University Press, 1924.

Will, George. *Statecraft as Soulcraft*. New York: Simon and Schuster, 1983.

Wittfogel, Karl A. *Oriental Despotism*. New Haven, CT: Yale University Press, 1957.

Wolfers, Arnold. *Discord and Collaboration*. Baltimore, MD: Johns Hopkins Press, 1962.

Woolsey, R. James. *Nuclear Arms: Ethics, Strategy, Politics*. San Francisco, CA: Institute for Contemporary Studies, 1984.

Wright, Quincy. *A Study of War*. Abridged by Louise Leonard Wright. Chicago, IL: University of Chicago Press, 1964.

Zahn, Gordon. *An Alternative to War*. New York: Council on Religion and International Affairs, 1963.

ARTICLES AND CHAPTERS IN FULL-LENGTH WORKS

Acheson, Dean. "Ethics in International Relations Today." *Vital Speeches of the Day* 31 (1 February 1965): 226–28.

Aikman, David. "Cambodia: An Experiment in Genocide." *Time*, 31 July 1978: 39–40.

Barrett, William. "Morality and the Present Peril." *Parameters* 11 (March 1981): 47–49.

Boorstin, Daniel J. "Myths of Popular Innocence," *U.S. News & World Report*, 4 March 1991: 41.

Bull, Hedley. Review of *Just and Unjust Wars*, by Michael Walzer. In *World Politics* 31 (July 1979): 588–99.

Bunting, Josiah. "The Conscience of a Soldier." *Worldview*, December 1973: 6–11.

Burtchaell, James T. "How Authentically Christian Is Liberation Theology?" *Review of Politics* 50 (Spring 1988): 264–81.

Catholicism in Crisis 2 (March 1984). S.v. "The Christian Soldier: A Symposium."

Childress, James F. "Reinhold Niebuhr's Critique of Pacifism." *Review of Politics* 36 (October 1974): 467–91.

Coll, Alberto. "Some Christian Reminders for the Statesman." *Ethics and International Affairs* 1 (1987): 97–112.

Cooke, Alistair. "Freedom and the Soldier." *Parameters* 10 (September 1980): 2–7.

Cropsey, Joseph. "The Moral Basis of International Action." *America Armed*, Robert A. Goldwin, ed. Chicago, IL: Rand McNally, 1963, pp. 71–91.

Cuomo, Mario M. "The Confessions of a Public Man." *Notre Dame Magazine*, Autumn 1984: 21–30.

Friedrich, Otto. "The Devilish Doctrine of Deniability." *Time*, 15 December 1986: 98.

Glover, James. "A Soldier and His Conscience." *Parameters* 13 (September 1983): 53–58.

Good, Robert C. "The National Interest and Political Realism: Niebuhr's 'Debate' with Morgenthau and Kennan." *The Journal of Politics* 22 (November 1960): 597–619.

Hartigan, Richard S. "War and Its Normative Justification: An Example and Some Reflections." *Review of Politics* 36 (October 1974): 492–503.

Henry, Carl F. H. "An Evangelical Appraisal of Liberation Theology." *This World* No. 15 (1985): 99–107.

Herberg, Will. "What is the Moral Crisis of Our Time?" *Intercollegiate Review* 22 (Fall 1986): 7–12. (Originally published in 1968.)

Howard, Michael. "The Causes of Wars." *The Wilson Quarterly* 8 (Summer 1984): 90–103.

————. "The Concept of Peace," *Encounter*, December 1983: 18–24.

————. "Ethics and Power in International Policy." *International Affairs*. 53 (July 1977): 364–76.

Johnson, James Turner. "Is Democracy an Ethical Standard?" *Ethics & International Affairs*. 4 (1990): 1–17.

Johnson, Paul. "The Heartless Lovers of Humankind." *The Wall Street Journal*, 5 January 1987: 16.

Kuntz, Paul G. Review of *Autobiographical Reflections*, by Eric Voegelin. *The Intercollegiate Review* 26 (Fall 1990): 47–50.

Lawler, Philip F. "Just War Theory and Our Military Strategy." *Intercollegiate Review* 19 (Fall 1983): 9–18.

MacIntyre, Alasdair. "The Privatization of Good: An Inaugural Lecture." *Review of Politics* 52 (Summer 1990): 344–77.

Maloney, Samuel D. "Ethics Theory for the Military Professional." *Concepts for Air Force Leadership*, R. I. Lester and A.G. Morton, eds. Maxwell AFB, AL: Air University Center for Aerospace Doctrine, Research, and Education, 1990, pp. 49–54.

Matthews, Lloyd J. "Resignation in Protest." *Army*, January 1990: 12–21.

McKenna, Joseph C. "Ethics and War: A Catholic View." *American Political Science Review* 54 (September 1960): 647–58.

Millett, Stephen M. "The Moral Dilemma of Nuclear Deterrence." *Parameters* 10 (March 1980): 33–38.

"The Morality of War." *Time*, 20 January 1967: 40–41.

Morrow, Lance. "Evil." *Time*, 10 June 1991: 48–53.

O'Brien, William V. "The Challenge of War: A Christian Realist Perspective." *The Catholic Bishops and Nuclear War*, Judith A. Dwyer, ed. Washington, DC: Georgetown University Press, 1984, pp. 37–63.

_____. "Just-War Doctrine in a Nuclear Context." *Theological Studies*. 44 (September 1983): 191–220.

Podhoretz, John. "Psychobabble Masks an Evil Deed." *Insight*, 15 September 1986: 72.

Roelofs, H. Mark. "Hebraic-Biblical Political Thinking." *Polity* 20 (Summer 1988): 572–97.

Sandel, Michael J. "Morality and the Liberal Ideal." *The New Republic*, 7 May 1984: 15–17.

Schlesinger, Arthur, Jr. "The Necessary Amorality of Foreign Affairs." *Harper's*. August, 1971: 72–77.

Solzhenitsyn, Aleksandr. "Men Have Forgotten God." *National Review*, 22 July 1983: 872–76.

Sondermann, Fred A. "The Concept of the National Interest." *Orbis* 21 (Spring 1977): 121–38.

Starr, Paul. "No Vietnam," *New Republic*, 18 February 1991: 8–10.

Stockdale, James Bond. "In War, In Prison, In Antiquity." *Parameters* 17 (December 1987): 2–9.

_____. "The World of Epictetus." *Atlantic*, April 1978: 98–106.

Strauss, Leo. "What is Political Philosophy?" *Journal of Politics* 19 (1957): 343–68.

Tellis, Ashley J. "Nuclear Arms, Moral Questions, and Religious Issues." *Armed Forces and Society* 13 (Summer 1987): 599–622.

Thompson, Kenneth W. "Beyond National Interest: A Critical Evaluation of Reinhold Niebuhr's Theory of International Politics." *The Image of Man*, M. A. Fitzsimons, Thomas McAvoy, and Frank O'Malley, eds. Notre Dame, IN: University of Notre Dame Press, 1959, pp. 435–51.

_____. "The Ethical Dimensions of Diplomacy." *Review of Politics* 46 (July 1984): 367–87.

Thompson, J. Milburn. "Moral Theology, War, and Peace: A Bibliographic Survey." *Choice* 23 (July–August 1986): 1637–45.

Tinder, Glenn. "Can We Be Good Without God?" *Atlantic*, December 1989: 69–85.

_____. "Christianity and the Welfare State." *Review of Politics* 49 (Fall 1987): 549–69.

_____. "Transcending Tragedy: The Idea of Civility." *American Political Science Review*. 68 (June 1974): 547–60.

Toner, James H. "Grant Us Peace." *Air University Review* 34 (November–December 1982): 105–13.

————. "Peacekeeping by Wishful Thinking." *Parameters* 17 (September 1987): 68–76.

————. "Sisyphus as Soldier: Ethics, Exigencies, and the American Military." *Parameters* 7 (1977): 2–12.

Toynbee, Arnold. "Is Religion Superfluous?" *Intellectual Digest*, December 1971: 58–60.

Tuchman, Barbara W. "An Inquiry into the Persistence of Unwisdom in Government." *Parameters* 10 (March 1980): 2–9.

Wells, Donald A. "How Much Can 'The Just War' Justify?" *Journal of Philosophy* 66 (4 December 1969): 819–29.

Wilkes, Paul. "The Hands That Would Shape Our Souls." *Atlantic*, December 1990: 59–88.

Will, George F. "The Meaning of Freedom." *Parameters* 13 (June 1983): 2–10.

Zoll, Donald A. "The Moral Dimension of War and the Military Ethic." *Parameters* 12 (June 1982): 2–15.

INDEX

Acheson, Dean, 12, 45, 47, 93–94
Acton, Lord, 4, 122–123
Aikman, David, 158
Almond, Gabriel, 46
Angell, Norman, 28
Anscombe, Elizabeth, 138–139, 143, 146
Anselm, St., 8
Aquinas, St. Thomas, 3, 10, 91–92, 106, 135, 145
Ardrey, Robert, 20
Aristotle, 8, 24, 86, 113, 165
Aron, Raymond, 42
Augustine, St., 2, 8, 66–67, 70, 130, 141
Axinn, Sidney, 98

Balance of power, idea of, 29, 31–32, 37–38, 53, 155
Barbarians, 78–7 9
Blainey, Geoffrey, 15–16
Bloom, Allan, 8
Brodie, Bernard, 15–16
Brogan, Denis, 44

Bunting, Josiah, 99–100
Burke, Edmund, 3, 163
Burns, James MacGregor, 55
Bush, George H. W., 11, 26, 45, 73, 95

Camus, Albert, 102
Canticle for Leibowitz (novel), 33, 172
Carr, E. H., 163
Carrighar, Sally, 20–21
Childress, James, 74, 76
Choice, freedom of, 7 5
Christ, identity of, 3, 11, 109–112, 130
Churchill, Winston, 147
Cicero, 18
Claude, Inis, 28, 32
Clausewitz, Karl von, 10, 18, 37, 54, 62, 73–74
Coll, Alberto, 165
Community, rebuilding, 86, 157–159
Conscience, 89–91
Cooke, Alistair, 160–161
Crabb, Cecil, 30
Cromwell, Oliver, 131

Crowl, Philip, 65
Cuban missile crisis, 24, 46

Dostoevsky, Fyodor, 123
Downs, Fred, 96–97
Duverger, Maurice, 157

Easton, David, 5, 114
Education, idea of, 3, 7, 88, 90, 154, 166, 168–169
Enlightenment, properties of, 159
Ethic of ultimate ends/responsibility, 163
Ethics, teleological, 3, 7–8, 37, 52, 102–103
Evil, existence of, 159–161

Faith, definition of, 7
Federalist, The, excerpts from, 29, 31–32, 51–52, 157
Fehrenbach, T. R., 54–55
France, Anatole, 2
Frederick the Great, 10
Freud, Sigmund, 21
Friedman, Thomas, 66–67
Friedrich, Otto, 163–164
Fromm, Erich, 22

Geopolitics, 43, 67
Glory (movie), 104
Gospels, 13, 107–109
Grace, 8, 166
Gray, J. Glenn, 99
Greeley, Andrew, 141
Griffin, Robert, 130–131
Guarding the guardians, 22, 115
Gurian, Waldemar, 169

Hadley, Arthur, 67, 75
Halle, Louis, 63
Henry, Carl F. H., 118
Herberg, Will, 159
Hobbes, Thomas, 2, 38, 125
Hoffmann, Stanley, 38, 43
Holmes, Oliver Wendell, Jr., 16, 96
Hook, Sidney, 145
Howard, Michael, 7, 15, 50–51, 52, 86, 95, 164–165
Human nature, 119–123

Huntington, Samuel, 66, 98
Hussein, Saddam, 17, 24, 49, 64
Huxley, Aldous, 12

Jacobinism, 140
John Paul II, 133, 138
Johnson, Lyndon, B., 44
Johnson, Paul, 67, 140, 166
Johnson, Samuel, 5
Jones, Jim, 7, 71, 109
Jus ad Bellum, 71–76
Jus in Bello, 76–79

Kaplan, Morton, 22, 29
Kellogg-Briand Treaty, 16
Kennan, George, 12, 39–40, 69, 146
King, Martin Luther, Jr., 93
Kirk, Russell, 5, 110–111
Kissinger, Henry A., 3, 6, 44, 47, 53, 56, 63, 66, 70, 153
Krauthammer, Charles, 5, 69
Kristol, Irving, 46

LaCroix, W. L., 134–135, 138, 143, 145
Lasswell, Harold, 5, 114
Law, 28, 75, 91–92
Leadership, definition of, 49; ordeal of, 46–49
Lee, Robert E., 12
Lenin, V. I., 114
Levi, Werner, 28
Lewis, C. S., 4, 113, 145, 158
Lewy, Guenter, 94–95, 146–147
Lex talionis, 134
Liberation theology, 116–119
Liddell Hart, B. H ., 85, 99
Lincoln, Abraham, 39, 72, 100–101, 168–169
Lippmann, Walter, 47, 50, 52, 140, 158
Lorenz, Konrad, 20

MacIntyre, Alasdair, 79, 156, 159, 166
Machiavelli, 5, 44, 101
Maritain, Jacques, 89, 125
Martino, Joseph, 146
Marx, Karl, 134
Milgram, Stanley, 22
Military power, definition of, 35

Mill, John Stuart, 7 9
Molnar, Thomas, 140
Montagu, Ashley, 20, 154–155
Montesquieu, 42, 12 2, 171
More, Sir Thomas, 72, 96
Morgenthau, Hans J., 4–6, 45, 48, 51, 63, 87, 95, 124, 153, 162, 166, 167–168
Mother Teresa, 119
Mueller, John, 70–71
Murray, John Courtney, 78–79, 145

Nation, definition of, 38–39; views of, 86–89
National interest, 40–43, 75
Natural law, 168, 172
Neuhaus, Richard John, 89–90, 157–158, 166
New Testament, great questions of, 125
Nicolson, Harold, 41
Niebuhr, Reinhold, 4, 6, 9, 30–32, 37–38, 52–53, 106, 130, 144
Norling, Bernard, 31
Novak, Michael, 118, 130
Nye, Joseph S., Jr., 93–94, 100, 146

Obedience, idea of, 115–116
Obligation, religious and political, 13, 92–96, 115–116, 135–137
O'Brien, William, 29–30, 54
Organski, A. F. K., and Jacek Kugler, 26–27
Original Sin, 31, 111–112, 154
Orwell, George, 5
Osgood, Robert, 42, 53–54, 74–75

Pacifism, millennial element of, 140–142
Pascal, Blaise, 167
Paul, St., 86, 90, 106, 136–137, 144–145, 154, 160, 167
Peace of Christ, 32
Pelagianism, 111, 142, 150
"Pereat mundus" argument, 63
Pershing, John J., 97
Pius XII, 79
Podhoretz, John, 160
Politics, definition of, 5–6
Pride, idea of, 113

Principle of Double Effect, 77
Prudence, 3, 124, 144
Public opinion, 49–51

Rand, Ayn, 156
Realism, Christian, 8–10, 31, 41, 44, 48, 51, 138, 142
Respondeat Superior, 77, 98–99
Ridgway, Matthew B., 97
Root, Elihu, 48–49
Rossiter, Clinton, 112
Rousseau, Jean Jacques, 4, 66

Schell, Jonathan, 17, 145
Schlesinger, Arthur Jr., 22, 45, 87, 156, 163
Seabury, Paul, and Angelo Codevilla, 65, 70, 73, 75
Sermon on the Mount, 134
Shame, idea of, 166
Sheen, Fulton John, 12, 50, 114
Silber, John, 92–93, 101–102, 162–163
Soldier's faith, 96–101
Solzhenitsyn, Aleksandr, 159
Speech, freedom of, 161
Stalin, 1, 146
State, definition of, 38
Stevenson, Adlai, 9
Strategy, 62–66

Tacitus, 11
Taillyrand, 9
Text, interpretation of (exegesis), 78, 108–109, 126, 133–137
Thompson, Kenneth, 145
Tinder, Glenn, 7, 38, 153–154, 157–158
Toynbee, Arnold, 23, 113
Tragedy, 2, 163–164
Tuchman, Barbara, 25
Tucker, Robert W., 74–75

Ulam, Adam, 42

Values, crucial or core, 43–46
Vicar of Christ, The (novel), 131–133
Voegelin, Eric, 7, 142

Walzer, Michael, 76

War, causes of, 19–32; definition of, 18–19; persistence of, 137–140; politics and diplomacy in, 59
War Lover, The (novel), 25, 30
Ways, Max, 40, 45–46
Weber, Max, 163
Weigel, George, 68

Weinberger, Caspar, 61–63
Wells, Donald, 77–78
Westmoreland, William C., 53
Will, George, 69
Wilson, Woodrow, 21, 26
Wisdom in government, 24–25
Wolfers, Arnold, 164

About the Author

JAMES H. TONER is Associate Professor of Political Science at Norwich University in Northfield, Vermont, where he teaches international politics and political philosophy. A graduate of the Infantry Officer Candidate School at Fort Benning, Georgia, he served on active duty as an Army officer from 1968–1972. He has contributed articles and reviews to a number of scholarly and defense-related journals, and he is the author of *The American Military Ethic: A Meditation* (Praeger 1992). From 1990 to 1992, he served as Visiting Professor of Political Science and International Relations at the U.S. Air War College, Maxwell Air Force Base, in Montgomery, Alabama.